Canning Mastery

My Complete guide to Water Bath and Pressure Canning. Delicious Recipes and Tips for canning safely

3 Books in 1

By
Linda C. Johnson

© **Copyright 2022 - All rights reserved.**

The content contained within this book may not be reproduced, duplicated or transmitted without direct written permission from the author or the publisher.

Under no circumstances will any blame or legal responsibility be held against the publisher, or author, for any damages, reparation, or monetary loss due to the information contained within this book, either directly or indirectly.

Legal Notice:

This book is copyright protected. It is only for personal use. You cannot amend, distribute, sell, use, quote or paraphrase any part, or the content within this book, without the consent of the author or publisher.

Disclaimer Notice:

Please note the information contained within this document is for educational and entertainment purposes only. All effort has been executed to present accurate, up to date, reliable, complete information. No warranties of any kind are declared or implied. Readers acknowledge that the author is not engaged in the rendering of legal, financial, medical or professional advice. The content within this book has been derived from various sources. Please consult a licensed professional before attempting any techniques outlined in this book.

By reading this document, the reader agrees that under no circumstances is the author responsible for any losses, direct or indirect, that are incurred as a result of the use of the information contained within this document, including, but not limited to, errors, omissions, or inaccuracies.

Table of Contents

BOOK 1 – Pressure Canning Without the Danger

INTRODUCTION 18

CHAPTER 1: CHOOSING YOUR PRESSURE CANNER 20

    Can I Use a Pressure Cooker? 20

    Can I Use a Water Bath Canner? 21

    Which Brand Is Best? 23

    Does Size Matter? 24

    Other Considerations 26

CHAPTER 2: THE PARTS OF A PRESSURE CANNER 28

    Gasket 28

    Weighted Gauge vs. Dial Gauge 29

    Vent Pipe 31

    Overpressure Plug 32

    Canning Rack 33

CHAPTER 3: PRESSURE CANNING PREPARATION 35

    Choosing a Recipe 35

    Preparing the Food 36

    Familiarize Yourself With Your Model 39

    Test Run 41

CHAPTER 4: HOW TO USE A PRESSURE CANNER 43

    Preparing the Pressure Canner 43

PRESSURIZING 44

DEPRESSURIZING 46

REMOVING THE CONTENTS 47

COMMON ERRORS AND HOW TO FIX THEM 49

CHAPTER 5: WHAT CAN CAN AND WHAT CAN'T CAN 51

WHEN TO USE A PRESSURE CANNER 51

VEGETABLE DO'S AND DON'TS 52

MEAT DO'S AND DON'TS 54

OTHER FOODS YOU CAN CAN 55

WHAT NEVER TO CAN 56

CHAPTER 6: PRESSURE CANNING VEGETABLES 58

HARVESTING 58

STORING VEGETABLES 59

VEGETABLES: RAW PACK VS. HOT PACK 60

MIXED VEGETABLES 63

CHAPTER 7: PRESSURE CANNING STOCK 65

WHAT IS STOCK? 65

THE BASICS OF STOCK SAFETY 66

CHICKEN BROTH VS. BEEF BROTH 68

TIPS FOR CANNING BROTH 69

CHAPTER 8: BONUS CHAPTER - PRESSURE CANNING MEAT 71

THE BASICS OF MEAT SAFETY 71

MEAT: RAW PACK VS. HOT PACK 72

MEAT PRODUCTS..73

POULTRY AND RABBIT..74

SEAFOOD 75

CHAPTER 9: CARING FOR YOUR PRESSURE CANNER.....................77

BASIC MAINTENANCE 77

PART REPLACEMENT 78

CLEANING 80

CARING FOR UTENSILS 81

STORING 82

CHAPTER 10: WHAT'S THE WORST THAT COULD HAPPEN? 84

BOTULISM 84

AVOIDING CONTAMINATION 85

UNDERSTANDING FOOD ACID LEVELS..87

WILL MY PRESSURE CANNER EXPLODE?..88

HOW TO SPOT DANGER...89

CONCLUSION 91

REFERENCES 93

BOOK 2 - The Essential Guide To Pressure Canning for Beginners

INTRODUCTION..96

CHAPTER 1: PRESSURE CANNING 101 98

BRANDS AND TYPES OF PRESSURE CANNERS 99

PARTS OF A PRESSURE CANNER 102

Pressure Regulator 103

Adjustable Pressure Regulator 103

Vent Pipe 103

Air Vent 103

Locking Bracket 104

Sealing Ring 104

Pressure Dial Gauge 104

Cooking Rack 105

Overpressure Plug 105

Jars, Lids, and Other Canning Equipment 105

Canning Jars and Lids 106

Utensils for Canning 107

A Canner 107

Kitchen Towels 107

Food Strainer or Mill 108

Water Bath vs. Pressure Canner 108

Important Considerations While Canning 109

Acidity 110

Temperature 111

Altitude 111

Risk of Botulism 113

Things to Remember 114

CHAPTER 2: HOW TO PRESSURE CAN 115

BASIC STEPS OF PRESSURE CANNING 115
    Step 1: Heating the Jars 116
    Step 2: Filling the Jars 116
    Step 3: Remove any Air Bubbles 116
    Step 4: Add the Lids 117
    Step 5: Lock the Pressure Canner Lid 117
    Step 6: Venting 118
    Step 7: The Right Pressure 118
    Step 8: Depressurize 119
    Step 9: Cool the Jars 119

ESSENTIAL PRACTICES 120

CHAPTER 3: LENTILS AND BEANS 122

DRIED BEANS 122
LENTILS WITH VEGETABLES 124
BAKED BEANS 127
CHILI CON CARNE 130
PORK AND BEANS 133

CHAPTER 4: TOMATOES 138

CANNING TOMATOES 138
SPAGHETTI SAUCE 140
TOMATO SAUCE 143

CHAPTER 5: MEAT 149

PORK 149

    Pulled Pork Barbecue 151

    Pork Meatballs 154

    Hamburger Patties 156

    Venison 159

    Sausage 161

    Beef Stew 163

    Sloppy Joe Filling 165

    Un-Stuffed Cabbage Rolls 167

    Corned Beef and Potatoes 170

    Burrito in a Jar 172

    Chicken and Gravy 175

    Chicken Marsala 177

    Apricot Chicken 179

    White Bean and Chicken Chili 181

    Bourbon Chicken 183

    Sweet and Sour Chicken 185

    Venison Stew 188

    Venison Spaghetti Sauce 190

    Spicy Turkey Burgers 193

    Turkey and Gravy 196

    Asian Turkey Meatballs 198

Chapter 6: Vegetables 204

    Green Beans 204

Ratatouille 206

Herbed Potatoes 209

Roasted Root Vegetables 211

CHAPTER 7: BONUS CHAPTER - SOUPS 215

Sweet Potato Soup 215

Carrot and Fennel Soup 217

Asparagus Soup 220

Vegetable Soup 223

Tomato Soup 225

Mexican Beef Garden Soup 228

Colorful Soup 231

Chile, Corn, and Chicken Chowder 233

APPENDIX 1 – ALTITUDE IN USA CITIES & CANADIAN CITIES 236

Appendix 2 - Measurement Conversion 239

Cooking Temperatures 240

Pounds to Kilograms 240

CONCLUSION 241

REFERENCES 242

BOOK 3 - Water Bath Canning for Beginners and Beyond

INTRODUCTION 251

CHAPTER 1 WATER BATH CANNING 101 255

What is Water Bath Canning? 255

WHEN TO USE A WATER BATH CANNER 257

WATER BATH CANNING EQUIPMENT 259

CHOOSING A CANNING RECIPE 260

OTHER HELPFUL TIPS 262

KEY CHAPTER 1 TAKEAWAYS 263

CHAPTER 2 HOW TO WATER BATH CAN IN 4 EASY STEPS 265

STEP 1: PREPARATION 265

STEP 2: HEATING 266

STEP 3: COOLING 269

STEP 4: STORING 270

KEY CHAPTER 2 TAKEAWAYS 271

CHAPTER 3 JAMS, MARMALADES, CHUTNEYS, AND JELLIES 273

JAM RECIPES 273

MARMALADE RECIPES 278

CHUTNEY RECIPES 284

IT TAKES TWO TO MANGO CHUTNEY 284

JELLY RECIPES 288

KEY CHAPTER 3 TAKEAWAYS 293

CHAPTER 4 DESSERTS 295

CANNING DESSERTS 101 295

FRUIT RECIPES 296

    Blasting Blueberries 296

    Rockin Raspberries 297

    Krazy Kiwi 299

Pie Filling Recipes 300

    Granny's Apple Pie Filling 300

    The Great Rhubarb Pie Filling 302

    Cherry Bomb Pie Filling 303

Fruit Sauce Recipes 305

    Lemon Zest Blueberry Sauce 305

    Awesomesauce Applesauce 306

    Cinnamon Pear Sauce 307

Key Chapter 4 Takeaways 309

CHAPTER 5 PICKLES 311

Pickling 101 311

Pickled Vegetables 313

    Dill With It Pickles 313

    In a Real Pickle Pickled Onions 315

    Rise and Brine Pickled Vegetable Mix 316

Pickled Fruit 318

    Perfect Pickled Peaches 318

    Picturesque Pickled Apricots 320

    Popular Pickled Fruit Cocktail 321

Relish 323

    Relished Dill Pickled Relish 323

    Relished Sweet Pickled Relish 324

    Relished Jalapeno Relish 326

  Key Chapter 5 Takeaways 327

CHAPTER 6 TOMATOES 329

  Tomato Recipes 329

    Dice to Meet You Diced Tomatoes 329

    Cherished Cherry Tomatoes 330

    Whole Lotta Whole Tomato 332

  Salsa Recipes 334

    Mild Salsa 334

    Spicy Salsa 336

    Salsa Verde 337

  Tomato Sauce Recipes 339

    Pasta La Vista, Baby Sauce 339

    Marinara Sauce 341

    Pizza Sauce 343

  Tomato Juice Recipes 345

    Tomato Juice 345

    Fresh From the Garden Vegetable Juice 346

    Bloody Mary 348

CHAPTER 7 CONDIMENTS 352

  Basic Condiments 352

    Knock 'Em Out Ketchup 352

    Better Barbecue Sauce 354

- Marry Me Mustard 356

ADVANCED CONDIMENTS 358

- Serenading Sweet Chili Sauce 358
- Horseradish Harmony 359
- From the Heart Honey Mustard 360

DRESSING AND SYRUP RECIPES 362

- You Won't Regret this Strawberry Vinaigrette 362
- Seriously Good Strawberry Syrup 363
- Best Blueberry Syrup Around 365

MORE SAUCES 366

- Can't Be Beat Cranberry Sauce 366
- Hot Hot Sauce 368
- The Chicken Wing Sauce 369

KEY CHAPTER 7 TAKEAWAYS 371

CHAPTER 8 BONUS CHAPTER - MEALS IN A JAR 373

MEAL PREPARATION 373

WHAT'S FOR BREAKFAST 374

- Apple Butter on Toast 374
- Greek Yogurt with Mango 376

WHAT'S FOR LUNCH 377

- Peach Salsa Tacos 377
- Cowboy Candy Over Salmon 379

WHAT'S FOR DINNER 381

    Spaghetti with Zoodles... 381

    Pickled Beets Salad... 382

  Key Chapter 8 Takeaways.. 384

CHAPTER 9 EVERYTHING ELSE YOU NEED TO KNOW 385

  Altitude 385

  Measurement Conversion 388

    Cooking Temperatures... 389

    Pounds to Kilograms.. 389

    EWG's 2021 "Dirty Dozen".. 390

    EWG's 2021 "Clean Fifteen".. 390

  Fruit and Tomato Canning Charts.. 391

  Pesticides 393

  What Can Go Wrong?... 393

CONCLUSION... 395

THANK YOU 398

GLOSSARY 399

REFERENCES.. 408

IMAGES 414

Your Free Gifts!

Out of all of the available literature on canning, you chose this one. Thank you. As a way to express my gratitude, I'm offering additional valuable resources for FREE to my readers.

Get Free Instant Access by clicking on or going to

www.customercore.eu

- **FREE GIFT:** My Ultimate Checklist For Canning Successfully

- **FREE GIFT:** My 5-Minute Cheat Sheet To Help You Can Safely

- **FREE GIFT:** My 17 Essential Items You Need To Can Successfully

- **FREE GIFT:** Is My Ultimate 35-Step Cheatsheet For Water Bath Canning Successfully every time

- **FREE GIFT:** Is My favorite (& secret) Pizza Tomato Sauce Recipe.

Before we start, I have a small favor to ask of you. When you finish reading this book, **would you please consider posting a review of this book on the platform?** Posting a review will help support my writing.

Thank you. I really appreciate it.

Just follow the relevant link below.

US- https://www.amazon.com/review/create-review?&asin=B0B7KCH351

UK- https://www.amazon.co.uk/review/create-review?&asin=B0B7KCH351

CANADA- https://www.amazon.ca/review/create-review?&asin=B0B7KCH351

MEXICO- https://www.amazon.com.mx/review/create-review?&asin=B0B7KCH351

BRAZIL - https://www.amazon.com.br/review/create-review?&asin=B0B7KCH351

SPAIN- https://www.amazon.es/review/create-review?&asin=B0B7KCH351

ITALY- https://www.amazon.it/review/create-review?&asin=B0B7KCH351

FRANCE- https://www.amazon.fr/review/create-review?&asin=B0B7KCH351

INDIA- https://www.amazon.in/review/create-review?&asin=B0B7KCH351

GERMANY - https://www.amazon.de/review/create-review?&asin=B0B7KCH351

Pressure Canning Without the Danger

Your Comprehensive Guide to Safely Using Your Pressure Canner. With Tips, Tricks, and USDA Guidelines to Help You Use Your Pressure Canner Without Risks!

Linda C. Johnson

Introduction

It is almost impossible to think of the pressure canner without considering its dangerous connotations. Many horror stories consisting of exploding lids and dodging boiling water have tainted the good name of the kitchen necessity. The pressure canner has been around for a long time and with that history comes the inevitable criticism. Just because your grandma's kitchen turned into an unwanted steam room doesn't mean yours will. The world has evolved and so has it's kitchen appliances. Today's pressure canners are not the faulty ones of the 1950's. Manufacturers were quick to learn that you can't make a profit if your product keeps exploding and thus intense safety measures were added to improve customer satisfaction. They just don't make them like they used to, and that is why your kitchen ceiling is safe from flying pressure canner lids.

The pressure canner, just like any other heavy equipment, should be handled with the utmost care and consideration. It is not a toaster. You can't just skim through the directions, push the on button and hope for the best. Just because this is the modern age of safety and precaution doesn't mean there haven't been any accidents. In contrast to this, it is not an impossible ten sided Rubik's cube. There is no reason to be intimidated. People have been successfully canning using a pressure canner for decades and will continue for years to come. As long as this balance of care and confidence is successfully navigated there will be no issue.

Still unsure if using a pressure canner is the right choice? Why bother canning at all when the nearest grocery store has a can of green beans for less than a dollar. There is a common misconception that simple, organic lifestyles such as canning are not as cost efficient. This misleading information stunts the growth of consumer independence from big corporations. Canning is an investment, whether it is used for business or just feeding your family. There's no doubt that pressure canners can be expensive, but so is the average monthly grocery bill. The amount of food thrown out due to spoilage is ridiculous: Hard earned money down the drain. Food prices are rising and, if the last fifty years are any indication, they are just going to get higher. Investing today saves you and your family from becoming just another victim of inflation.

Another important benefit to using a pressure canner is knowing exactly what is in your family's food. Even with F.D.A. regulations, there's no way of knowing every single ingredient that goes into the canned goods at the grocery store. With every new food related research study, it's understandable that canning would be part of a new trend. Not only are you freeing yourself from the hold that major chains have on the American family, but you are expressing the freedom of choosing what you want to eat. Whether it's no gluten, all gluten, keto friendly, paleo, or coma-inducing levels of sugar, the choice on what you eat is all yours.

Consumer liberation is an obvious choice, however, the important question still remains. Will my pressure canner explode? The answer: Probably not. That is perhaps not the most reassuring answer, but the truth is that something can go wrong: Mostly happening when we're not being safe. Even with all the technical advances in the world, the pressure canner is not foolproof. That's why this book exists, to keep the kitchen nice and tidy. Blunders will occur, but the best part about mistakes is that they never have to happen twice. Luckily, someone somewhere has already made those mistakes so now you don't have to.

This ambiguous answer might not be enough so to put it plain and simple, the pressure canner is not a dangerous appliance. A car causes far more fatalities and disasters in a year than the pressure canner could in all the time of its existence. Does that mean cars should become obsolete? Of course not. As long as everyone abides by the laws of traffic and is careful, there's no reason to fear vehicles of any kind. It's when people don't that crashes happen. The pressure canner is just as safe as you make it, and by choosing to read this book you've already proven that you're smart and capable enough to be perfectly safe.

Chapter 1:
Choosing Your Pressure Canner

Can I Use a Pressure Cooker?

No. Well, maybe. If you're making a delicious beef stew, then by all means use a pressure cooker. However, if you plan on canning that beef stew, then a pressure canner is required. Despite their similar names the two appliances are not interchangeable. Canning food is not as easy as placing it in jars and heating it up. There are many safety procedures put in place to make sure the food is safely edible. If these aren't followed, it runs the risk of dangerous toxins contaminating the canned food that can lead to serious illness and possibly death.

The confusion between these two appliances is understandable: Besides their names, pressure cookers and pressure canners have similar processes as well. Pressure being the key word. Both are sealed pots that build up pressure through the use of steam. In addition, the two contraptions have a kindred history. Cookers have the same unfortunate reputation as canners, stemming from past unsafe manufacturing errors. It was through the technology of pressure cooking, that the canning community discovered this new and safe way to can low acid foods. The canner is a modified version of the cooker, and it's main purpose is preservation rather than immediate consumption.

The other difference between the pressure canner and the pressure cookers is the size. Most pressure cookers, like the instapot, are smaller and only hold about four or less quarts. Pressure canners are larger, and are capable of canning seven quart jars or even up to 24 half pint jars at a time. This size difference completely changes the heat up and cool down process and because of this, canning in a pressure cooker can lead to an under processed result. Even the largest pressure cookers aren't capable of recreating the environment that is needed to stop contamination.

Since pressure cookers are not manufactured with the purpose of canning, they are missing integral parts to the process. Many cookers will not have gauges that measure the pressure inside the pot. Without this feature there is no way to know if the food is safe to consume. Even in the rare case that a pressure cooker does have a gauge, they are not always very reliable because the process of pressure cooking isn't as exact as pressure canning is. It is very important to know just exactly how much pressure is being put on the jars and their contents when canning.

Manufacturers may claim that their pressure cooker is safe for canning, but it's important to research further into this claim and make sure the cooker is USDA approved for pressure canning. If the cooker is smaller than 16 quarts then there is no safe way to convert canning recommendations. Even with a large enough cooker that has an adjustable gauge, most USDA approved recipes are going to call for a pressure canner to avoid any possible mistakes. Ultimately it's the customer's decision, but considering the possible deadly repercussions, I cannot recommend using a pressure cooker as a pressure canner.

Can I Use a Water Bath Canner?

No. Well maybe. A water bath canner is a perfectly valid way to can food products, unlike the pressure cooker which can be dangerous. Water bath canning is not the same thing as pressure canning, however. There are two common methods to canning due to the fact that different foods require different circumstances to be safely preserved. Pressure canning utilizes steam to create high levels of heated pressure that sterilizes the jars. Water bath canners can not reach the same temperatures and are only used for products that don't need high heat to be processed.

Unlike the pressure canner, a special water bath canner is not actually required for water bath canning. All that is needed is a large pot, a lid and a rack to hold the jars at the bottom. However, there are pots that are manufactured specifically for water bath canning. Pressure canners only use about 1-3 inches of water compared to the water bath method where the jars are completely immersed in the boiling water. Because of this, preserves in water bath canners can only reach the temperature of the water. It is during the cool down time that jars become sealed and the food within them becomes safely preserved. The time in which this takes place is usually specified in the recipe.

Knowing what type of food requires a water bath versus what type requires a pressure canner is very important. A water bath canner only reaches temperatures of 212 degrees Fahrenheit, whereas a pressure canner can heat to 240 degrees Fahrenheit. This can be the difference between enjoying delicious preserved food or suffering through food poisoning. Water bath canning is only really used for fruits, fruit products like pie filling or chutney, vinegar, and condiments. Pressure canning is for vegetables, certain kinds of meats, and broth. When following a canning recipe, make sure to double check what canning method is required.

So what is the difference between these two groups of foods? Water bath canners are used for acidic food, while pressure canners work for non-acidic food. Whether a food is acidic or not is reliant on its pH levels. Acidic food such as fruit have lower pH levels while meat and vegetables have alkaline or neutral levels. Both acidic and non-acidic food can kill dangerous bacteria at the temperature of a water bath canner, but *Botulinum* spores survive this process. Acidic food naturally kills these spores however, non-acidic food cannot and so a pressure canner is required for extra protection.

Some vegetables can be canned using the water bath method without the fear of *Botulinum spores*. *Botulinum* spores can be killed by lowering the pH level of the vegetables and making them more acidic. These low or extreme pH levels can be achieved by pickling the vegetables. To pickle the vegetables, simply submerge them in vinegar and that will make them more acidic. It should be acknowledged that this process will change the texture and taste of the vegetables. Meats and broth can only ever be safely processed through a pressure canner.

Which Brand Is Best?

When it comes to pressure canners, there are two brands that dominate the market, and with any good feud between two retail juggernauts comes the inevitable question. Which brand is best? Pepsi or Coke, Apple or Android, All-American or Presto? The answer is whatever you prefer. Apologies for this unsatisfactory answer, but both All-American and Presto pressure canners have their pros and cons. Ultimately, it is the customer's decision on what model makes them feel most comfortable. For first time pressure canner owners it is important to know what you're looking for and what brand is best for you.

All-American pressure canners come in a variety of sizes, which is perfect for people who plan on making large batches at a time. Their largest size will can 19 quart jars at a time, while their smallest holds only four. With this variety of sizes comes a variety of prices. Be prepared to spend more money for larger canners. All-American canners should only be used on a gas range instead of an electric one, so there is no stove damage. A feature of the All-American that makes them more user friendly is their weighted gauge. Instead of having to manually adjust the heat, weight on the valve regulates the pressure.

Presto pressure canners only come in two sizes which are the 16 quart liquid capacity model, and the 23 quart liquid capacity model. The Presto brand canners work with both gas and electric ranges. This fact, along with their small size, makes Presto more versatile than the All-American canners. The gauge is a dial gauge instead of a weighted one, and the pressure must be manually handled. This is better for people who wish to can in higher altitudes. Newer models have a button feature that drops down to inform you when the canner is safe to open.

As far as price goes, the Presto brand runs cheaper, and is more commonly available in stores such as Walmart. Presto canners do require the additional expense of replacing the rubber gasket around the inside of the lid. Gasket replacements are not very expensive however, and are only needed every few years. Keep in mind location when choosing between the two brands as well. High altitude places will prefer the presto while lower altitudes can enjoy the weighted gauge feature of the All-American. The decision between the two is also dependent on batch sizes. Investing in a larger All-American pressure canner will be the smarter option for those who have a good amount of canning orders to do in a short time. Presto canners are better for casual canning. Both brands are well built and last a long time.

Just because All-American and Presto are the most well known brands on the market, does not mean they are the only brands. Mirro, while not as popular, is the only brand other than the two aforementioned brands that is most recognized by professionals in the field of canning. Mirro, like Presto, only comes in two sizes: Both of these sizes have weighted gauge features like All-American canners. Fagor was another common brand until it was discontinued in 2018.

Does Size Matter?

When buying a pressure canner it's very important to choose a size that is going to work best for your canning experience. Size does matter: Different canning projects are going to require different size models. Is this a business opportunity, or do you just want to feed your family fresh carrots in the winter? It is also important to keep in mind when you're not using your pressure canner. Do you have the space for the biggest All-American model or would a smaller Presto fit in the cupboard better? These are just a few things to keep in mind before choosing a size of pressure canner.

To be considered a pressure canner by the USDA, the pot must be able to hold at least four quart jars. Presto and Mirro pressure canners start at an internal total volume of 16 quarts and those are the most commonly considered smallest canners. The smallest All-American model however, holds an internal total of 10 quarts. That does not mean the All-American model isn't a pressure canner though, because they do follow the USDA rule of being able to hold 4 quart jars. Anything smaller than this is considered a cooker and is not approved for canning by the USDA.

The University of Wisconsin Extension Service suggests only using a 16-22 quart pressure canner and believes anything less to be unsafe. All-American has two pressure canners under this limit at 10 and 15.5 quarts. It is essential to understand that All-American does not recommend using their canners under 16 quarts for smoked fish, as they do not have suitable processing times. Considering that both the Mirro and All-American brands make canners larger than 22 quarts, this is a strange limitation to put on the max volume of a pressure canner. In fact, using a pressure canner that is bigger than is required is not actually going to cause any danger.

Both Presto and Mirro start at 16 quarts although this size does have its limitations. The 16 quart models of each brand are just as wide as the 22 and 23 quart canners, but they lack their counterpart's height. Their smaller size slows down the canning process since you can not stack a second layer of half liter jars. Larger canners can also be used for water bath canning, but there just isn't room for this process in a 16 quart pressure canner. Their cons are outweighed by the fact that they do heat up and cool down faster than the larger canners.

Despite there being no safety issue in using a larger pressure canner for a smaller job, that doesn't mean bigger is always better. Keep in mind how efficiently you are using energy. Using a bigger pressure canner will increase your energy cost per jar, and considering one of the main goals of canning is to lower the cost of living, this is something to avoid. Remember that a bigger canner will also increase your carbon footprint, so if you plan on canning a lot, you might want to think about purchasing two canners in different sizes.

Other Considerations

Even if you know what brand and size you are looking for, there is still a lot to consider when buying a pressure canner. Most importantly how much they cost: Price varies on size and brand, but pressure canners range anywhere from 100 to 600 USD. Presto will usually be cheaper than Mirro or All-American, since it is more widely available. While pressure canners are a smart investment, it can be daunting to spend this much money on what could be considered a seasonal appliance. Mirro, Presto, and All-American are all very durable brands with available replacement parts, which makes buying a pressure canner second hand no problem. Just make sure to double check everything is in working condition or easily fixable before purchasing using this cheaper option.

Once again, make sure you have a distinct idea of what you're canning for before you purchase anything. If you are starting a home canned goods business, you are going to need a large and dependable pressure canner. A 600 dollar, 41 quart canner is a good idea because you can make the money back and the investment will pay off quicker. If you just want to can peas from your personal garden once a year, a smaller and cheaper model will do just as well. You should do what makes the most sense for your canning lifestyle.

Not everyone is able bodied, and unfortunately not all pressure canners are created with this in mind. The weight of the model you choose is very important. Since they are built to withstand pressure and hold jars, racks, and water, they are very heavy. The bigger the canner, the heavier it gets. Knowing your physical ability will help you choose a model that you can use with little to no issues. Your stove top should also be a factor in your model's weight. Large canners can easily crack a glass stove top. You don't want to ruin your kitchen before you have even had the chance to start canning.

Luckily, most pressure canners come with sets, but if you are buying second hand, sometimes you won't have everything you'll need. The following utensils are a mandatory investment every canner needs. Pressure canners always come with their own racks that sit at the bottom of the pot and hold the jars. You will also need jars as the whole point of pressure canning is to put food in jars. Another must have are canning tongs or jar lifters which will help to remove the jar from the rack when the pressure canner is finished cooling down. There are many kits available online with a variety of utensils that will make the process of canning much easier.

Even with all this information, choosing a pressure canner may still be an intimidating task, so here are some of my recommendations: If you are a beginner and only want to dabble in canning, I suggest a 16 quart Presto model. If you've been canning for a while and want to feed your family through the winter, either 22 quart Presto, 23 quart Mirro, or even a 25 quart All-American should work depending on the size of your family. If you have a year round canning business, a 30 or 41 quart All-American model is a good investment.

Chapter 2:
The Parts of a Pressure Canner

Gasket

A gasket is a rubber ring around the rim of the pressure canner lid. Its purpose is to seal in the contents and allow the canister to pressurize. It does this by stopping the steam from leaving the top of the kettle. Depending on your brand and model, gaskets are a very important feature and should be well taken care of. After every use, they need to be removed from the lid and thoroughly cleaned. Not only will this keep them in better condition for a longer time, but it will also sterilize the surface and stop the spread of any possible bacteria.

With time, the gasket becomes worn, and it is important to watch out for the rubber hardening or stretching. When this happens the gasket needs to be replaced to prevent any possible accidents. The recommended time in which to replace the gasket is anywhere between one and five years. Anything more than five years is often seen as pushing the gasket to its limit and unsafe in the canning community. The NCHFP says that you should wait no more than two years in between replacements. It also depends on how often the pressure canner is being used. Canners that often take on larger loads should have new gaskets every year.

While the brands Presto and Mirro require rubber gaskets to function, not all pressure canners use this part in their product. All-American pressure canners are the only brand to not have gaskets at all and instead seal metal to metal. The absence of the gasket doesn't make it any less safe however, and the metal to metal seal is more user friendly making the lid easier to open and close. While the other brands may have the minor inconvenience of replacing the gasket every few years, the price of said replacement is by no means a financial burden. On Amazon, a pack of rubber gaskets is available for under ten dollars.

With the need to replace the gasket every few years, you may feel tempted to stock up on them. Preparedness is often a virtue, but not necessarily in this case. Rubber gaskets are made from a fragile material, and even when they are not being used they are still subject to natural erosion. The verdict on how long you should keep a spare gasket or if you should even keep one at all is undecided. Some sources say they can last up to five years as long as they are kept in a cool and dry area. The brand Presto recommends buying them fresh and not using stored gaskets.

Your pressure canner will likely never explode; However, if it does, you might want to check the state of your gasket. It is widely considered the whole system's weakest link. Back in the days of old, before safety precautions were put in place, regulators would become clogged and place extreme pressure on these gaskets. The rubber gasket could not withstand these conditions for very long and would snap during the canning process. Pair this with the malfunction of a lid latch and thus the origin for the horror stories of flying pressure canner lids is born. Something like this happening today is very unlikely.

Weighted Gauge vs. Dial Gauge

A pressure gauge is supposed to monitor and help regulate pressure inside of the canner. There are three different models of gauges that you can find on a pressure canner. The first and oldest is a dial gauge that is used to measure the pressure within the pot. The downside to this is that it can't control the pressure. A weighted gauge is the opposite: It controls the pressure but can't measure it. Lastly is a dual-gauge, which is a hybrid of the two. It has a dial for reading the pressure levels, but also utilizes weight to regulate that pressure.

A dial gauge has a watch face design that is used to display numbers relating to the amount of pressure being applied. Since a dial gauge can't control the amount of pressure in the pot, it requires a more hands on approach. You need to adjust the burner heat to change the pressure. This is helpful for higher altitudes because they require different pressure to properly process. It is possible for dial gauges to become inaccurate with age or if they are bumped around. In consideration of safety, it is fine if the food is cooked with too high of pressure, but the quality will be lackluster.

Dial gauges need to be checked at least once a year. This is generally carried out at the start of canning season, after the pressure canner is taken out of storage. This can be done by taking it to your local extension service. If you don't have a local extension service it will be unwise to invest in this type of gauge. You can also do it yourself if you have the dual-gauge feature. If the gauge is off by more than two when tested at 11 pounds then it should be replaced. Anything under is fine as long as you adjust to the difference with the heater when you are cooking. Also, if the glass on a dial gauge breaks or goes missing, it's time to get a new one.

If a dial gauge is manual, then a weighted gauge can be considered an automatic regulator. There are three settings of weights for this gauge and they are 5, 10, and 15. When the pound per square inch or PSI is reached this gauge will signal this by jiggling and making a rattling noise. Despite the fact that weighted gauges come in 5, and 10, the desired pressure is actually slightly over that. They are at this weight because weighted gauges don't release at exactly this PSI. That's why recipes are different for dial gauges and read to release pressure at 6 and 11 pounds.

The dual-gauge is just using both methods. Since weighted gauges are less hands on, the dial gauge is mostly there to keep track of where the PSI is at. It can be a back up if something goes wrong, but to be honest, it is kind of useless. Modern Presto canners are mostly dial gauge, but they've made their pot compatible with dual-gauges. The weights are sold separately. This is helpful for people who prefer the dial gauge way, but aren't close enough to a local extension service to get their dial checked every year.

Vent Pipe

The vent pipe is located on the lid of your pressure canner. It is a small opening where steam and pressure are vented out from the pot during the canning process. This is where the weighted gauge is placed. It will jiggle on top of the vent pipe when the weight is reached, making a rattling sound. The vent blows out steam automatically when the pressure attained is above 15 PSI. The vent pipe is one of the most important pieces and the pressure canner should never be used if this is damaged in any sort of way.

To clean the vent pipe, you will need a pipe cleaner or a string to pull through the vent opening. This piece is harder to clean, but it doesn't require you to remove it from the lid. Make sure not to use too much soap or other cleaning supplies that can dry and clog the vent. Don't try to clean the vent pipe with a toothpick or anything similar, as it can break and become lodged inside. Before using the canner, it is always smart to check if anything is clogging the vent pipe. To do this, hold the lid up to a light source so it is easier to see inside.

If the vent pipe is bent or damaged, you will need to replace it. You can also replace it if the inside has become corroded with rust or other foreign objects. Every pressure canner is different and so the method of removing the vent pipe will vary. No matter the brand, you will need a wrench to unscrew it from the lid. If it is stuck, you can use olive oil as lubricant. Make sure to wash your new vent pipe before you screw it in. It should be a relatively easy replacement that your owner's manual can help with. New vent pipes aren't expensive either, so there's no need to worry about putting a hole in your pocket.

There are some problems to look out for when it comes to the vent pipe's functions. Modern pressure canners have an overpressure plug that releases when the vent pipe fails, so there's no reason to be afraid if something goes wrong. You might be alarmed if condensation starts to appear under the regulator. This is normal because the pressure regulator starts off at a lower temperature than the lid. If it continues it could loosen the vent pipe, though. If you notice a lot of moisture during a process, feel free to tighten the vent pipe back up with a wrench once it is finished.

Overpressure Plug

The overpressure plug is a small, black piece of rubber that acts as a safety precaution when the vent pipe fails. When the overpressure plug is new it should be soft and pliable. This is important for its function, so make sure to replace brittle overpressure plugs as soon as you can. If the vent pipe becomes obstructed, the overpressure plug pops out of its hole on the lid and allows for the steam to exit the canner. This is the only safe way to release pressure when the vent pipe is no longer doing its job. When the canning process begins, it is normal to see a small amount of steam leaking from the area around the plug. This will stop once it seals.

To clean or replace the overpressure plug, you are going to need to pop it out of the opening on the lid. It should be fairly easy to do with a gentle push. To put the plug back in it's spot, flip the lid so the inside is facing you. The domed side of the plug should go first into the hole from this side. Push it in until it is even against the lid. If it isn't sealed right, steam will leak and ruin the PSI of the canning process. Some overpressure plugs will read TOP on the dome side. This should be visible from the top side of the lid.

Before each use of your canner, you will want to double check that the overpressure plug is still in good condition and capable of sealing in the pressure. It will also need to be cleaned in between loads. Since the plugs are made out of rubber like gaskets are, they are susceptible to the same problems. They can dry out quicker if they are regularly washed. Make sure to dry them off completely before putting them back in because you don't want the hole to rust over. Keep them away from direct exposure to high heat as well. A stovetop could easily melt the rubber and make them deteriorate faster.

Overpressure plugs need to be replaced at least every three years. Most canners suggest replacing them when you are replacing the gasket because both parts are made from rubber that cracks and deforms at the same pace. They need to be replaced as soon as they start to deform. Overpressure plugs are the last line of defense. If they are not in the condition they need to be, the canner could explode from too much pressure and no release. Replacements are easy to get and available for a decent price online.

Canning Rack

When you buy a pressure canner, it will usually come with a canning rack. If you have purchased yours second hand or your model just didn't come with one, you will want to invest in a canning rack. They sit at the bottom of the pot and hold the jars during the canning process. Jars can not touch any side of the pot or else they will not evenly heat up. This guarantees heat circulation and evenly canned food. It also keeps the jars from touching each other. The last thing you want is for your jars to break or chip during the process which can happen if they are not evenly dispersed.

It is common for canners to double deck within a load. This means having two rows of jars on top of each other. The National Center for Home Food Preservation has okayed double decking for both pressure canning and water bath canning. You can use a second rack for this, but it isn't necessary as long as the jars are staggered for weight distribution. There are special racks made for double decking to make it easier for certain size jars. Double decking does not change the amount of water to put in the pot or how long it takes to can.

Just like any canning equipment, remember to wash it after every use and then thoroughly dry it to prevent rust. Like the pressure canner, you can use steel wool to get stubborn stains off. Unless it is made from a non-metal, then you should use a more appropriate cleaning method. When it is time to store the canning rack, keep it in a dry area away from the humidity. You can wrap it in a paper towel to keep the dust off of it. If you have a metal canning rack, they will likely rust eventually and have to be replaced.

There are several different types of canning racks: The most popular are the ones made from stainless steel. These will last a very long time and come in a variety of different sizes that will suit your canner's model. There is also the aluminum canning rack that is similar to the stainless steel one. They are just as common and durable, and happen to be the cheaper option. If you want to avoid rust, you can buy a plastic rack. The downside to this option is that they aren't as durable, which is probably why they're not as common as their metal counterparts. Lastly, there are silicone racks. These are easy to clean like the plastic rack and can be used in pressure cookers too.

Whichever type of canning rack you get, make sure you fit it to the size of your model. This will just be simpler if you buy a canner that already comes with a rack. They are easy to buy though, so you don't have to worry if it's not the most financially beneficial decision for you. If you're overwhelmed by all the choices, I will suggest buying an aluminum pressure rack. It is just as durable and reliable as stainless steel but for a cheaper price. Some people don't buy canning racks at all and get very creative with DIY racks. If you'd rather research ways to do that, it is safe as long as it doesn't fall apart.

Chapter 3:
Pressure Canning Preparation

Choosing a Recipe

Choosing a recipe should be the easiest part of using a pressure canner, right? Just use one of your grandmother's old recipes that have been passed down for generations. If it worked for your ancestors then it should work for you. Unless it doesn't and you're unlucky enough to contract botulism. The truth about using an old family recipe is that you don't actually know what safety protocols whoever wrote it was following. That doesn't necessarily mean that you have to give up on generations of canning traditions. Just make sure it aligns with the USDA's canning guidelines. It's always better to change your dear, old, departed Grandma's recipe than to join her.

Not everyone comes from a long line of canning ancestors. First generation canners have to rely on their own resources to find suitable recipes. Thankfully we live in the age of the internet and a safe and tasty meal is only a few clicks away. With a boatload of information comes a boatload of confusion however, so be careful choosing a recipe online. Only use recipes that are specific to pressure canners. The two methods of canning, the water bath method and the pressure can method, require different treatments and preparation for the jar's contents and should not be used interchangeably.

You should also only choose recipes that are on or below your level of expertise. There are plenty of available canning recipes for beginners online or at your local library. If you aren't comfortable with the recipe you may become distracted, which is the last thing you want to be when operating heavy equipment such as the pressure canner. It is best to start with simpler recipes and work your way up to more complicated ones.

This rule applies to new canners as well. If you aren't comfortable with your new model, don't start off with an expert level recipe even if you have years of experience.

While the internet can be a wonderful place for new canners to find and share delicious recipes, this is not always the case. Not everyone on the internet is a pressure canning scholar, even if they claim to be one. Always make sure the recipe you choose comes from a reliable source. In this case, a reliable source refers to any recipe that aligns with the guidelines from the USDA. I suggest reading through these guidelines before choosing a recipe, so you know what to look out for. It is best to further research specific recipes if you are uncertain if they follow these guidelines.

Lastly, pick a recipe that is actually achievable for your appliance and supplies. If you're using a recipe that calls for fresh meat, but all you have is frozen chicken breasts from the grocery store, then maybe look for a recipe that fits your ingredients better. You don't want to be overzealous with your canning either, especially if you have an older pressure canner. You certainly don't want to overwhelm the machine and accidentally send it into an early retirement because you wanted 300 jars of fresh peas. It also helps to know how many jars and lids you'll need so there won't be any potential extra waste.

Preparing the Food

Before you even touch the pressure canner, your first job is to make sure that the food is ready to be canned. Different food requires different preparation, so make sure to thoroughly research your meal before you start. Have a clean preparation area, as cross contamination can lead to bacteria growth. This is especially vital if you plan on canning more than one type of meat. It is important to know the pH levels of what you are canning as well. You could pressure can acidic food with little to no problem, but it is unnecessary since a water bath canner is perfectly safe.

Most canning resources are going to recommend the freshest of ingredients. Do you have to follow this advice? Technically no, but the fresher the food the better the taste. It also has a longer shelf life than over-processed food does. Fresher food has more health benefits as well, so I have to highly recommend following this advice. Remember to carefully examine your vegetables before canning, as you don't want bruised or potentially rotting food. If you discover a brown spot or some kind of lesion, you don't have to throw away the whole piece, just cut off the bad part.

Prior to placing the food into jars, you should know whether you want to cold pack or hot pack. Cold pack is often referred to as raw pack and is the process of putting unheated food into the jars. The jars still need to be warm though, so whatever syrup, water, or juice you add should be boiled beforehand. Hot packing is the process of using freshly boiled food. Before adding hot packed food to the jars, let it simmer for a few minutes. The syrup, water, or juice added to the hot pack still needs to be boiled, as well.

Raw packing is mostly used for pressure canning, while hot packing is best for the water bath method. This is because hot packing is the superior way to get rid of any air within the food tissues by boiling it first. Food contains 10-30% more air before it is canned, but this air would cause discoloration quickly within the jars. Raw packing only lasts about two to three month in storage before they become discolored. This is unfortunate but also the only safe way to can non-acidic foods. Hot packing also shrinks the food which allows for more room in the jars.

It is suggested to start to can your prepared food as soon as possible. With unnecessary exposure to air comes the browning, bruising, and ultimate loss of flavor that we are looking to avoid. With fruits, you should always keep your cut up pieces in a water-diluted ascorbic acid bath. This will help to keep them fresh and acidic. Vegetables don't require this however, as they are not acidic, and are canned in pressure canners only. Non-acidic food such as meat and vegetables still need to be protected from oxygen and other enzymes, and therefore should be rushed for maximum freshness.

Jar Preparation

Despite its name, pressure canning isn't putting food into cans. This is probably because the word jarring isn't very aesthetic, with its negative connotations of being shocked or disturbed. The act of putting food into jars is relaxing and positive, so it needs a name that aligns with its values. Even though it's called canning, do not put aluminum cans in a pressure canner: It won't work and it's not safe. Some people have used steel cans, but it's a complicated process and there isn't that much reading material available for it. Pressure canning, especially for beginners, should only ever be done with jars

Remember that not all jars work in pressure canners. Since pressure canners reach higher temperatures than water bath canners, not all jars are compatible with both methods. The mason jar brand Ball is most widely approved for pressure canning use. Commercial jars, like for spaghetti sauce that you can find at the grocery, should not be used in a pressure canner: These are one use jars. The lids are usually one piece and aren't safe for a second use, while the glass isn't made to withstand the heat. They also don't come in the same sizes as mason jars and will not fit into the canner the same way.

Mason jars usually last around ten years. Anything more than that and you might face chipping issues. While antique jars may look pretty and are in good condition, it is not safe to use them in a pressure canner. Most jars that are from the 70's or earlier aren't made out of tempered glass and can't survive the temperatures inside of a pressure canner. If a jar cracks inside of the pressure canner, the product within it cannot be used, and so investing in new jars is always the better option. Mason jars are usually available in bulk for a reasonable price.

Always clean your jars before and after use. You don't want any dust or debris clinging to the sides of your jar ready to contaminate your food. Hot water and white vinegar is great for getting rid of any unwanted, filmy residue. You can also just run it through the dishwasher. Watch out for soapy jars because it will make your food taste like soap. After you have finished cleaning, the jars need to be sanitized: Which is not the same thing. The sanitizing step can be skipped if the food's pressure canning process takes more than 10 minutes. Sanitizing is just boiling the jars in water for 10 minutes. Make sure to remove the jars with tongs when they are done sanitizing so you don't accidentally burn yourself.

The jar lids should still be cleaned as well, but they don't need to be sanitized. Mason jar lids come in two parts: The screw band and the lid. The lid is made from metal and rubber and comes into direct contact with the food. That is why they need to be thrown out and replaced after one use. The metal screw bands are reusable and can be washed with warm water and dish soap. They do need to be completely dried however, as a wet screw band could affect the seal and allow bacteria to get in. Keeping them dry will also prevent rust.

Familiarize Yourself With Your Model

Pressure canners are not the type of thing to just jump into the deep end with. While modern canners are very safe, there is the very small chance of something unfortunate happening. That's why it is vital for you to familiarize yourself with your pressure canner before you start using it. If your canner is brand new, it will come with written directions: This will be your holy scripture. Read it, preach it, live by it. If your pressure canner is second hand and it doesn't come with directions, you can likely find instructions for it online as long as you know the brand and model.

Understanding your model's size capacity is often overlooked. The instructions should say how many jars will fit inside your canner. If for some reason it doesn't, don't make a guess and go with it. Look it up online by your pressure canner's brand and model.

Jars will usually be described in the sizes of quarts or pints. Only use these size jars as anything else hasn't been approved upon by your brand for that model. Never over stuff your pressure canner or it could result in broken glass. The only thing worse than hot steam going everywhere is hot steam *and* glass.

No matter what brand you choose, all models are different. As long as your pressure canner isn't from the 1950's, you should have a thoroughly enjoyable experience using your model. To ensure this, you need to know how all of its pieces work. Some models have gaskets, while some don't and close metal to metal. Brands have different moving pieces like, for instance, All-American are weighted gauge canners while Presto is available in dial gauge styles. These require different approaches and should not be treated as the same thing. Not every recipe is going to take this into account, and that is why reading your directions is so crucial. Know your model and how it works.

Knowing your model also requires you to know the utensils that come with it. Canning utensil kits usually come with more things than you'll know what to do with. Don't waste space in your kitchen, learn how to utilize all these tools. Whether it is a tong or a jar wrench, your canning experience will be so much easier. If your pressure canner didn't come with a kit because it's second hand or it just wasn't part of the deal, investing in one will be a smart idea. Kits save so much time and prevent possible accidents.

The most important part of knowing your pressure canner is knowing when the process is done. Recipes will tell you how long a specific food will take, but you will still have to wait until the depressuring is finished. With most models, the dial gauge will read zero and that's when you'll know the pot is safe to open. This isn't always the case, though, and that's why reading your owner's manual will help you avoid any mistakes. Some newer pressure canners have features that lock the lid until the pot is fully depressurized. It is possible that an older model pressure canner doesn't even have a gauge and you will have to time it yourself.

Test Run

The exact process for a test run is explained in Chapter 4, where we will go over how to actually use your pressure canner. These are just tips to pull off your test run as smoothly as possible. Now you may be thinking, "Do I even need a test run? How complicated can this even be?" Pressure canners aren't actually that complicated at all, but they can be if you don't know what you are doing. That's why a test run is the perfect place to find your footing and to become comfortable with your equipment before starting on larger, more complicated loads.

Before your test run, go through your chosen recipe again. Read it as many times as it takes to fully understand what it is telling you. Cooking times and the amount of pressure applied are not recommendations. They are the difference between safe and deadly. Hopefully the recipe you choose has been tested time and time again for optimal taste as well. The recipe will also give you tips on whether to hot pack or raw pack the food. Pay close attention to this because it affects the preparation for the water that goes in the pressure canner before you start cooking.

You should also start small for your test run. Adapt the recipe or choose a different one that requires a smaller amount of jars. Hot packing recipes don't use as much due to shrinkage, but they do take a little more prep time. If you start with a smaller amount of jars, it will be easier to focus on the pressure canning itself. If you have a large canner, don't worry about utilizing all the space. Fewer jars won't change the outcome and it will still be safe to eat. Don't make this a habit though as it is a waste of energy.

A test run should be done with an easy product to can. The food that I highly suggest starting off with is green beans. Green beans are very versatile when it comes to planning meals. They are the perfect side to nearly any entree. It is also one of the most simple vegetables to pressure can. You have the option to either hot pack or cold pack green beans. Since the minimum is only two quart jars at a time, you can hot pack them and not worry about a larger load. Corn and carrots are other great vegetables to start off with, however, you don't have to do your first test run with veggies. Meat and stock are not that much more complicated and are just as versatile.

Now that you've reread your recipe and know exactly what food and how much you're cooking, you are ready to start your test run. This may seem daunting, but it is highly unlikely anything will go wrong. The pressure canner is very safe as long as you are using it properly. Your main focus through your test run is paying attention. Pay attention to the gauge. Pay attention to the timer. Pay attention to your appliance as a whole. If anything does happen to go wrong, you will be way ahead of it as long as you've been paying attention.

Chapter 4:
How to Use a Pressure Canner

Preparing the Pressure Canner

After you've prepared everything else, it is time to prepare your canner. The first step is inspecting the pot. The pressure canner should never get dirty with food since it's in jars, but if it has just been taken out of storage it could be covered in dust. The pressure canner can be cleaned with hot, soapy water. Make sure to thoroughly rinse the soap off and then dry it. Don't forget to wash the lid and gasket, as well. After you check the canner for dust, make sure to check for any natural wear and tear. If you are uncertain about any corrosion, don't use it. It is better to be safe than sorry.

The canning rack will be the next thing to inspect. Even if you have just bought your pressure canner and canning rack, you should still give it a thorough cleaning as you don't know where it has been. The jar rack can be cleaned in the same way as the pot with hot and soapy water. If you are having trouble removing stains, using steel wool will work better than using a regular sponge. You will not want soapy steam, so make sure the rack is completely rinsed off. After it has dried, place it at the bottom of the pot.

You will then add water to the pressure canner. You do not want this water to have soap or any other strange particles in it: That is why everything is thoroughly rinsed out before it is used. In the water bath method, the pot is filled to cover all the jars, but a pressure canner uses less water. The goal of the pressure canner is to boil this water into hot steam. In most cases the water is two to three inches deep. Some pressure canners have different qualifications, though, so you should always double check the owner's manual.

Your jars should already be cleaned and if you prefer, sanitized. Follow your recipe and jar your ingredients in a timely manner to optimize freshness. Before putting on the lids, make sure there are no air bubbles that could possibly lead to food spoilage. You will want to wipe the rim of the jar after adding the food to make sure nothing can stop the jar from sealing. Place the lid flatly on the top of the jar and screw down the band. This should be tight enough that it will stay sealed, but not too tightly that it can't be opened again. When the jars have been securely tightened, place them gently at the bottom of the pot in the canning rack.

Before the canner can start pressurizing, you will need to close the lid. How this can be done will vary from brand to brand. If you have a Mirro or Presto brand, double check that your gasket is in good condition and ready to be used. If you are uncertain on how to close your lid, check the owner's manual. It is very important that the lid is fastened shut: The last thing you want is for the top to pop off in the middle of the canning process. Some models have mechanisms that close the lid until the canner is done depressurizing. If you have one of these models, make sure this feature is in working condition and has properly sealed the pot without any leaks.

Pressurizing

Congratulations, you have made it to the process of pressurization! Times vary when it comes to processing so it is important to pay attention to your recipe and follow it closely. Of particular consideration is your altitude. There are three steps to the pressurizing process which I refer to as vent, plug, and rattle. Before you begin, make sure you have whatever regulator your pressure canner uses nearby because you will need it. Also make sure you have some sort of timer so you don't accidentally over-process your canned goods. Remember to pay attention, too, as this is the most dangerous part to mess up at.

Finally after all the work of preparation, you can turn the pressure canner on. The heat needs to be turned on high. Give the canner a few minutes to warm up. Once it is hot enough, steam will start coming out of the vent pipe. You want this steam to be coming out in a steady stream. This is the start of the pressurizing process. Get a timer and set it to ten minutes because that is how long you should let the pressure canner vent. It is possible for steam to be present around the lid lock, which will pop up around when the pressure canner is done venting.

Next, you will place your regulator on top of the steam spout. If you have a weighted gauge regulator, make sure it is set at the right weight. The weight you should use will usually be specified in your recipe. Keep in mind, different altitudes have different requirements for the amount of weight you should put on it. Oftentimes, it is anywhere between 10 to 15 pounds of pressure. If you don't have a weighted gauge model just pay attention to your dial gauge. Be careful when you place the regulator on the steam spout as it can be very hot: Oven mitts will keep you safe from the heat.

The next step is more waiting: Eventually the regulator will start to rattle. It shouldn't take that much time for this to occur, though. Take out the timer again and set it to the recipe specified canning time. Once more, you should adjust the time to your altitude provisions, since that can affect processing times. Depending on your type of pressure canner, you may have to wait until the regulator starts to rock and then adjust the heat to achieve the stable rattling noise. If you have a dial-gauge canner, wait until the gauge reads 11 pounds to start timing.

If for any reason your pressure goes below the recommended amount, you need to bring the pressure back up and start the timer over again. This loss of pressure will result in unprocessed food. If you find the pressure going above the recommended amount, your jars may lose liquid. This will result in less full jars and possibly discoloration. **It is imperative that you do not open the pressure canner at any point in the pressurizing process.** The pot is full of boiling hot steam that can burn you or anyone else nearby. If this does happen, seek medical attention immediately.

Depressurizing

Don't open the lid just yet: Your pressure canner is still full of hot steam that has the potential to cause a serious burn. You have just completed the pressurization process, but that doesn't mean you are done just yet. The pressure canner needs time to cool down. This is the process of depressurizing where the steam is released in a safe way. Depressuring doesn't require as much care and attention as the process of pressurizing, but it is still very easy to get hurt. Have your oven mitt ready because the regulator and other parts of the pressure canner may still be hot.

The first step to depressurizing is to turn off the heat. From here the pot will slowly start to cool down. It is important that you don't try to rush this process in any way. If you try to force the pot to cool down, it could result in spoilage. Now, if you're wondering how one would even attempt this, there are two common ways people mess up the cooling process: One way is to use cool water on the canner. This has the capability to warp the shape of the pressure canner lid. The second way is opening the vent pipe before it is ready. This will mess with the sealing process and ruin the goods.

Depending on your model, there are different ways to know when the pressure canner is fully finished depressurizing. Some models have a safety valve that will drop down when the process is complete. Not all models are this convenient, though, and some have to rely on the dial gauge. The dial gauge will read zero pounds pressure after everything has cooled down. Dial gauges aren't always the most reliable, however, so proceed with caution. The time in which a pressure canner takes to cool down varies depending on how old the model is. Older models have thicker walls and take longer than the newer, thin-walled pressure canners. If your pressure canner doesn't have a dial gauge or a safety valve, you'll have to time it yourself. These are usually heavier models and take about 30 minutes to depressurize.

Now it is time to remove the pressure regulator. Even if the dial gauge is at zero, you should still use an oven mitt for this because steam will come out of the vent pipe. You should not remove the regulator if it is still rattling. If your dial gauge is at zero and it's still rattling, then you probably have a broken dial gauge. In that case, the jar's contents are not safe to eat and should be either reprocessed as soon as possible, or just thrown away. Don't open the lid as soon as the steam stops as this could still result in a possible accident. Wait 10 minutes from the time you removed the regulator for optimal safety.

The depressurizing process has finished and you can safely remove the lid from the pot. Since opening and closing the lid is different from model to model, consult your owner's manual if you are unsure on how to do this. After you unfasten the lid make sure to lift it in a way that protects yourself from any possible steam escaping the canister. You have succeeded so far and it would be a shame to end this positive experience with a burnt face. You also don't want to accidentally burn your hands so use your trusty oven mitt when handling the lid.

Removing the Contents

The last part of the canning process is removing the jars from the canner. Let's not get too ahead of ourselves yet though, because the pot is still very hot. The jars should be left in the pressure canner for at least ten minutes after the lid has been removed. This gives them enough time to cool slightly. The jars are still going to be way too hot to touch with your bare hand, but it will still be safe to remove them. Don't try to speed up the natural cooling time with cold water or you could accidentally break the jars.

When the ten minutes are up, use a jar lifter to remove the contents of the canner. Jar lifters or tongs come in canning kits and can be found online for a decent price. Do not use your hand. This should be done very carefully, so only lift one jar at a time; To the best of your ability try to avoid tilting the jar, as its seal is still fragile. The jars should be carefully placed on a kitchen towel or wire cooling rack, away from any cold draft. Placing the jars on a cold surface could lead to breakage. Leave about one inch of space in between the jars so they are not touching.

The jars should be left to cool for the next 12 to 24 hours. At no point before this time should the lids be tightened or touched. The sealing process is completely finished when the jars are entirely cooled. Once this time period has passed, test the seals by pressing on the lid. If it pops up or down something went wrong with the sealing. Just because the sealing failed doesn't mean the food has to be thrown out. You can refrigerate it but make sure it is consumed as soon as possible. Before you get ready to store the jars, take off the screw bands. They are no longer needed to keep the jar closed and you can reuse them for another time.

Date the lid of the jars with a permanent marker so you can know when they go bad. The lid will be discarded later, so you don't need to mark the jar's glass every time. It will also be helpful to label the jar with its ingredients just in case you forget later on. Most people store their canned goods in their basement but it doesn't matter where you put them as long as it is cool and dry. It is also important that it is out of direct sunlight as that can spoil the food faster. For optimal quality, canned goods should be used within one year. If the label on a canned good has disappeared, rubbed off, or is unreadable in any way, there is no safety risk but the contents might not taste as good.

After the jars have been removed from the pressure canner and it has cooled to a reasonable temperature, you can start washing it. Before and after use, the canner, lid, and gasket all need to be washed, rinsed, and dried. It is very important to completely dry these pieces to avoid mold and rust. The screw bands should also be washed before they are put in storage. Your owner's manual should have a complete guide to the safe storage of your pressure canner, but we'll go over it in Chapter 9 as well. Once clean up is finished, feel free to enjoy one of your delicious canned meals.

Common Errors and How to Fix Them

Even if you did everything perfectly according to the recipe, the owner's manual and the USDA guidelines, mistakes can still happen. Not everything is your control and that's okay because most errors can be fixed. Pressure canners have a lot of moving parts that need constant upkeep. If one thing goes under the radar, the whole process can be messed up. Not everything can be checked before you start pressure canning and by the time you realize something is wrong, it can be too late to save the food. This is unfortunate, but it is also not always the outcome.

One of the worst things that can happen is an inaccurate dial gauge. If you realize that your dial gauge is off by a couple pounds then it's time to get a replacement. Don't trust food that was canned with an inaccurate dial gauge. If it's over-processed it is going to be inedible, but if it's under-processed it could be contaminated with dangerous bacteria. Dial gauges should be checked for accuracy at least once a year. This can be done by going to your local county extension service. If it is off by under two pounds, it can still be used just make sure to consciously adjust it.

Another side effect of the natural wear and tear of moving parts is having a stuck lid. Even after everything has cooled and your pressure canner is safe to open, it won't open. This is a rubber gasket problem: When gaskets get old they start to harden making the lid more difficult to open. Lubricant can be a temporary fix, but it is time to get a new gasket. They are available online for a reasonable price. If you really need to use your pressure canner and can't wait until the replacement comes in, you can rub the gasket with olive oil and it shouldn't stick anymore. To get the lid unstuck, tap it gently with a hammer and repeat every few minutes until it comes off.

Sometimes when removing the jars you might notice some air bubbles floating to the top. This doesn't mean your food hasn't been processed correctly or that something went wrong with sealing. It is actually quite common and there is no reason to be upset. Air bubbles are normal to see up to after two hours post pressure canning. You should only start to worry when it's been a couple days and there are still air bubbles. At that point, the food is probably fermenting and should be thrown out. It is likely that something did go wrong with the sealing process so you might want to check the jar for cracks.

Another common problem people find when they remove the jars from the canner, is a loss of liquid. You filled up the jars to the recommended spot, and yet now they look less full. Once again this is a normal occurrence and is called siphoning. There's no reason to be alarmed unless the jar is less than half full of liquid. If this is the problem then something did go wrong and the jar is probably not sealed. Always check the lid after the jars have cooled even if the jars are more than half full. If the jar hasn't sealed, make sure to refrigerate the contents.

Chapter 5:
What Can Can and What Can't Can

When to Use a Pressure Canner

As previously discussed there are two methods to canning. The water bath method uses boiling water to heat and seal in the food while the pressure canner uses steam. The water bath method can be used in any large enough pot while pressure canning can't be safely performed without an actual pressure canner. A pressure canner can heat to 240 degrees Fahrenheit. This is around 30 degrees higher than the capacities of a water bath canner that only reaches temperatures of 212 degrees Fahrenheit. These are the only two recommended ways to can food. Under no circumstance should a pressure cooker be used to can food as they are not big enough.

When it comes to the decision on whether to use a pressure canner or a water bath, it is not really up to you. It all depends on the acidic level of your food. Acidic cuisine doesn't require high temperatures and can kill off bacteria all on its own. Non-acidic food has to be processed in a pressure canner or it has the possibility of becoming contaminated with deadly bacteria. How can you tell if a food is acidic? Well you could guess, but that is not very safe. Good thing this chapter will provide a comprehensive list of what can can and what can't can in a pressure canner.

Water bath canners are primarily used for fruit and fruit products. Fruit is acidic and does not require a pressure canner for safe consumption. The same goes for other acidic food such as salsa, pickles, and relish. Vegetables, on the other hand, should not be eaten unless they are canned in a pressure canner. Meat and stews should also only be processed with a pressure canner. Not all fruit is ready for a water bath straight from harvest. For instance, figs are considered to be low-acid fruits but as long as you add a little bit of lemon juice to your concoction, a water bath canner will be fine.

The age-old question is finally answered when it comes to deciding on a canning method. Is a tomato a fruit a vegetable? Technically, scientists have already decided that it is fruit. Seeing as the tomato can safely be processed in a water bath canner, the canning community must concur. Since they are so multifaceted when it comes to meal planning, tomatoes are a popular choice for many canners. They are very acidic to start off with but oftentimes, for extra safety, lemon juice is added to the jars to make them process better in the water bath.

You don't need to pressure can fruit but there isn't really danger to it. The worst case scenario is that the fruit doesn't taste as good as it could have. There is a serious danger to water bath canning vegetables or meat though. There is a way to change the acid levels in vegetables if you really want to use a water bath canner. Pickling the veggies is a common way canners bypass this rule. This can be done by fermenting them in a bath of vinegar. It is not recommended to pickle meat as an attempt to water bath can it.

Vegetable Do's and Don'ts

Many vegetables come out of a pressure canner delicious and ready to eat. This will not always happen though. It is important to listen to your recipe because different vegetables need to be prepared in different ways. There are several things to account for before you start canning. Vegetables are non-acidic and you will have to use a pressure canner with them if they are not pickled. That doesn't mean starch levels and amount of nutrients is the same across the board. Flavor, health, and even the shape or form of the vegetable should be considered before you pick a recipe.

There are some vegetables that are favorites to can among canners and they are green beans, carrots, and corn. They make for the best side dishes and are very versatile when it comes to choosing a recipe. They are also very cheap and easy to experiment with when you are first starting your canning journey. Carrots are some of the healthiest vegetables packed full with important dietary vitamins. If you are interested in the health benefits of carrots make sure to find a recipe that doesn't add unnecessary starch. Corn, in addition to some other favorite veggies like potatoes and peas, are very starchy. This means they are healthy in moderation only. Potatoes are usually hot packed to limit the amount of starch seeping into the jar during processing.

Spinach has been found to be one of, if not, the healthiest vegetable. Not only are they full of vitamins, but they are also enriched with antioxidants that fight off cancer and other chronic diseases. Beets are another wonderful choice, but they have a flavor that works better for a more mature pallet. Peppers make a great addition to any salad and sauce. Asparagus is another powerhouse of health and provides a delicious flavor for fewer calories. There are many, many other vegetables that work wonders in a pressure canner but that doesn't mean all do.

All vegetables can be safely processed in a pressure canner but that doesn't mean they are going to taste good. Any and all pressure canned vegetables will not pose any risk to your health as long as the process is done correctly. Most problems arise from the vegetables that are naturally soft. Squash is not a good choice for a pressure canner despite their healthy nature. They can be pickled but a pressure canner's high heat will not work well with the squash's texture that will become edible mush. More vegetables that are subject to mush are cauliflower, broccoli, eggplant, artichoke, and olives. These will do better being pickled and then being processed with the lower heat of a water bath canner. The only time cabbage should be canned using any method is as sauerkraut in a water bath canner. Lettuce should only be eaten fresh as any attempt to preserve the veggie will result in sub-par flavor.

Meat Do's and Don'ts

Meat Do's and Don'ts are pretty simple. You can can anything that isn't rotten meat. All meats are not created equal however, and will require different processing times and PSI. Always double check the recipes because one little mess up can cause contamination. Botulism is more common in vegetables, but that doesn't make meat immune so it is important to only ever use a pressure canner. Meat can not be pickled to use in a water bath canner like veggies can. According to the USDA, there is no safe way to raise the acidic level of any kind of meat.

Does it matter if the meat isn't fresh? Well, it won't change whether or not the meat can be canned in a pressure canner. Frozen meat can still be canned as long as it is still good to eat. Most recipes are going to call for farm fresh meat, though. This is because it will taste better. Food that is frozen loses its flavor quickly. If you don't have the stomach to supply fresh meat yourself, don't worry. Local butchers shops are always the best bet for fresh beef and poultry. Most supermarkets have a deli counter as well. If you live by a body of water, you could find a nearby fishmonger.

If you enjoy hunting, canning is a great way to keep your big game safe to eat for longer. A large buck can easily last you a year if it is canned properly. You should always find a recipe that matches whatever you bring home. A recipe for venison will not work for rabbit meat. Hunting and canning have often come hand and hand so many animals that you can legally hunt have a readily available recipe. As long as you have a license to hunt it, then there's no limit to what you can't can. However, good luck finding enough shelf space for a full-sized black bear.

If you have a vegetarian or vegan lifestyle, you might be wondering what meat alternatives can be canned. This is all dependent on what the meat alternatives are made from. While many alternatives are advertised as plant-based, they can also include ingredients that won't work in any method. The brand Beyond Meat has most of their available food marketed as plant-based, but this isn't just vegetables and includes grains. Grains cannot be processed in a canner and shouldn't be used as an ingredient for a canning recipe. Anything that includes soy, will also not work. Which means tofu and Impossible burgers can't be canned either.

Other Foods You Can Can

Pressure canning isn't just for meats and vegetables. It is for canning anything that is non-acidic and can't fight off the *Botulinum* bacteria itself. The only other group of food that really falls into this category is soups and stocks. Most soups are made with meat or vegetable products anyway, and so they have much of the same principles when it comes to canning. Make sure to follow a tested and trusted recipe since soups often have a mixture of ingredients. Meat and vegetables don't usually have the same processing times or PSI, but when they are together in soup they have to. Don't be your own guinea pig, let someone else find the middle ground for this.

Some things, as we will go over in the next section, should never be canned in a pressure canner. Do not use these in your soups or stocks. These ingredients can always be added in later when you are ready to eat the food. Not only is it potentially dangerous, but it's also just going to ruin the flavor. This means some of your favorite soups such as cream of mushroom and chicken noodle can not be canned. Noodles and anything that works to thicken the soup should be added later. Rice is another popular soup ingredient that can't be put in a pressure canner either.

Stock and broth are better and healthier when they are homemade rather than store bought. If you want to lower your sodium intake, homemaking and canning your own is a great way to do this. Broth that is made with meat will likely have higher amounts of fat. Before canning this type of broth, you are going to want to strain as much of this fat out as possible. If this is not done, the fat from the meat could float to the top of the jar and discolor the contents after the broth is canned. It could also turn the food rancid if it goes bad.

Mushrooms are another non-acidic food that can be pressure canned. While mushrooms are often seen as vegetables and are technically classified as such, I placed them in this category because they are not plants. However, they are the best food to have at a party. You know, because they are FUNGI. Get it? Anyway mushrooms are great to can due to their numerous health benefits. Just remember to be careful washing them as it may ruin the flavor and reduce its nutritional value. They also work really well in soups or stocks if you want to enhance the taste.

What Never to Can

Even though it is recommended to water bath can fruits, you can still use a pressure canner on them. The following foods can absolutely, under no circumstance, go through this method. Not only is it dangerous, but it will just result in the worst possible flavor outcomes. The first food, despite being non-acidic, is boiled eggs. Most people choose to preserve their eggs by pickling them, but unlike vegetables this doesn't make them ready for a water bath canner. In any method, the eggs are going to be overcooked and turned into a rubbery mess. Eggs can be used in a canner as an ingredient like, for instance, if you are canning lemon curd.

Milk, however, should never be used as an ingredient in something being canned. Milk is non-acidic which means it is the perfect place for the botulism bacteria. Even if it is processed in a pressure canner, the fat in milk preserves the *Botulinum* spores that will later turn into the toxin that has been known to kill. This is why dairy should never be canned in general. Anything else that comes from a cow that isn't meat, like butter, cheese, and cream should never see the inside of a canner. Dairy needs a great deal of heat to process and even if this temperature is reached, the food becomes inedible. Yogurt, sour cream, and even soy are off the table.

Grains don't make for very good canned goods either. There is little to no oil in grains, making them very dry. For other food, this is good because you don't want the oil to seep out after canning and ruin the product. It doesn't work the same for grains, though. Pressure canners will dry grains out further and destroy their nutritional value. It will also just ruin the flavor. Grains don't hold heat like other non-acidic foods, so their interior will not reach temperatures high enough to kill bacteria. This means you can not safely can any food that has rice, oats, bread, barley, crackers, dough, biscuits, or wheat.

Other foods that should be avoided are sweets with a lot of fat such as caramel and marshmallows. Like grain, they won't heat up properly, which allows for bacteria. Cornstarch and flour break down acid which is important for killing *Botulinum* spores. Pasta and noodles are made from flour and will just turn to mush. Nuts are too oily and this works against them as a protective layer to *Botulinum* spores. Lard has too much fat and it holds up well if it is frozen anyways. If you have canned any of these in the past and haven't gotten sick, you got lucky. Just because the potential is there doesn't always mean you'll get poisoned. Try to avoid these mistakes in the future because eventually you will lose at botulism roulette.

Chapter 6:
Pressure Canning Vegetables

Harvesting

Hardcore canners have their own garden where they can get the freshest of ingredients. This isn't mandatory for most recipes, but they will recommend it. There's no denying that fresher vegetables are better, if not just for the taste alone. They last longer, have more nutrients, and if you garden them yourself, you know what pesticides were used. Most grocery stores do offer an assortment of fresh vegetables, but keep in mind you don't always know if they are ethically sourced. You should always check them for bruises and brown spots before you make a purchase. Avoid the frozen isle, as there isn't much nutritional value there.

If you've decided that gardening is the best option for you, you will need to master the art of harvesting. Just because something looks ready, doesn't mean it always is. Every vegetable has its own peak for maturity. This will be the most opportune time to harvest. Picking before this could mean a less than favorable flavor. Picking after this peak could mean working with rotten food. When a vegetable has reached its largest stage that doesn't mean it is necessarily ripe. Other vegetables can be harvested before they are ripe. That's why you need to thoroughly research your veggies before you plant them.

If you are planning on pressure canning your vegetables, don't bother planting broccoli, cabbage, or cauliflower. They will lose their shape and become inedible mush. I suggest starting with carrots, peppers, and spinach. All of these have wonderful health benefits and are adaptable to most meals. Carrots are ready to be harvested when they are one inch in diameter. Spinach leaves are ready when they are at a length of four to six inches. Don't cut the crown if you wish to get several harvests out of the plant. Peppers come in different colors so you know what type you have for harvest. Bell peppers will be green and the usable hot peppers may be red or yellow when they ripen.

It is very important to keep your garden healthy. You can do this by avoiding bruising or damaging your produce while it's still on the vine. Stems and vines are fragile, so stepping on or injuring them, especially while they are wet, opens them up to potential diseases. This is why you should only harvest when it is dry out. If vegetables aren't being easily removed from their vine, use a clean knife instead of tugging at it as this could result in damage. Vegetables will still continue to grow way past their harvest date so make sure to keep up or they can quickly become overgrown.

Storing Vegetables

Most recipes are going to call for the freshest of produce and you should always try to can your vegetables as soon as possible. The farther you get from their harvesting date, the less nutrition and flavor you'll have. Sometimes, though, life doesn't go according to plan and you are going to need to store your vegetables. Fresher vegetables harvested from a home garden do better during storing than store bought vegetables. Not everybody has time or the space for a garden, though, so if you plan on storing store bought vegetables make sure they are damage free with little to no bruising.

There are several reasons as to why you might need to store vegetables before canning them. Just because something is in season, doesn't mean you have the time. If you have to wait a couple days after procuring your vegetables to can them, a refrigerator should be fine, but sometimes it might be weeks. Weather doesn't always permit either. Root vegetables like potatoes and carrots can be kept in the ground for longer, if need be. However, in wet and cold seasons they need to be quickly harvested. Another reason could be a recipe calls for mixed vegetables, but their harvest dates don't match up. You might need to store some spinach while you wait for your peppers to ripen.

There are a couple methods to storing vegetables safely. You can use your basement as long as it is cool and well ventilated. If you want to avoid the produce drying out, try placing them in moist sand. If you have room in your backyard, you can make an outdoor pit. Simply dig a hole and place an upright garbage can or wooden barrel in it. Make sure the top is four inches above the dirt. You'll want to dig a small moat around the perimeter to keep water out. Next, cover it in a foot of straw, grass clippings, or sawdust. The last step is placing a plastic cover over it. This should keep them cool and ripe for a couple of weeks.

Keep an eye on your stored produce. Just because these methods have worked for some people, doesn't mean something can't go wrong. Watch out for rot and remove any vegetables that show signs of going bad. A rotting vegetable can contaminate any vegetable nearby, so if you don't want to ruin the rest of your produce check them frequently. Clean the storage area thoroughly to avoid any unwanted contamination. If a vegetable looks shriveling, it's time to use it before it goes bad. Once a vegetable is taken out of storage it should be used right away.

Vegetables: Raw Pack vs. Hot Pack

Should vegetables be hot packed or raw packed? Oftentimes you won't have to make this decision yourself. Whatever recipe you choose, it is likely that it will say what is required of the specific meal you are planning. It is smarter to trust a well tested recipe than to make the decision on your own. However, in the case that the recipe doesn't specify what method to use, do not fret. There are ways to figure out what will work best for you. To make this decision you have to understand what each process is used for and what it does in relation to vegetables.

Hot packing is often used for water bath canning. It helps reduce the amount of oxygen and shrinks the food so you can get more contents into the jar. Hot pack canned goods keep their color and fresh flavor longer than their raw pack counterparts. This is because the food is boiled and then is left to simmer for a few minutes before it is placed in the jars for canning. The boiling is what removes the air and results in high quality food. It's important to make sure the jars aren't cooled before going into the canner or it runs the risk of coming out under-processed.

Raw packing is the process of canning the food without cooking it in any way first. Hot liquid is added over the contents before the jars are sealed. The food should be packed tight because it will start to shrink during the pressure canning process. There are four vegetables that are the exception to this rule and they are corn, potatoes, Lima beans, and peas. These veggies will expand and will need the extra room. Placing raw pack jars into a hot canning pot can break the glass so be wary of the temperature of the water inside your pressure canner.

Comparing the end result between the two methods, hot packing seems to be the more quality choice in relation to shelf life. Due to the fact that most vegetables shrink during the process, there ends up being empty space at the top of the jar where the air escapes to. This addition of air will lead to discoloration usually within three months. Hot packing however, is more work. This may seem worth it for better quality, but pre-boiling the vegetables is going to change the taste and texture anyways. Raw packing is usually recommended for specific food that is susceptible to losing its shape if it is hot packed.

Most vegetable canning recipes are going to recommend raw packing instead of hot packing. The USDA guidelines specifically state that raw packing is more suitable for vegetables. Does this mean you should only raw pack vegetables? No, there are a few deviations from this guideline. Potatoes should always be hot packed due to their starchy nature. If the starch isn't boiled out, it could leak from the potatoes and gelatinize the contents of the jar. Some canners also just prefer hot packing since the food becomes more pliable and is easier to fit in jars. This may be a better option for people with less jars to fill and don't want to waste anything.

Plain Vegetables

Plain vegetables must be pressure canned to avoid potential foodborne illness. If you want to make them safe for a water bath canner, you will need to pickle them by fermenting them in vinegar. This will not only change the acidic level, but also the taste. Before you place the vegetables in jars for pressure canning you should wash them, especially if they are garden fresh. Vegetables should be only rinsed off: If they are soaked in water, they will lose nutrition. When you are preparing the vegetables, be very gentle. Produce is fragile and you don't want to cause any bruising.

Carrots should be rinsed and peeled and rinsed again in preparation of the canning process. If you are canning baby carrots, they can be done whole but regular carrots should be sliced or diced. To hot pack carrots, boil them for five minutes before placing them in jars and pouring boiling water over them. To cold pack them just skip the part about pre-boiling them. Your recipe will tell you how long they should be processed and how pressure should be applied.

Corn can not be canned on the cob because it won't fit in the jar. You'll need to husk it, remove the excessive silk, and wash it before boiling it for three minutes. The corn can't be removed from the cob if it isn't boiled first. You can simply cut the kernels off but don't scrap them or you could ruin their form. You also have your choice of hot packing or cold packing them

If you want to can hot peppers, use gloves. You can wash your hands afterwards, but you really don't want to touch your face at any point during the preparation. They'll need to be washed as well. Since peppers come in all sizes, the little ones can be kept whole. You are going to want to slice up the bigger ones though. Remove their seeds and the core. Peppers should only be hot packed due to their thicker skin.

Potatoes should be washed, peeled, and then washed again. Potatoes can be left whole if they are very small but otherwise they should be cut up. Potatoes are very starchy which means, just like peppers, they should only be hot packed. You can get rid of this excess starch by boiling them for a couple of minutes depending on the size of your slices.

When you are jarring your vegetables, no matter what type they may be, only use the recipe recommended sizes. You can use smaller ones, but they might over cook. Just make sure to still follow the processing time listed. Larger jars are where the real safety issues come. Some vegetables will shrink during the canning process because of water loss, so keep that in mind when you pack them into the jars. In contrast to this, some will grow so make sure to know what you are working with and how they will react.

Mixed Vegetables

What's better than pressure canning one veggie at a time? Pressure canning mixed vegetables. This can and has been safely done for as long as the pressure canner has been around. The most common combinations are carrots, peas, green beans, corn, tomatoes, and summer squash, but as long as you can can it, feel free to be creative. While tomatoes are considered a fruit, they pair better with veggies. If you plan on doing so you'll have to use a pressure canner. The acidic nature of tomatoes is not going to make corn any more safe in a water bath canner.

Make sure to pick the right recipe when it comes to mixing vegetables. The more complicated a process is, the more important it is to find a well trusted source to get your recipe from. If you are using a recipe and plan on making any sort of substitution, be careful that it won't drastically change the outcomes. For instance, if you're mixing carrots and potatoes, but the recipe calls for carrots and green beans to be cold packed, then you're gonna need to change that too.

Pressure canning mixed vegetables is going to take a longer preparation time. Make sure you know what to do for each vegetable. Pay attention to your recipe as it will help you navigate and prevent possible confusion from this. Some of the same rules may apply, like rinsing instead of soaking, and what size pieces to cut them into. Depending on your choice of vegetable, you might have the decision on whether to cold or hot pack them. This might be done together or separately. If you are combining potatoes or peppers with non-starching food, you'll still need to hot pack it.

The PSI and processing times are going to change, too. Different vegetables are going to require longer times that can overcook other vegetables. The tested recipe is going to try its best to avoid this, but it still can be a possible side effect of canning mixed vegetables. Make sure your recipe is specific to your type of canner and altitude as well. You don't want to put all this work in for nothing.

Chapter 7:
Pressure Canning Stock

What Is Stock?

Surprisingly, there's been much debate on the difference between stock, soup, and broth. The average Joe probably thinks they are all the same. Are they right? The answer is actually still up in the air. Most chefs tend to agree that soup could be either broth or stock as long as they are served as a dish with added ingredients such as vegetables, meats, and grains. Another term that gets thrown around with this topic of conversation is bouillon. Is this another predecessor to soup like the other terms? Yes, it is because bouillon is just another word for broth.

So, what's the difference between stock and broth? In the eyes of a classically trained chef, stock is made from bones and vegetables like onions, carrots, or celery. It can be made from any animal, but most come from the bones of chicken or cows. It has seasoning and its flavor comes from roasting the bones. Stock's most defining feature is its very thick texture. In cooler temperatures, this thickness becomes gelatinous. This is because of the collagen in the connective tissue of the bones. Stock isn't usually eaten as is and works as a base to start off soups and sauces.

Broth is the byproduct of actual meat. It is liquid that meat has been cooked in and uses the same vegetables as stock. It also doesn't matter what meat is being used in the liquid. Chicken is the most common type of broth, but beef is a close second. As for what part, once again, the answer is any. Some people make it with a whole chicken carcass. Whereas stock has a viscous texture, broth is more watery. It is also made with seasoning and can be served just as it is. Broth can be a base and be actual soup.

The main difference between the two is that broths are made with meat, and stocks are made with bones. Here is where it gets confusing, though. The term bone broth is just another name for stock and isn't considered a broth by professional chefs. If broth or stock is prepared vegetarian style, they are the same thing because veggies don't have bones or meat. When it comes to canning these foods, none of this information makes a difference. Stock, broth, or soup are considered non-acidic and should always be canned using a pressure canner.

The Basics of Stock Safety

You don't have to butcher your own chickens to make homemade broth or stock, but you can. The healthiest and best flavored broths come from free range chickens. Most chickens are slaughtered at 47-days old. Make sure you fully pluck and clean the chicken before using it's carcass. Chickens tend to be clean animals, but that doesn't mean they don't get sick. If it's going to be butchered, the animal needs to be in perfect health. It's also important to prepare the meat in a timely manner. Don't wait for the chicken to rot before you start cleaning it up.

Sometimes killing a chicken just isn't for you or maybe you just don't have the space to raise them. It takes a lot of work that may seem unnecessary when you can get fresh meat from your local butcher. This is the easier alternative if you prefer beef stock anyways. Frozen meat can be used to make broth and stock but it's not going to taste as good so make sure to use fresher meat. You should also know what farm your meat is coming from and how they raise their livestock. As stated above, free range chickens are often the preference.

Since stocks and broth can be made from just about any type of meat, going to the butcher or raising your own chickens are not the only options. Stock can be made from any leftover meat you have around the house. You can use the remains of a half eaten rotisserie chicken, steak bones, shells from any type of seafood, or even the last piece of fried chicken from a combo meal. Will these make top quality broths? Probably not, but you can try it. As long as the meat hasn't been sitting out and has started to spoil, you can use whatever meat product you want.

Stocks and broths have a lot of fat in them. To reduce this you can chill the broth for 12 or more hours. In this time, the fat will float to the top and all you have to do is skim what you don't want off. You can always keep the fat and use it for cooking or additional flavors. Leaving the fat in might raise your cholesterol, but won't cause any problems as long as you eat the broth within the first six months after it is canned. If you're worried that the fat might grease up the lid and ruin the seal, rub vinegar around the rim.

The Benefits of Canning Stock

Despite what gourmet chefs say, you can pretty much do whatever you want when it comes to making stock. Throw some meat, veggies, and seasoning into some water and let it simmer. If you are a vegetarian, you don't even have to use meat. It is completely up to you on what type of stock you want. This means you can control the flavor, the nutrition, and the amount made. It is pretty easy to make too much stock and that is where the blessing that is canning comes in. Stock is made from non-acidic foods and has to be canned in a pressure canner.

Since broth and stocks are pretty easy to make and work well as a staple to most diets, many people can them by the gallon. This is no problem as long as you have the room and your canner has the capacity to do so. It might take a lot of time, but at least you'll have a year's supply. Then you'll only ever have to make it once a year, so in a way it saves you time and money spent on ingredients. Store bought bone broth can get a little expensive, so having it readily available without the worry of spoilage is also another financial benefit.

Perhaps, most famously, bone broth has a lot of health benefits. The gelatin protein found in bone broths works to help regulate the digestive system. Bone broth may help with certain gut issues, too, such as IBS, but not much research has been done on the subject. The intestines can directly affect the immune system, and so consuming bone broth can possibly protect you against certain food borne illnesses. Drinking bone broth will not shield you from botulism though, so don't try to can it in a water bath canner. In one research trial with mice, bone broth helped to increase microbial diversity.

Another health benefit of stock is its collagen properties. Collagen is often used as a supplement in skin care routines to look younger and more refreshed. Consuming a large amount of bone broth has shown to increase levels of the amino acids that create collagen. This has led to claims that stock can have anti-aging effects. Another benefit of collagen is its improvement of pain and stiffness of joints in patients with osteoarthritis. The gelatin found in collagen has even been found to prevent exercise injuries.

Chicken Broth vs. Beef Broth

Bone broth has recently gained popularity in the health-conscious community. It has even replaced coffee as a morning supplement in some households. With all the new research coming forward about it's miraculous properties, it makes one wonder which broth is better, chicken or beef? As far as flavor is concerned, that is up to you. When it comes to meat, chicken and beef have always been at odds. They are both commonly found in American meals and have proven themselves versatile. No matter which broth you prefer, you will still reap the health benefits.

Starting with chicken, it is the easier option to make due to it being the number one consumed meat in the U.S. and Canada. Chicken bones are more readily available than cow bones. They are less dense, so it doesn't take as long to cook chicken broth up. Chicken bones are what are linked to the joint relief properties recorded in patients with osteoarthritis. It also produces amino acids that make collagen and repairs skin damage. Despite the limited research into its reproduction of collagen available, chicken broth has several celebrity endorsements. Chicken broth has more protein, but it also has more cholesterol.

Beef has a longer cooking time due to the density of cow bones. Since they aren't as available as chicken bones, they are more expensive. The health benefit most related to beef broth is regulating intestines and promoting gut health. Beef has more amino acids that produce glycine. Glycine is good for your gut because it fights inflammation. Glycine also helps you sleep and relax, which is shown to boost your mood by increasing serotonin. Beef's flavor is often considered to be more bold than chicken flavor. Some people find this more satisfying.

In the end, it might just come down to what you're in the mood for. Sometimes chicken sounds better than beef and other times it's the opposite. As far as benefits go, chicken has beef beat. It has more protein, hydrating electrolytes and muscle building amino acids. However, if you have high cholesterol, you are going to want to go with beef. You should also go with beef if you want to fight seasonal depression with a warm mug of bone broth. Older people might prefer to look younger with chicken broth's age-defying magic. I find that with all these potential benefits, the best solution is to drink both.

Tips for Canning Broth

Here is a tip that might be controversial to some world renowned chefs. The difference between broth and stock doesn't matter. It shouldn't limit how you choose to prepare this dish. Add meat to your bone broth, add bones to your meat broth. Don't have any meat products at all and just use vegetables. They are both nutritious and there's no reason why you can't have seasoning and a thick texture. It's safe and makes the stock taste better. It feels almost pretentious to pretend that they are different. Do whatever works for your pallet.

While fat isn't the worst thing to eat, it is one of the worst things to can. Your broth will go bad within six months, but it could also go bad right away. The grease in fat can ruin a seal and then the stock that was supposed to last a year won't even last a week. A little bit of fat is going to be inevitable, but it shouldn't affect the final product. If you want to avoid your broth going rancid, removing the fat with the previously mentioned method is your best choice.

With any food that is going to be canned and stored for almost a year, fresher ingredients are better. You can buy bone broth from the store with the intention to can it, but homemade stock will usually taste better and have a longer shelf life. It also has more health benefits. If you do decide this is the best option for you, you are going to need to find a recipe for canning bone broth that most closely resembles the ingredients you used. Seafood stock is going to have a different processing time than vegetable stock.

It's very easy to can a lot of stock but you should only do this if you need a lot of stock. Canning by the gallons is going to take up a large amount of space. Space that can be used for carrot, potatoes and spinach. Your caning pantry should be diverse. One main point to canning is to be able to eat foods that are out of season and to add an assortment of nutritious foods that wouldn't be available otherwise. Stock is healthy but only eating stock will stunt your diet.

Chapter 8: Bonus Chapter - Pressure Canning Meat

The Basics of Meat Safety

Fresh meat makes the best meat. If you are not providing your own meat, make sure to only purchase from the meat counter at the grocery store or your local butcher shop. Purchasing from the frozen aisle will result in less flavor. At the store, it is best if you purchase the freshest food last. Make sure the product is cold because warm temperatures can cause rapid deterioration of the product. Pay attention to the sell-by-dates listed on the packaging. Meat that is within two days of it's sell-by-date should be canned right away.

Canning should be done as quickly as possible but this isn't always an attainable goal. If you plan on refrigerating the meat, do this as soon as you return home. If meat is exposed to room temperature for more than 30 minutes, it can start to go bad. Only purchase from grocery stores nearby or keep the meat in an ice cooler during transportation. If you are freezing meat, make sure to protect it from freezer burn with a thicker layer of packaging. Keep in mind frozen meat loses its flavor and won't taste as good when canned.

When it is time for preparation, you can not defrost meat at room temperature or bacteria can grow. Place them in the refrigerator so it will stay cold as it defrosts. You can also defrost the meat by putting it in cold water. Make sure it is in an airtight bag though because you don't want to contaminate the meat with unwanted moisture. If you are short on time, a microwave can also work. However, the meat should be cooked directly after this to prevent any bacteria that can thrive off the warm parts of the meat.

If you are planning to can the meat with vegetables, do not share utensils between them. Clean anything that has touched the meat before it works with the vegetables. They should not be prepared within five feet of each other to avoid cross contamination. You will also need to wash your hands after touching the meat. Meat can only ever be safely canned in a pressure canner because it is non-acidic. A water bath canner will not be hot enough to kill the *Botulinum* spores.

Meat: Raw Pack vs. Hot Pack

Choosing whether to raw pack or hot pack meat is very similar to choosing a method for vegetables. For safety reasons, meat can only ever be canned in a pressure canner. A water bath canner does not get hot enough to kill off the potential bacteria of botulism and other dangerous contaminations. The raw pack method works best with most food used in a pressure canner and so it's likely that most recipes will suggest this. Just because this is what is recommended by the USDA doesn't mean this is the only option. Meat can be safely hot packed and choosing to do so will not lead to any serious repercussions.

The choice is up to you and that's why knowing the pros and cons of each method is paramount to your food enjoyment. Once again, hot packing anything will take more preparation. Instead of boiling the food like you do with vegetables or fruit, meat is precooked in some way. This is mostly just basic browning of the meat and since the pressure canner reaches a high level of heat, you don't need to cook it all the way through. After the meat is cooked and placed in the jars, boiled broth, drippings, water, or tomato juice are added on top.

Raw packing meat, just like raw packing vegetables, is a much simpler process. Cut up the meat however you want to and if desired add salt. Canned meat is usually cut into cubes, strips or regular chunks. Raw packing meat doesn't require liquid because liquid is naturally stored within raw meat and is cooked out during the hot pack process. Not all meat has enough liquid to cover all the contents in the jar and that is when discoloration happens. Since there is no liquid added with the raw packing method, leave two to three centimeters of space in between the top of the jar and the meat. This room is for the meat's liquid secretion and prevents the jars from becoming too full.

Whichever method you choose, the processing time is the same. This means that if you're short on time, a raw pack method might be the better option for you. However, if you have a finite amount of jars, once again hot packing will be better since the meat shrinks when it's cooked. Raw packed meat also ends up looking less full in comparison because of this. Hot packing also allows for the separation between meat and fat. Raw packs often have more fat at the top of their jars that can make the food go rancid.

One worry you might have about raw packing is whether the meat will be fully cooked. The answer is yes, you can eat the meat directly from the jar after processing. Unlike vegetables, raw packing is said to have a better taste and texture compared to hot packing. There is only one meat where the choice isn't yours and that is ground beef. Ground beef must be hot packed because its consistency is too clumpy and won't cook all the way. Make sure to shape the ground beef and cook it just enough that you won't have to worry about it congealing into a dense mass.

Meat Products

Meat products refers to any meat that does not fall under the category of seafood or poultry such as beef, venison, lamb or pork. Meat has high levels of fat and that needs to be removed before the canning process begins. If this fat isn't removed, the jar might not seal. If it hasn't been done already, bones will need to be removed. Wild meat will have a stronger flavor which means it should be soaked in brine for one hour. The ideal ratio of this brine will be one tablespoon of salt per quart of water

Meat can be cut into cubes, strips or chunks depending on whatever you prefer. These pieces should be no more than one inches wide to ensure even cooking throughout the meat. If you are canning wild game make sure you will have enough jars and lids. It is also important to have an assortment of canned goods so it is necessary to have room in your canning pantry for more than just this meat. Only can as many jars at a time as is recommended in your owner's manual.

Cold packed jars full of meat often lose water so to ensure it cooks and doesn't become discolored, hot packing is usually the best way to prepare meat products. The choice is up to you, though. If you want to hot pack, start by pre-cooking the meat. You can roast it, stew it or brown it until it is rare. Add salt and pack it into hot jars. You should leave a one inch headspace at the top. Before you close the jar, add in your choice of boiling liquid. The raw process is the same procedure, except you skip the precooking stage.

Whether you are using a weighted gauge or a pressure gauge canner, it will usually take 90 minutes to process if you have quart jars. Pints only take 75 minutes. The PSI will change depending on your altitude but anywhere under 1,000 feet is doing 11 PSI for a dial gauge and 10 for a weighted. Anywhere that is above 1,000 feet in a weighted gauge will raise to 15 PSI. Jar size does not affect PSI.

Poultry and Rabbit

Poultry is defined as the meat that is harvested from domestic fowls. This includes goose, chicken, duck, turkey and game bird. Rabbit meat can and should be canned the same way as poultry. For the best taste, you will want to procure the meat from a free range farm. Poultry should be chilled 6 to 12 hours before it is canned. Rabbit needs to be soaked in salt water for an hour before it is canned. The ratio of this salt water bath should be one tablespoon of salt per quart of water. You should also remove any excess fat to ensure the sealing process works correctly.

Because their bones are small, poultry and rabbit meat can be canned with or without bones. This will change the processing time for the two products. Cut the poultry or rabbit meat into small pieces that fit into whatever jar size you will be using. Poultry and rabbit have similar procedures to meat products when it comes to hot packing or cold packing. To avoid any liquid loss, hot packing is recommended but not mandatory.

To hot pack poultry or rabbit meat, you can boil or bake until they are about two-thirds done. Fill the jars, leaving a 1-1/4 inch headspace. If you want to enhance the flavor, you can add a teaspoon of salt. Add less if you are using pint jars. Lastly add hot broth and make sure to keep the 1-1/4 inch headspace. Cold pack is exactly the same without the precooking or the addition of broth.

If you have a dial-gauge pressure canner process the jars at 11 PSI at altitudes below 2,000 feet or at 12 PSI for altitudes of 2,001 to 4,000 feet. If you have a weighted gauge pressure canner, you should process jars at 10 PSI for altitudes below 1,000 ft. For altitudes above 1,000 feet, 15 PSI is ideal. Both raw pack and hot pack will take 75 minutes for pints and 90 minutes for quarts if you took out the bones. Processing times for poultry and rabbits that still have bones are 65 minutes for pints and 75 minutes for quarts.

Seafood

Unlike poultry or meat, seafood doesn't have one method to properly cook everything.

You will have to pay special attention to what your recipe says to do because everything is specialized. The processing time for seafood is also much longer than their counterparts. Where pints take about 75 minutes for meat, they take 110 minutes for some seafood. This is because seafood is at a higher risk for botulism than meat or poultry especially if it is shell bearing. Whether a fish is smoked or not will change the processing time.

Some sources approve of using the quart jar but most recipes favor the pint jar for canning seafood. Smoked fish should always be canned in pint jars only. A popular jar for seafood is the half pint jar, nicknamed the salmon jar. If you decide to can in a quart jar, venting times will need to be extended to 30 minutes. Smaller pressure canners such as the All-American 10.5 quart and 15.5 quart models are not permitted to safely can smoked fish. Smoked fish should not be thoroughly cooked before canning or you run the risk of drying it out.

If you are worried about discoloration, you can add lemon juice to the fish before canning them. This won't help preservation but it will keep the fish from turning dark. When preparing the fish, cut off the head, tail and fin. The bones will become soft and edible. You have the choice to remove or keep the skin on. If you want the jar to look more aesthetic, you can have the skin facing out but if you want an easier clean turn it in.

Fish can be frozen before they are canned like other meat but when it comes to defrosting them, it can only be done in a fridge. It is important to rinse the thawed fish off when it is done to get rid of any icicles. Another thing you should do is avoid reprocessing seafood. If a jar doesn't seal the first time around, the second time will just overcook it. At this point, there is no other option than to dispose of the jar's contents.

Chapter 9:
Caring for Your Pressure Canner

Basic Maintenance

Maintenance for your pressure canner can come in all forms. Whether it is cleaning, replacing parts, or even just double checking that everything is working, maintenance is a vital part of the canning process. Canning is often seasonal work done when the product is ready to harvest. This means that for a good amount of the year, the pressure canner is not being used. This time is just as important as the productive period when it comes to maintenance. Pressure canners can be expensive and that's why purchasing one should be an investment. If you don't keep it from getting ruined, then it won't last as long as it can.

A simple maintenance tip is cleaning before and after every use. This may be annoying to do every time, but it is better to be safe than sorry. Dirty pots are the perfect breeding ground for bacteria that you don't want anywhere near your food. It's not just the pot that you should clean, either. The lid and gasket will need a thorough rinse. Rubber is not as durable as metal and keeping it clean is one way to make it last as long as possible. Make sure to remove the canning rack from the pot and clean it separately so you don't miss any spots.

Every so often, you will need to spend money on replacements. The most common of these replacements is the biennial gasket replacement. Some gaskets can last five years but waiting two years in between changes is more often recommended. As previously stated, rubber is not a strong material and once it starts to crack, the chances of your pressure canner blowing a gasket rises. Since this is the most common replacement, gaskets are very cheap and easy to find. If you have an All-American brand pressure canner, you won't have to ever worry about getting new gaskets since they have a metal to metal seal feature.

Another thing that you should do to keep up with maintenance is annual dial gauge checks. If you over-process your jars due to an inaccurate dial gauge the taste is more than likely going to be sub-par. If you under-process your jars you could die. This may sound dramatic, but unfortunately it's true. While botulism is very rare, it is still a serious condition that should be avoided at all costs. Your local extension service can help with your annual check. If you have a weighted gauge then you won't have to worry about this potential problem.

Maintenance can be boring and repetitive, but canners that are well cared for can last up to several decades. There are many moving parts, which means there is a lot of work to be done to keep these machines safe. Make sure to thoroughly read your owner's manual to find any other things you should be regularly doing to care for your pressure canner. Maintenance also depends on your model so if you are not someone with a lot of time to do this, you can always buy a model that seals without a gasket and uses the weighted gauge feature. No matter what model you have, you should still always clean it frequently.

Part Replacement

It is important to know when to call it quits on your pressure canner parts. The signs are different depending on what needs to be replaced. If you are confused on whether or not something needs to be changed, your trusty owner's manual should give you an idea. If your model has any rubber, they are going to need to be replaced more often than any of the metal parts. The main indicator for rubber is a brittle texture, while metal should be replaced if it has completely rusted over. To avoid accidents, don't use pieces that exhibit these signs.

Once you know what you're replacing, you can usually find a new one online by looking up your brand and model. Presto pressure canners will often have a model number stamped on the side or on the bottom of the pot. This number will tell you exactly what type of part you will need to match your pressure canner. If you don't have a Presto, the owner's manual will have or say where you can find the model number. You don't want to just guess your model number because the wrong part could cause the canning process to go south.

Since gaskets are the most often replaced part, you should know how to do it. The first step is taking off the old gasket and cleaning the groove. This is an easy spot for residue to hide, so make sure to scrub at any leftover soap or potential rust. Before the new gasket is installed it needs to be washed with warm, soapy water. Rinse it and then let it soak for 10 minutes to increase it's pliability. It needs to be completely dried so it won't rust the groove. When installing the new gasket, work it in with one section of the groove at a time.

You should also replace the pressure plug every time you change the gasket since they are both made out of rubber. Much of the process of changing this out is the same as the gasket. You should remove the old piece and clean the air vent out thoroughly. Clean the new plug in the same way with soapy water and dry it to prevent rust. Different canners will require different ways to insert the new plug into the vent. Carefully read the instructions before you attempt to do so as to avoid accidentally ruining the new plug.

With all these required replacements, you might be wondering how much they cost. The price of a pressure canner can be upwards of 200 dollars and it might seem like a continuous drain on your wallet to keep it working. The only reason why the actual canners are that expensive is because they last a long time. Most replacement parts are very cheap and easy to find online. Whether it is a gasket, a pressure plug or dial gauge, you can find it for under 20 dollars on Amazon or from your brand's direct website.

Cleaning

All the parts of the pressure canner need to be cleaned. We've gone over cleaning the vent pipe and safety valve, but what about the actual lid? Unless you are using your pressure canner as a cooker, there shouldn't be any food sticking to the inside of the lid, but you still check to make sure it is perfectly clean. Your type of gauge will tell you if soaking the lid is a good idea or not. A dial-gauge can rust or corrode if it is ever immersed in water. Also avoid holding the dial-gauge upside down when your lid is being washed or it could end up collecting moisture and ruining the dial's capability to tell pressure.

Certain chemicals such as lye, scouring powder, or baking soda can stain aluminum pots and should never be used to clean your pressure canner. When your canner is in the cooling process let it come down to low temperature naturally. Adding cold water can warp the shape of your canner and make the lid no longer close correctly. This will make the pressure canner unsafe to use. Never leave any liquid or food in the pot for extended periods of time. If your pot is made from aluminum it will likely absorb any strange odors that will be difficult to get rid of.

Mineral deposits are an unfortunate occurrence, but they're not the end of the world. A dark line around the perimeter of the canner can be removed with a mixture of water and cream of tartar. This should be measured as one tablespoon of tartar for every quart of water. Fill the pot with this mixture so that it is covering the mineral deposit. Heat this on the stove until it boils the stain away. Add more cream of tartar if it doesn't work. Once it looks like it has cleared up, empty the canner and wash it with hot, soap water. The last step is to rinse and dry thoroughly

This process can be tedious after a while but there are ways to prevent mineral deposits from forming in the first place. Adding two tablespoons of white vinegar to the canner's water before you start pressurizing should do the trick. Sometimes the cream of tartar method for cleaning the pressure canner doesn't work and you have to do it several times to see results, so it's better to prevent this than fix it later. Preventative care initiatives like this one are an important way to make your pressure canner last longer and work more efficiently.

Caring for Utensils

Jars and their lids are probably the most essential utensil to the canning process. You can't can if you don't have a can to can the canned goods in. We've already gone over basic jar care in Chapter 3, but a reminder to clean and routinely check for cracks doesn't hurt. Also, remember to throw away the tops after one use, but you can reuse the jar and screw band. Jars aren't the only canning utensil that requires care and attention: Don't forget to consider the needs of other equipment, so that you won't have to keep spending money to replace items that can easily last you years.

Tongs are just as susceptible to rust as any other metal part of the canner. Always dry them off completely before putting them in storage. If they do start to rust, you can always use water and baking soda to break down these deposits. Scrub with a wire brush afterwards. If your tongs touch any food and it isn't properly washed off, they could grow mold. Soapy water and some light scrubbing after use will help to prevent this. Other metal equipment, such as a steel funnel should be subjected to this same care routine.

Some of your equipment might have rubber handles or other parts made from this material. As we have gone over multiple times, rubber is not as strong as metal. It needs a more gentle cleaning ritual. Don't use any brushes that are made from metal or they will rip it up. A regular, soft, yellow sponge will do just fine. Don't put the rubber near any high temperature heat sources or it could melt. Worn down rubber is an easy spot for bacteria to grow so make sure to either replace that part or if need be, the whole thing.

Canning is very messy at times and so you're going to need kitchen washcloths to wipe down jars and countertops where the food is prepared. You could use paper towels, but they're not very good for the environment. It is also financially beneficial to work with reusable supplies. Fabric can easily develop mold or spread bacteria so don't use dirty cloths. This goes for oven mitts as well. There's a lot of hot surfaces that you might have to touch so you'll definitely need one of these. Don't forget to wash it after you use it.

Storing

When the harvest season comes to an end, it's time to put your canning equipment away until next year. Pressure canners are meant to last decades, but that doesn't mean you can just put it anywhere and it will be in perfect condition a year later. They require care and a good amount of attention. You won't want to start off the next canning season with a rusty pressure canner and broken utensils. Even if you have the perfect location to keep the canner, there's still a whole procedure to follow before you can store it. Skipping any step could shorten your equipment's lifespan.

Clean the entire pot for good measure. Any leftover residue can make the pot rust and develop mold if you give it enough time. You'll also want to dislodge anything that might be trapped in the vent pipe with a pipe cleaner. The overpressure plug should be removed and the area should be scrubbed for rust. Remember to put the plug back in though, as you don't want to lose such a small piece. Don't forget about the utensils. The canning rack, jars, jar lifter and other special canning equipment need to be washed and dried before it is ready to be stored.

The appliance is still not ready to be stored until you've checked everything's condition. Any rubber piece needs to be looked over for breakage or any brittle parts. If you need to replace a gasket, wait until next year so that it isn't already a year old by the time you get to use it. The dial gauge doesn't need to be checked at the local extension service until right before next harvest season. You should still look for cracks in the glass or other damage. The pot and lid should be inspected for any signs of rust because that needs to be taken care of as soon as possible.

After everything is checked over and cleaned, it is finally time to store your canner and canning supplies. Crumple up some clean paper towels and put them in the bottom of the pot with the rack. This will work to absorb moisture and unwanted odors. The lid can be placed on top of the canner upside down. Don't seal it on or that might lead to mold growth. Jars should be stored without their lids and placing them upside down will limit dust deposits. Pressure canners need to be stored in clean and dry areas. Follow all these steps and you'll be ready for the next canning season.

Chapter 10:
What's the Worst That Could Happen?

Botulism

So, what is the worst that could happen if you don't use a pressure canner safely? Death. The most dangerous thing to worry about isn't an explosion, it is a foodborne illness. If your jars are not properly sealed, you run the risk of creating the perfect environment for the *Clostridium botulinum* bacteria. This bacteria produces a serious toxin that causes the illness of botulism. The toxin is produced in food, wounds, and baby intestines. Luckily this is a rare condition, but it should still be taken seriously. If, for whatever reason, you may believe you have contracted botulism, seek medical attention immediately.

The bacteria that causes botulism isn't actually that dangerous. It's naturally found in many different places and isn't found to cause any illness. It's the spores created by the bacteria that become dangerous. The spores are produced to protect the bacteria in harsh conditions such as low oxygen or low acid levels. Since pressure canners are used for non-acidic food products, there's always the possibility for these spores to spawn. When the spores themselves are consumed, it is still unlikely to get sick with botulism. It's only when the spores grow and produce the toxin that problems arise. As long as the food is properly canned, the spores won't grow or produce the toxin.

Botulism has clear signs and symptoms to look out for. If you fear you might have consumed contaminated food, pay attention to your eyes. If your vision is blurry or you feel like you are seeing double, these are red flags. More optical issues include difficulty moving your eyes or drooping eyelids. Another area you should pay attention to is your stomach. If you are nauseous, vomiting, or having other stomach related issues botulism is a possibility. Other symptoms include muscle weakness and problems with breathing, swallowing, and speech. It is possible to not show signs of all of these symptoms and still have botulism.

If you do seek medical attention, the doctor will likely perform a series of tests before diagnosis. These include a brain scan, a spinal fluid examination, and nerve and muscle function tests. However, the only way to know for certain is a specific laboratory test. Depending at what stage you are at, treatment will vary. You will firstly be administered an antitoxin drug to stop any further damage from the toxin. This is not a cure all though, and won't reverse the effects you've already suffered. Botulism attacks the nervous system and can cause paralysis. Most patients slowly recover, but this can take weeks or even months. In the case of a patient with breathing issues, a ventilator may be administered until they can breathe on their own.

Less than 5 of every 100 people with botulism die. This is far better than in the past when the survival rate was only 50%. The most common complication of botulism is respiratory failure. Many problems can arise from long term paralysis as well such as infection. Years after their diagnosis, some patients still report shortness of breath and fatigue. Pressure canners were created precisely to avoid this illness. As long as you pay attention to the USDA's safety protocols in relation to the pressure canner, you will never have to deal with this food poisoning.

Avoiding Contamination

The most important toxin to look out for is botulism, but fortunately it and other contaminants can be easily avoided. There is no way to taste, see, or smell the botulism toxin, but one little bite can kill you so it's important to know other ways to avoid this deadly mistake. Always remember to sterilize everything: One contaminated tool and it's all over. Sterilizing couldn't be more simple, just place your jars, tongs, and lids in boiling water heated up on the stove. This will kill any dangerous bacteria and make your work space safe for canning. Jars should be immersed in boiling water for at least ten minutes.

The USDA provides a complete guide to home canning that should be scrupulously followed. During the canning process, cutting corners is highly dangerous. No amount of money, resources, or time is worth your life. Canning beginners shouldn't even buy a pressure canner before reading these techniques. Even if you have a lot of experience with canning but are just getting back into it after taking time away, don't trust your memory. Review the guidelines, they are there to keep you safe. Other reading material about canning safety can be provided by the National Center for Home Food Preservation or your state and county extension services.

A sure-fire way to make sure your food isn't contaminated is to use the right equipment. Low acid foods need to be pressure canned. A pressure cooker or just using the water bath method will not have good results. Even if the cooker has a feature for canning, the size difference between the two appliances makes it unsafe. Pressure canners can be expensive, but so are hospital bills. It's also important to make sure your equipment is in working condition. Before each use, always check the gauge's accuracy and that the gasket isn't starting to crumble. If you are unsure how to check your gauge, county extension services can do it for you.

Just because you can't physically see botulism doesn't mean you can't see the signs of contamination. If you pick up a jar off your shelf and it looks swollen or the lid is bulging, do not eat its contents. Whether you canned it months ago or yesterday, the food has gone bad and is no longer safely edible. Avoid eating discolored, or foaming substances. Always trust your nose when it comes to canned goods. If a jar's contents smell rancid or moldy, throw it out. In fact, if you have any reason to doubt the food's safety then throw it out.

Jars are the most important indicator for any possible contamination. Through every part of the canning process make sure your jars are in good condition. One little scratch isn't going to make a difference but a chip on the rim could completely affect the sealing process and allow bacteria to grow. Also keep in mind that just because jars are reusable doesn't mean their lids are. Most lids are not manufactured with the ability to reseal jars after they've already been used. Once again, if the jar isn't sealed bacteria can grow and produce the botulism toxin.

Understanding Food Acid Levels

Knowing the difference between a water bath canner and a pressure canner is the first step to not contracting botulism. A water bath canner is for acidic food and a pressure canner is for low or non-acidic food. This basic fact is helpful, but how can you tell what foods are acidic and what aren't? Well it's pH levels, of course. To anyone who doesn't study agriculture or food safety, this means nothing. What are pH levels? Taste isn't always an indicator for whether foods are acidic. You have to look at it on an atomic level. Acid releases free hydrogen ions and pH levels are just a scale to measure these free hydrogen ions in food.

This scale is pretty much useless if you don't know how to read it. It ranges from zero to 14, zero being the most acidic and 14 being non-acidic. For better understanding, battery acid is a zero while liquid drain cleaner is a 14. The pH level seven is considered to be neutral. This is the acidic level of pure water. If a level is above seven, it is called alkaline. Most food that can be processed in a pressure canner isn't actually alkaline and sits at a range a little lower than seven. Alkaline will sometimes also be called basic.

Food with a pH level above 4.6 needs to be pressure canned or it can become the breeding ground for *Botulinum* spores. This rule was made specifically because of this bacteria. Fruits can usually kill these spores, but meat and vegetables can't. It's usually a safe bet to only pressure can foods with high pH and only water bath food with low pH. With any rule comes the exception, so make sure to research your product before you start to can it. This rule doesn't always take into account food viscosity, taste, or heat transfer properties though.

Not all foods that are considered to be acidic should be canned in a water bath canner alone. Tomato, the most indecisive of produce, requires an addition of lemon juice. This is because their pH levels are near 4.6. Other borderline foods such as the papaya and figs have a similar pH level and also need a supplement to increase their acidic levels. Cantaloupe and watermelon have pH levels that match some kinds of meat. Pressure canning these isn't recommended though, because it will ruin the flavor. They can only be water bath canned once they've been pickled.

Will My Pressure Canner Explode?

No. It can, but it won't because you know how to avoid it. You have purchased a pressure canner that is not older than your grandparents, and therefore should have a release valve. You also frequently clean your equipment, so you never have to worry about dirt or other unwanted particles blocking the safety valve. If you own a dial-gauge, you get it checked every year so you won't accidentally apply too much pressure in your pot. You've also read through your owner's manual and keep it around in case something goes wrong. Most importantly you've read this book. The only way your pressure canner is going to explode is if you let it.

There are three common defects, all of which you can avoid. The first problem that can cause an explosion is an unsealed lid. If a lid isn't sealing, don't turn it on. You don't want the steam to escape in an uncontrolled way or for the lid to go flying. There are numerous reasons as to why a lid won't shut. The canner can be too full or something may be lodged in the gasket. Something could have warped the pot as well.

In this case, you'll have to get a new pressure canner.

The next problem is a faulty gasket. Gaskets seal the canner's lid. If you gasket breaks in the middle of a load the lid can pop off and you can get burned. This is unlikely to happen if you replace your gasket every year. If this happens and you have a new gasket, you may have gotten the wrong size. Make sure to look up your make and model in your pressure canner owner's manual. The last defect and most unlikely is insufficient venting. This only happens when something clogs both the overpressure plug and the vent pipe.

It's unlikely that your canner will come with a manufacturing error that causes any of these problems, but it is possible. Make sure to check all your parts are working after you purchase the canner even if it's not second hand. You might get a good settlement, but you'll also get burned so it is always better to be safe than sorry. An explosion is probably not going to cause any more damage than within a 10 foot radius, so if you notice steam isn't coming out properly, turn the appliance off and run away.

How to Spot Danger

You can store most home canned goods for up to one year. Anything older than this should be swapped out for something new. This is why labeling your products with the date they were canned is very important. Always have a well-organized canned goods storage so you know when something is about to go over one year. Does this mean you can't eat canned food that is older than a year? No, you can. Once it is properly canned, the food is technically edible forever as long as the seal isn't broken. Is it going to taste good forever? No. Quality and nutrition drop after one year.

If you want your canned goods to retain their quality for as long as possible, have a regulated temperature between 50 and 70 degrees Fahrenheit where you store them.

Anything higher than 95 degrees will shorten the shelf life. The food won't become toxic but it will spoil. If you think your food has spoiled, don't taste test it. Jars that are stored without screw bands will have a clear indication of something wrong. As a rule of thumb, If the seal is broken, the food has gone bad. Bacteria and yeast break the seal by producing gas that swells the lid.

Just because a jar is unopened, doesn't mean it is still safe. There are several ways to tell if an unopened jar of food has spoiled: If the jar looks swollen because the center of the lid is raised, it is probably bad. Lids should have a concave center. Food shouldn't still have rising air bubbles a couple days after canning either. This means it has not been properly sealed and air is somehow still getting in. The most obvious sign will be the discoloration of the product.

Mold is easy to spot and will look somewhat like cotton spores. When you open the jar make sure nothing is out of the ordinary. Don't just check the food either, something nasty could be hiding on the underside on the jar's lid. Mold can come in a variety of colors like green, white, blue, or black. Spurting liquid and foam can also be a sign of spoilage. Try not to inhale any of it before throwing it away. You can also smell if something's wrong. Even if everything looks fine, jars with unnatural odors should not be trusted.

Conclusion

You did it! You learned how to use a pressure canner safely. Congratulations, the horror stories stop with you. There aren't going to be any holes in your kitchen ceiling thanks to your smart choices. A pressure canner is no longer an object to fear, but instead an appliance for you to master. Now that you know how to properly prepare and can food products you no longer have to wait for your favorite veggies to go into season. Never again will your meat products spoil before you can consume it all. Throwing away leftovers will be a thing of the past.

Clearly, there is a lot to consider before you start your canning journey. Whatever size, brand, or model you choose, make sure you are comfortable with using it. The first step to safely using a pressure canner is to trust your appliance. If you have valid worries about the condition of your canner, don't use it. As cliche as it may be, always remember it is better to be safe than sorry. Modern pressure canners are built with your safety in mind, but that does not mean accidents can't happen. Know your model and its integral parts. That way, if something is wrong, you can easily identify and fix it before something bad happens.

Pressure canning isn't as difficult as it may seem. Once you get a hold of its process and precautions, it will be second nature. Always listen to the recipe, but first make sure it aligns with the USDA's food protocols. If it is telling you to pressure can strawberries, it is probably not a good recipe. In addition, being comfortable with the canning process does not mean being careless. Always be alert when the pressure canner is being used. Mistakes only happen when we let them, which means there's no reason to fear when we're being safe.

There are so many fun and interesting recipes you can use with a pressure canner. Once you've become comfortable with your model, feel free to be creative. While canning can be a job, it should also be enjoyable. Now that you know how to be safe when using your pressure canner there should be nothing stopping you from experimenting with different meals. There are so many avenues to explore whether it be with meat, broths, or vegetables. You can even learn how to use the water bath method with your pressure canner. Just make sure to thoroughly research the safety precautions and not just rely on what you know about the pressure canning method.

Lastly, thank you. Whether your pressure canning to make money or just for fun, you are helping to eliminate unwanted waste. Even if it's not on purpose, canning is still a sustainable lifestyle that helps the planet. The amount of produce that is thrown away everyday is almost sickening. Being mindful of what you use and what you need develops a healthy relationship with food and protects our environment. By making the decision to can, you are taking accountability for your waste and making a difference. Thanks to people like you, the world is becoming a better place. Good job!

References

Centers for Disease Control and Prevention. (2019). About botulism. CDC. https://www.cdc.gov/botulism/general.html

Chihak, S. (2020, April 6). Master pressure canning at home in 9 simple steps. Better Homes & Gardens. https://www.bhg.com/recipes/how-to/preserving-canning/pressure-canning-basics/#:~:text=A%20pressure%20canner%20is%20a

Chihak, S. (2020, April 27). Save your produce up to a year when you master water bath canning. Better Homes & Gardens. https://www.bhg.com/recipes/how-to/preserving-canning/canning-basics/

Cooks, C. (2020, July 22). All American vs Presto pressure canners. Corrie Cooks. https://www.corriecooks.com/all-american-vs-presto-pressure-canners/

Cash, J. (2015, December 22). Picking your pressure canner — All American or Presto? Backwoods Home Magazine. https://www.backwoodshome.com/picking-your-pressure-canner/

Fillmore Containers. (2015, August 7). Which jars are safe for pressure canning? (Updated). Fillmore Container. https://www.fillmorecontainer.com/blog/2015/08/07/which-jars-are-safe-for-pressure-canning/#:~:text=A%20Pressure%20Canner%20brings%20jar

Go Presto. (2019). Pressure canner care maintenance. Go Presto. https://www.gopresto.com/downloads/canning/PressureCannerCareandMaintenance.pdf

Healthy Canning. (n.d.). Pressure canner brands. Healthy Canning. https://www.healthycanning.com/pressure-canner-brands/#Typical_pressure_canner_brands

Meakin, C. (n.d.). Chicken vs. beef bone broth: Which is better for you. Bluebird Provisions. https://bluebirdprovisions.co/blogs/news/best-bone-broth

Meredith, L. (2020, September 17). Boiling water bath and pressure canning - When to use which. The Spruce Eats. https://www.thespruceeats.com/boiling-water-bath-versus-pressure-canning-1327438

National Center for Home Food Preservation. (2009). National Center for Home Food Preservation | How do I? Can meats. NCHFP. https://nchfp.uga.edu/how/can_05/strips_cubes_chunks.html

National Center for Home Food Preservation. (n.d.). National Center for Home Food Preservation | UGA Publications. NCHFP. https://nchfp.uga.edu/publications/uga/using_press_canners.html

Neal, J. (2015). Causes of pressure cooker explosions and how to avoid them. Watts Guerra

LLP. https://wattsguerra.com/product-liability-lawyers/causes-of-pressure-cooker-explosions-and-how-to-avoid-them/

Phelan, K. (2019, August 29). 4 canning dangers to be aware of. Homestead Survival Site. https://homesteadsurvivalsite.com/canning-dangers/

Philpotts, R. (2021, November 26). Top 7 health benefits of bone broth. BBC Good Food. https://www.bbcgoodfood.com/howto/guide/the-health-benefits-of-bone-broth

Preserve & Pickle. (2019, July 26). Buying a pressure canner - Guide to choosing & using a pressure canner. Preserve & Pickle. https://preserveandpickle.com/buying-a-pressure-canner-guide/#Considerations_When_Buying_A_Pressure_Canner

Rebekah. (2019, August 15). The ultimate list of what you can (and cannot!) can. J&R Pierce Family Farm. https://jrpiercefamilyfarm.com/2019/08/15/the-ultimate-list-of-what-you-can-and-cannot-can/

Sakawsky, A. (2021, August 9). How to use a pressure canner safely. The House & Homestead. https://thehouseandhomestead.com/how-to-use-a-pressure-canner-safely/

Schmutz, P., & Barefoot, S. (2011, August 20). Canning foods—The pH factor. Home & Garden Information Center | Clemson University, South Carolina. https://hgic.clemson.edu/factsheet/canning-foods-the-ph-factor/#:~:text=The%20acidity%2C%20or%20pH%2C%20of

Swanson, M. (2012). Using and caring for your pressure canner PNW 421. A Pacific Northwest Extension Publication. https://www.rollingprairie.k-state.edu/health-nutrition/food_preservation/Caring%20for%20your%20pressure%20canner.pdF

Thomas, C. (2021, February 10). Canning bone broth or stock (Chicken, beef, or vegetable). Homesteading Family. https://homesteadingfamily.com/how-to-can-broth/

Treadaway, A., & Crayton. (2019, May 21). Wise methods of canning vegetables. Alabama Cooperative Extension System. https://www.aces.edu/blog/topics/food-safety/wise-methods-of-canning-vegetables/

University of Illinois Extension. (n.d.). Storing vegetables - Taste of gardening - University of Illinois Extension. University of Illinois. https://web.extension.illinois.edu/tog/storing.cfm

Zepp, M. (2021, May 4). Canning jars and lids—An update. Penn State Extension. https://extension.psu.edu/canning-jars-and-lids-an-update

The Essential Guide To Pressure Canning for Beginners

All-In-One cookbook with Safe, Easy, and Delicious Recipes for Meals in a Jar! Successfully Can Meat, Soup, Vegetables, and So Much More!

Linda C. Johnson

Introduction

"Food is a passion. Food is love."

Hector Elizondo

If you have always wanted to start canning at home but did not know how to start or what to do, then keep reading…this is the book for you!

You see, canning is not very difficult once you know what it involves. Even if you have never tried your hand at canning, it is easier than you might think. The first step to getting started with canning at home is to understand what pressure canning is, and the simple but important steps to be followed. Once you do this, you can start enjoying your favorite foods with your whole family all year long. Pressure canning is a food preservation process that involves using a special appliance called a pressure canner to seal the contents within a jar. From wild game, poultry, and beef to soups and stews and vegetarian ingredients, lots of different foods can be canned. All you need to do is understand what pressure canning is and how it works.

The concept of canning is nothing new and it has been around for decades. That said, with modern advancements and development, canning has become easier than ever before. It is also an incredibly efficient, safe, and practical means of preserving tasty meals in a jar. By using the different recipes given in this book, you can quickly rustle up healthy and filling meals. This book will also introduce you to the basic process of pressure canning, the equipment and tools involved in it, and an understanding of how this process works. It will also introduce you to a variety of factors that influence pressure canning. Once you are armed with all this information, you will be introduced to the different steps to be followed to start canning food at home.

In this book, you will learn about preparing meals in a jar and learning to can different types of foods. Whether it is meats, vegetables, or even stews and soups, they can be canned. So, do not stifle your creativity and instead, let it run wild. With the right safety information, practice, and patience, you can become a pro at canning within no time!

Are you wondering how I know all this? Well, I believe a little introduction is needed. Hello, my name is Linda Johnson and I have been canning for as long as I can remember. I grew up on a beautiful farm in rural Kansas. From a young age, I have been interested in gardening, farming, canning, food preserving, horse riding, and walking. I am not just passionate about canning but love sharing the goodies with my loving family and other loved ones. I am primarily a homemaker and a mother but I certainly know my way around the farm too.

I started sharing my tips and tricks for canning with others along with my preferred recipes. All the positive feedback I started receiving motivated me to compile my knowledge and experience into this book. I can imagine how intimidating canning might seem to a beginner. Well, you do not have to worry because I have got you covered. In this book, I will introduce you to everything you need to learn as a beginner. The information shared will ensure you aren't unknowingly following any unsafe canning practices. I believe canning is one of the best means to preserve food and avoid food wastage. And I am certain you can become an excellent canner within no time! Canning is extremely useful and simple to do once you get the hang of it. You can consume healthy and wholesome convenience food without any artificial preservatives. Also, this is more economical than any store-bought variant.

Even if you are just getting started, this book will act as your guide every step of the way. The tried and tested recipes given, coupled with simple instructions will turn you into a canning pro within no time! You will discover helpful information needed for creating perfect food storage options.

If you are ready to jump into the world of home canning, then there is no time like the present to get started!

Chapter 1:
Pressure Canning 101

"Food is a necessary component to life. People can live without Renoir, Mozart, Gaudi, Beckett, but they cannot live without food."

Grant Achatz

What is the first thing that pops into your head when you hear the words pressure canner? Chances are you think about a stovetop cooking pan with a lid and a noisy whistle. Well, you are probably thinking of a pressure cooker and not a canner. Chances are we most commonly use these two words as synonyms, but they are not. Even though they share some similarities, they don't refer to the same kitchen equipment. Usually, pressure cookers are used for cooking large cuts of meat quickly. These cooking appliances are like large saucepans. On the other hand, pressure canners are not meant for processing or cooking food but instead storing them through a process known as canning. The jars with food should be placed in the pressure canner and the pressure within it helps seal the jars. Usually, pressure canners are much larger than a cooker and can hold anywhere between 7 and 24 jars at any point.

Pressure canning is a wonderful technique used for food preservation using special kitchen equipment known as a pressure canner. This process helps extend the shelf-life of certain cooked foods. A pressure canner is a large pot with a lid that snugly fits it. It also has a weighted or a dial gauge to check the pressure building up within the pot. The added pressure created within helps sterilize the jars and ensure the food within them is pathogen-free.

I could write a whole book on Pressure Canning 101 basics and safety. In fact. I have! It's called **"Pressure Canning Without the Danger** - Your Comprehensive Guide to Safely Using Your Pressure Canner. With Tips, Tricks, and USDA Guidelines to Help You Use Your Pressure Canner Without Risks!". I encourage you to read it as it covers in much greater detail the topics I write about in this chapter.

Brands and Types of Pressure Canners

When it comes to pressure canners, there are two brands that dominate the market, All-American and Presto. Both All-American and Presto pressure canners have their pros and cons. Ultimately, it is the customer's decision on what model makes them feel most comfortable.

All-American pressure canners come in a variety of sizes, which is perfect for people who plan on making large batches at a time. Their largest size will can 19 quart jars at a time, while their smallest holds only four. With this variety of sizes comes a variety of prices. Be prepared to spend more money for larger canners. All-American canners should only be used on a gas range instead of an electric one, so there is no stove damage. A feature of the All-American that makes them more user friendly is their weighted gauge. Instead of having to manually adjust the heat, weight on the valve regulates the pressure.

Presto pressure canners only come in two sizes which are the 16 quart liquid capacity model, and the 23 quart liquid capacity model. The Presto brand canners work with both gas and electric ranges. This fact, along with their small size, makes Presto more versatile than the All-American canners. The gauge is a dial gauge instead of a weighted one, and the pressure must be manually handled. This is better for people who wish to can in higher altitudes. Newer models have a button feature that drops down to inform you when the canner is safe to open.

As far as price goes, the Presto brand runs cheaper, and is more commonly available in stores such as Walmart. Presto canners do require the additional expense of replacing the rubber gasket around the inside of the lid. Gasket replacements are not very expensive however, and are only needed every few years. Keep in mind location when choosing between the two brands as well. High altitude places will prefer the presto while lower altitudes can enjoy the weighted gauge feature of the All-American.

The decision between the two is also dependent on batch sizes. Investing in a larger All-American pressure canner will be the smarter option for those who have a good amount of canning orders to do in a short time. Presto canners are better for casual canning. Both brands are well built and last a long time.

Just because All-American and Presto are the most well known brands on the market, does not mean they are the only brands. Mirro, while not as popular, is the only brand other than the two aforementioned brands that is most recognized by professionals in the field of canning. Mirro, like Presto, only comes in two sizes: Both of these sizes have weighted gauge features like All-American canners.

A pressure gauge is supposed to monitor and help regulate pressure inside of the canner. There are three different models of gauges that you can find on a pressure canner. The first and oldest is a dial gauge that is used to measure the pressure within the pot. The downside to this is that it can't control the pressure. A weighted gauge is the opposite: It controls the pressure but can't measure it. Lastly is a dual-gauge, which is a hybrid of the two. It has a dial for reading the pressure levels, but also utilizes weight to regulate that pressure.

A dial gauge pressure canner uses a dial to display the pressure that is present within the canner. As the temperature, as well as the pressure, builds up within the canner, the dial rises. Some gauges can show a half or a 1 pound increase in pressure while others are only marked for 5 pound increments. These pressure canners come in handy if you want to determine the pressure increments at higher altitudes. For instance, the pressure required for meats and vegetables is around 11 pounds if the altitude is less than 2000 feet. Unless you carefully monitor the gauge and adjust the heat, you cannot maintain the desired pressure within the pot. The gauges of these canners should be checked at least once a year to ensure their accuracy.

Similarly, a weighted gauge pressure canner uses a weight that regulates the pressure building up or present within the canner. These pressure canners have a single flat disc that has different markings for pressure such as 5 and 10. Some models of weighted gauge pressure canners have metal rings that can be stacked to regulate the pressure within the canner. For instance, if only 10 pounds of pressure is needed, two rings of 5 pounds each can be added. As the pressure starts building within the pot, the pressure causes the weight to jiggle. This is also an indicator the desired temperature is achieved within the pot. Some weights will jiggle a few times while others do it continuously. At altitudes of over 1,000 feet, don't forget to increase the pressure by 5 pounds.

The dual-gauge is just using both methods. Since weighted gauges are less hands on, the dial gauge is mostly there to keep track of where the pound per square inch or PSI is at. It can be a back up if something goes wrong, but to be honest, it is kind of useless. Modern Presto canners are mostly dial gauge, but they've made their pot compatible with dual-gauges. The weights are sold separately. This is helpful for people who prefer the dial gauge way, but aren't close enough to a local extension service to get their dial checked every year.

Parts of a Pressure Canner

A pressure canner consists of several parts that are specially designed to help regulate the temperature as well as the steam pressure present within the canner. Understanding the different parts and the specific functions they perform will leave you better equipped to use your pressure canner. In this section, let's look at all the different parts of a pressure canner.

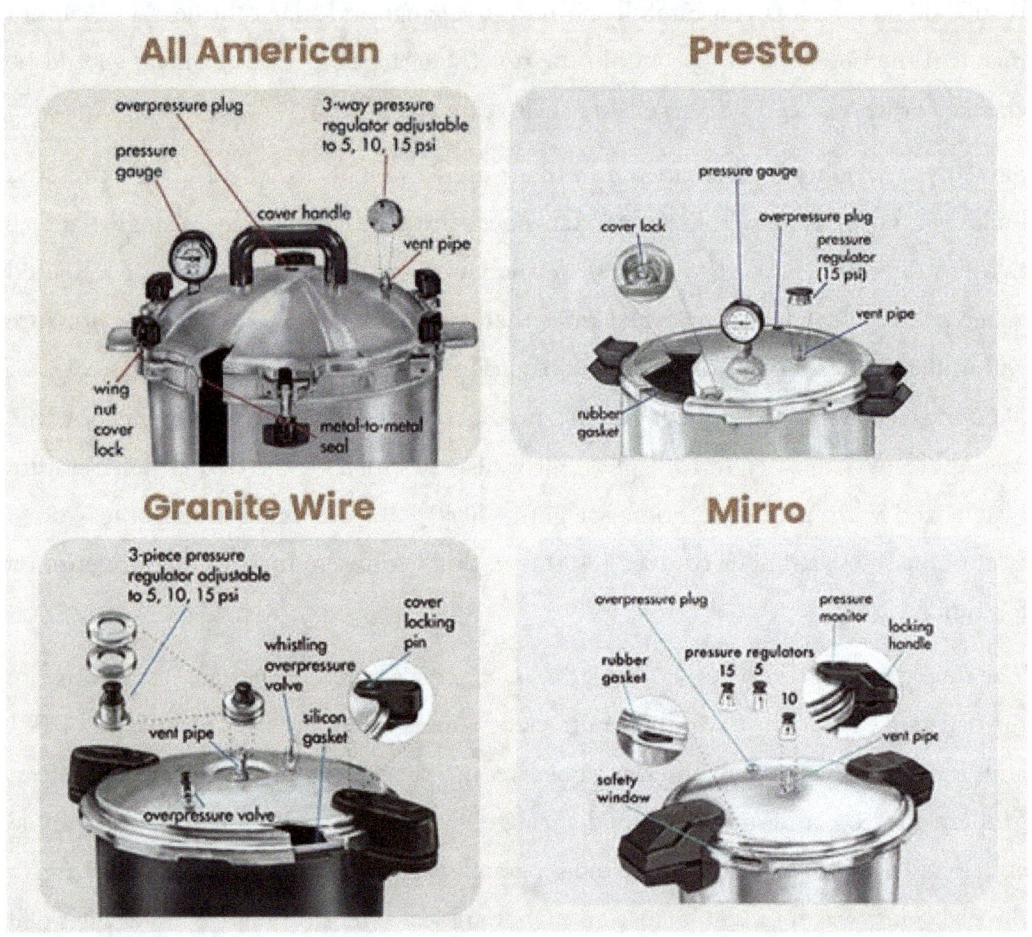

Pressure Regulator

This part helps maintain and regulate the pressure within the canner. A peg usually holds the regulator in place. This feature ensures the pressure does not exceed 15 pounds within the canner.

Adjustable Pressure Regulator

Some pressure canners have adjustable regulators to adjust the pressure within the pot. Such regulators give you the option to decide whether the pressure within the pot should be 5, 10, or 15 pounds. If the pressure regulator starts a gentle rhythmic rocking motion, it signals that the ideal pressure is maintained within the pot.

Vent Pipe

The vent pipe is an important part of a pressure canner because it helps release excess pressure in the pot. It is a small opening where steam and pressure are vented out from the pot during the canning process. In some models, the vent pipe might be present on the lid itself. Ensure that you always check the vent pipe after every use because, at times, food or foam can clog it which prevents it from functioning effectively.

Air Vent

The air vent is essentially a visual indicator of the pressure that's building up in the canner. Once sufficient pressure is present within the pot, the cover locks itself. This means opening it becomes impossible in any type of pressure canner. This is also a safety feature put in place to ensure the device is always closed under extreme pressure. The cover lock and air vent drop when the pressure inside the canner reduces.

Locking Bracket

The locking bracket is present within the body of the pressure canner. This engages with the air vent to ensure the cover cannot be opened when pressure is present within the pot. All the pressure canners that were manufactured before 1978 do not have this feature.

Sealing Ring

The sealing ring helps seal pressure within the body of the canner to ensure the pressure doesn't escape. It fits right around the pressure canner's cover and offers a tight pressure seal. It's present between the lid and the body of the pot. Sufficient pressure will not build within the canner if this ring is broken or not in place. It can handle the heat only from the pressure canner for as long as there are no tears or cracks in it.

Pressure Dial Gauge

The dial gauge is a readable dial with a pointer that indicates the pressure present within the canner. You cannot use this to regulate the pressure. Instead, it is simply used to check the pressure within.

Cooking Rack

The cooking rack is used for elevating food away from the liquid present in the pot. It also helps separate foods that you don't want to mix. You can use it for sterilizing as well. The cooking rack makes sure the jars or containers do not touch the bottom or the walls of the canner.

Overpressure Plug

Another safety feature added is an overpressure plug. Any food clogging the vent pipes makes it difficult for the excess pressure to be let out of the body. In such instances, the steam will be automatically redirected from the overpressure plug. This plug usually pops out in case this happens. Heed it as a warning that you need to release the pressure from the part.

Jars, Lids, and Other Canning Equipment

Canning at home is not only easy but is a rewarding activity, too. Whether it is delicious meat or vegetables, canning comes in handy. Once you have the required equipment, you simply need to follow the canning instructions given in the subsequent chapters. Here we will identify the equipment you need to can successfully.

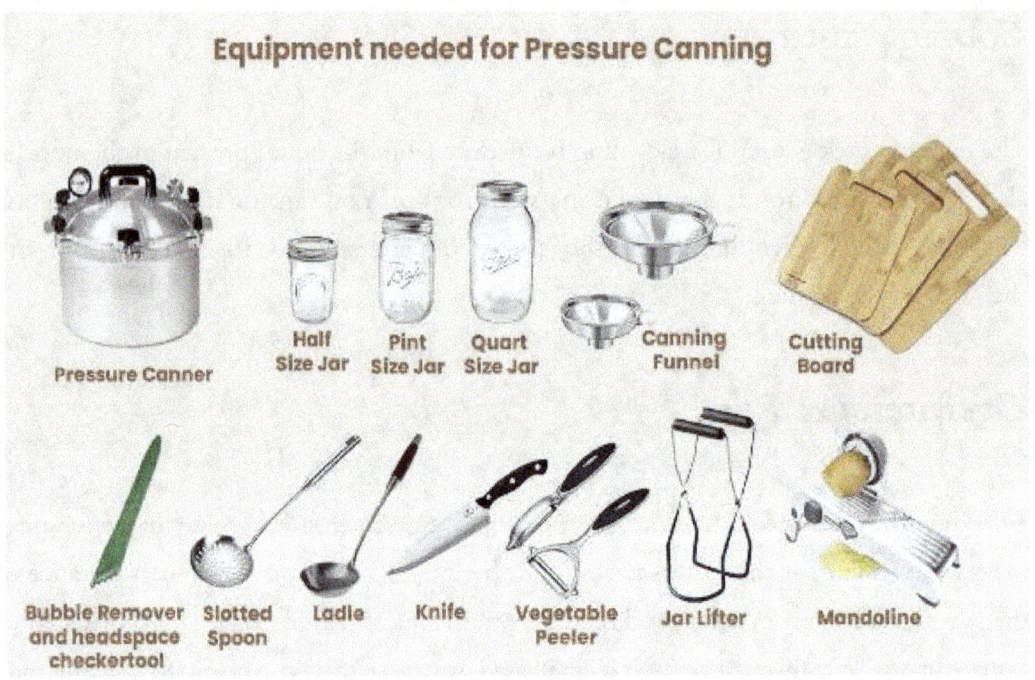

Canning Jars and Lids

You cannot start canning without the required jars and lids. These days a variety of canning jars are available in different shapes as well as sizes. Depending on the items you want to can, the size of the jar will vary. These jars are good for repeated use provided you thoroughly clean and sterilize them. They are typically made of glass and can have a wide or regular mouth.

The lids of the canning jars have two parts—bands and lids. These are usually made of metal and fit the size of the jar's mouth. As long as the bands are in good shape, they can be reused but not the lids. You should never use the lids a second time; however, the bands can be used repeatedly.

Utensils for Canning

Using a canning funnel makes things easier, especially to transfer liquids or semi-solid foods into the canning jars. Depending on the ingredients you are canning and the portions, the size of the funnel needed will vary.

You will also need a ladle for spooning the ingredients into the jars. Always opt for a stainless steel one because they are not only durable but are resistant to melting as well.

Once the jars are filled and you have put the lid on, it is time to put them in a pressure canner. This is where jar lifters come in handy. Using a jar lifter ensures you can do this process without accidentally dropping the jars or burning yourself. A jar lifter looks quite similar to a pair of metal tongs. The only difference is, they have a rubber coating on them and are ideal for lifting hot jars in and out of the pressure canner without any difficulty.

A Canner

You need a pressure canner for pressure canning. In the previous section, you were introduced to different types of pressure canners and you can opt for one depending on your needs and requirements. Pressure canners can be used for almost all types of foods regardless of their acidity unlike water-bath canners. You will learn more about the differences between pressure and water-bath canners in the subsequent sections.

Kitchen Towels

Regardless of what you are doing, you will need plenty of kitchen towels. This is a must-have for any kitchen project but is especially needed while canning. You can use them for setting hot jars on the counter and for cleaning the countertop too. A clean towel should be used for wiping the rim of the jar before you seal them. This prevents contamination. It also makes things look clean and tidy.

Food Strainer or Mill

If you want to grind or puree foods for canning, you will need a food strainer or mill. These items also come in handy for other purposes and not just canning. Whether you are making homemade apple sauce or tomato puree, investing in one of these is a good idea.

Water Bath vs. Pressure Canner

If you opt for the right canning method, the ingredients of your choice can be preserved safely and stored in your pantry for prolonged periods. However, this process becomes a little complicated if you are unsure of the method you are using. This is why it's important to understand the two different kinds of canning methods. The first one is known as water bath canning and the second is known as pressure canning. A boiling water-bath canner does not require any special equipment apart from the canning jars you need for storing food. On the other hand, pressure canning, as the name suggests, requires a pressure canner. Now that you know a pressure cooker is not the same as a canner let's learn the difference between water-bath canning and pressure canning.

If you want to opt for water-bath canning, you simply need a large pot that has a rack placed at the bottom. Whether it is a pot that's used for making soup or stock, any large pot can be used in this process. Fill the canning jars with the ingredients of your choice leaving the headspace recommended in the recipe and ensure the lids are secured tightly. Once the lids are in place, immerse these jars in boiling water for a specific time suggested by the canning recipe. Once you remove the jars from the boiling water of the water bath, let them cool down. In this process, a vacuum seal is formed between the jar and its lid. When it comes to using a water bath for canning, remember that the temperature of the water does not go beyond its boiling point.

On the other hand, a pressure canner is specifically designed for the purpose of pressure canning. It is a specialized piece of equipment that has various parts such as a pressure gauge, screw clamps, and a vent to ensure the pressure within the canner is not restricted to the temperature of boiling water. So, when the jars filled with food are placed in it, they are heated beyond the boiling point of water. A wonderful thing about a pressure canner is regardless of the pH of the food, you can pretty much can anything you want. If you are trying to can foods that are alkaline or low in acid, opt for a pressure canner. Even though botulism-causing bacteria cannot survive the temperature of boiling water (212°F), the spores can. Unless the temperature is greater than 212°F, the risk of botulism cannot be eliminated. This is where a pressure canner steps into the picture. You will learn more about how a pressure canner neutralizes the risk of botulism in the next sections.

Important Considerations While Canning

If you have a canner and other equipment, canning at home is easy. That said, certain external factors are also responsible for the longevity of the food you canned. Three important factors that home canning enthusiasts must pay attention to are altitude, temperature, and acidity. These three factors make all the difference between a successful attempt and a poorly canned jar of food.

Acidity

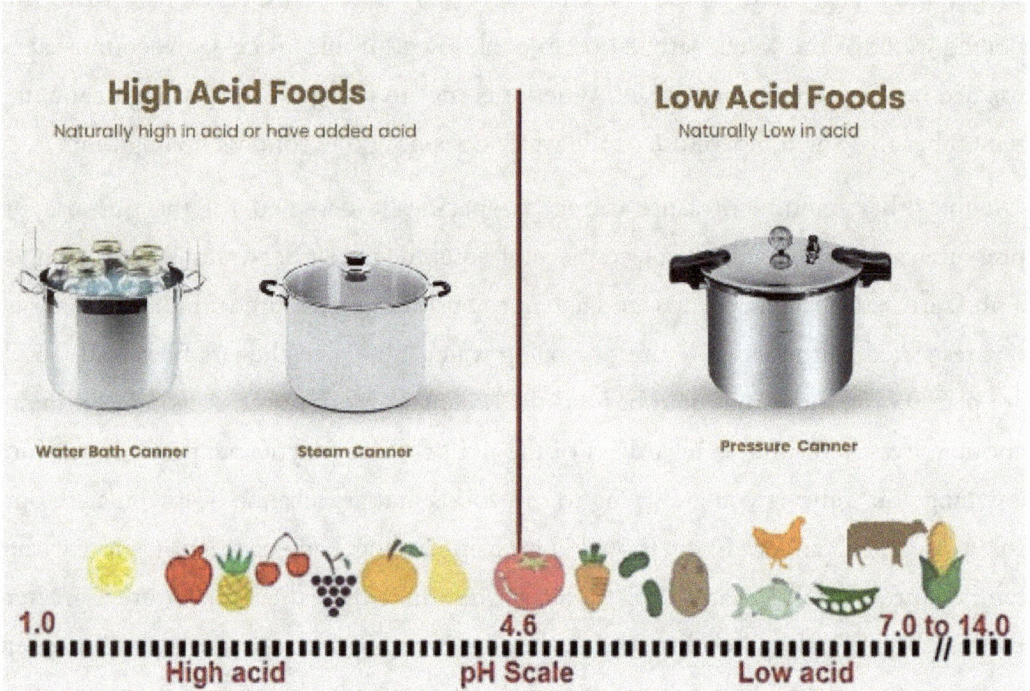

To determine how acidic or alkaline things are, a scientific measure known as the pH scale is used. The markings on this scale extend between 0 to 14. If the pH is between 0-6, it is known to be acidic, with 7 being neutral and above that is what is known as basic or alkaline pH. The stronger the acidic pH, the closer to 0. Are you wondering what this has to do with canning? An important benefit of pressure canning is it helps eliminate botulism-causing spores and bacteria. Acidity plays a vital role here. Common foods that are low in acidity score are milk, fresh vegetables, red meats, seafood, and poultry. Their pH is above 4.6. Any other ingredient with such a weakly acidic pH must be sterilized at temperatures between 240-250°F to ensure the harmful spores are killed. This is perfectly attainable while using pressure canners. The only exception to this is tomatoes because of their high acidity. Other high-acid foods such as jams, pickles, fruits, jellies, and such usually have a pH lower than 4.6. These can be canned using a regular water bath canner.

Temperature

The boiling point of water is 212°F. Regardless of the time spent boiling the water, it will not exceed this temperature. After the water reaches its boiling point, evaporation starts. This is a primary reason why water-bath canning is not the best method for preserving and canning low-acid foods. When water is heated up in a closed container, the temperature increases. This is due to the added pressure in the form of evaporating water. Due to this simple mechanism at play, pressure canning is ideal for any type of food. While using a pressure canner, there is an additional 10-11 pounds of pressure that increases the water beyond its boiling point and brings it up to 240°F. This is the temperature desired for destroying botulism-causing bacteria and their spores. It effectively halts their germination cycle by destroying all their traces from the food within the jars.

Certain factors reduce the temperature present within the pressure canner. One such thing is an inaccurate dial reading or low temperature of the air present within the canner. This is one of the reasons why the canner must be allowed to vent for at least 10 minutes. This helps expel the cold air present within. Before you place the weight or the pressure regulator, ensure that you let the pressure canner vent for a while. If the pressure canner has dial gauges, then make sure you check the gauges annually to maintain their accuracy.

Altitude

The next important external factor that you must pay attention to while home canning is the altitude. It's repeatedly mentioned that the boiling point of water is 212°F. However, did you know that this is the boiling point of water at sea level? When the altitude increases water can boil at a lower temperature. This is why you need to pay attention to altitude while canning. The time or temperature has to be changed accordingly depending on the altitude to ensure harmful pathogens are not present in the jars you are canning.

Altitude in Feet	Weighted Gauge in Pounds	Dial Gauge in Pounds	Weighted Gauge in Kilopascal	Dial Gauge in Kilopascal
0-1,000 (0-304 m)	10	11	69	76
1,001-2,000 (305-609 m)	15	11	103	76
2,001-4,000 (610-1,219 m)	15	12	103	83
4,001-6000 (1,220-1,828 m)	15	13	103	90
6,001-8,000 (1,829-2,483 m)	15	14	103	97
8,001-10,000 (2,439-3,048m)	15	15	103	103

This table shows the pressure required at various altitudes to reach 240°F (115° C) inside the pressure canner. Once the correct pressure for these altitudes is applied, the processing time is the same at all altitudes.

As the altitude increases the time taken for canning along with the temperature to be maintained during this process will increase. While using a pressure canner, the time taken for canning prescribed by most recipes will stay the same. That said, the pounds of pressure that need to be applied have to be increased. If you are using a weighted gauge pressure canner and are at an altitude of over 1000 feet, then food is normally sterilized at 15 pounds pressure. If the altitude is between 1,000-2,000 feet, 11 pounds of pressure is sufficient to attain the same results. However, the pressure must be increased to 12 pounds if the altitude is between 2,000-4,000 feet. Similarly, for an altitude of 4,000-6,000 feet, the pressure needed is 13 pounds whereas it is 14 pounds when the altitude is between 6,000-8,000 feet.

Learning about this is needed because the cooking time is crucial to ensure the ingredients are properly sterilized and processed. Depending on the altitude of the area you reside in, the recipes given in this book must be adjusted.

Risk of Botulism

Botulism is a type of food poisoning that's caused by a specific strain of bacteria known as *Clostridium botulinum*. Spores of this specific bacteria are commonly present on all food surfaces. Chances are you have heard of the risk of botulism in canned foods. It usually occurs upon the consumption of improperly canned food. It probably makes canned food seem risky but with a few safe practices, you can eliminate this health hazard.

If the spores of this bacteria are present on all surfaces, then shouldn't eating any food be harmful? Well, the thing is, these spores are harmless when present on the surface of fresh foods. Understand that there is a difference between harmless spores and a full-blown infestation of the bacteria. Under the right conditions, these spores germinate, multiply, and diet. This cycle keeps repeating until they have fully contaminated the food. As these bacteria multiply and die, they release a toxic compound causing botulism. This renders the food unfit for consumption.

The absence of oxygen and low temperature are the two external factors the spores of botulism-causing bacteria need to develop. The ideal temperature for their germination is between 70-120°F. Canned foods meet both these basic needs. Therefore, you need to be extra careful while canning foods, especially ones with low acidity. When food is canned using a pressure canner, the pressure within the canner helps increase the temperature of water beyond its boiling point. The temperature within it can be up to 240° F, which is sufficient to destroy the spores of this harmful bacteria.

Things to Remember

Here are some simple points you must remember while using a pressure canner:

- If you are using a dial gauge pressure canner, ensure the gauge is checked for accuracy. You should do it once a year. Ideally, get the dial inspected right before the canning season.

- If you are using a weighted gauge pressure canner, the units of pressure exerted by it are 5, 10, and 15 pounds. Depending on the altitude, the pressure required will vary. For instance, if you need 12 pounds of pressure, opt for the next closest weight, which is a 15-pound weight.

- One important thing that you must not forget while using pressure canners is to always check the vent openings after and before every use. A visual check helps ensure nothing is obstructing the vent. You can also run a string through the opening. If the vent is clogged the pressure within the canner will become too high. This, in turn, means the overpressure plug can blow. To ensure there isn't an accidental explosion while using a pressure canner, check the vents.

- As the altitude increases pay extra attention to the pressure within the canner. At higher altitudes, the pressure within the canner is lower, and therefore the temperature is lower too. Whenever you are using a canner at a higher altitude, increase and adjust the pressure accordingly.

- If there is any air trapped within the canner during the process the temperature reduces. This, in turn, increases the risk of under-processing. The simplest way to avoid this is by allowing the pressure canner to vent for 10 minutes.

Chapter 2:
How to Pressure Can

"To eat is a necessity, but to eat intelligently is an art."

François de la Rochefoucauld

Learning about pressure canning and how your pressure canner works is the first step toward becoming a successful home canner. Now, it is time to get to the interesting part of canning — learning about the process involved.

Basic Steps of Pressure Canning

Now that you have all the required equipment and tools, it is time to start pressure canning. It might sound intimidating, especially if you are trying it for the first time, but it is not. Once you go through the steps discussed in this section, you can become a pro in no time.

Step 1: Heating the Jars

This step helps sterilize the jars before they are ready for canning. Place the empty jars without their lids in the canner. Do not place the lid on the canner. Pour hot water into the canner such that the jars are completely immersed in it and the water is about an inch above the jars. Ensure you use hot water and not boiling water. Turn on the heat and let the water come to a boil over high heat. Once the water comes to a rolling boil within the canner, turn off the heat after 10 minutes. Carefully remove the jars from the canner and set them out on a clean surface to dry. Ensure you use tongs or a lifter for removing the jars, because they can be quite hot. Wipe the jars thoroughly with a clean cloth.

Step 2: Filling the Jars

Once the jars are sterilized, it is time to fill them! ensure they are still warm at this stage. Never fill jars when they are cold because it increases the risk of contamination. While filling the jars, ensure you leave about an inch of headspace between the food and lid to create a vacuum seal. Don't tightly pack the jars because this can cause the food to expand and bubble out during the canning process.

Step 3: Remove any Air Bubbles

Now, chances are there will be some air bubbles within the jar. You might not even see them at times. Use a thin and flexible spatula, to remove air bubbles. To do this, simply slip in the spatula and move it around to release any trapped air. If there is any more space, you can top it up again.

Step 4: Add the Lids

Once you have filled the jars, don't forget to wipe their rims. Do this before adding the lid. Set the lid in place and screw it tight. This is crucial to ensure that air does not enter the jar.

Step 5: Lock the Pressure Canner Lid

As and when you start filling the jars, place them in the pressure canner. While doing this, there should be sufficient water in the canner so that only a few inches of them are covered. Ensure the jars are not submerged. Set the lid of the canner in place and twist so the handles lock.

Step 6: Venting

Now, it is time to turn on the heat and let steam start building up in the pressure canner. You will see a full head of steam blowing out of the vent. Let it go on for 10 minutes before adding the regulator on top of the steam spout.

Step 7: The Right Pressure

If you have a weighted gauge regulator, make sure it is set at the right weight. The weight you should use will usually be specified in your recipe. Keep in mind, different altitudes have different requirements for the amount of weight you should put on it. Oftentimes, it is anywhere between 10 to 15 pounds of pressure. If you don't have a weighted gauge model just pay attention to your dial gauge. Be careful when you place the regulator on the steam spout as it can be very hot: Oven mitts will keep you safe from the heat.

You need to let the pressure canner reach the required pressure for canning. If it has a safety valve, it will pop up showing that sufficient pressure is there within. If for any reason your pressure goes below the recommended amount, you need to bring the pressure back up and start the timer over again.

Never open the lid of the pressure canner if its regulator starts rocking. The pot is full of boiling hot steam that can burn you or anyone else nearby. Adjust the heat so it starts making a constant rattling sound. If the recipe has a specific time, adjust it accordingly.

Step 8: Depressurize

Once the time prescribed by the recipe is up, it is time to turn off the heat. Do not make the mistake of opening the lid right away. Ensure the safety valves are back in their place before attempting to open the lid. Even if you feel a slight resistance, give it a while longer to fully depressurize. Remove the regulator and then open the lid such that the steam isn't directed at you.

Step 9: Cool the Jars

Using a kitchen towel or jar lifter, carefully lift the jars out of the pressure canner. Usually, letting them stay in the pot for up to ten minutes ensures they are relatively cool before removing them. Do not try tightening the lids at this stage. Set the jars on a kitchen towel or a wire rack to let them cool down. Usually, it is recommended to leave the jars undisturbed for 12-24 hours. Do not try to tighten the bands on the jar lids or push down on the flat lid until the jar is fully cooled. If any jars seem improperly sealed, refrigerate them immediately if not consumed right away.

After all this, do not forget to spend some time cleaning the pressure canner, cleaning the canner's pot, the gasket, and the lid. Remove the safety valves and clean, wash, and dry them too.

Once you complete these nine steps, you have successfully completed canning your first batch at home! Yes, it is as easy as that! You simply need to pay attention to the temperature, pressure, and time limits prescribed by the recipe of your choice!

Date the lid of the jars with a permanent marker so you can know when they go bad. The lid will be discarded later, so you don't need to mark the jar's glass every time. It will also be helpful to label the jar with its ingredients just in case you forget later on. Most people store their canned goods in their basement but it doesn't matter where you put them as long as it is cool and dry. It is also important that it is out of direct sunlight as that can spoil the food faster. For optimal quality, canned goods should be used within one year.

Essential Practices

When it comes to canning, there is a learning curve. It takes consistency, effort, and practice to get the hang of canning techniques. If you want stellar results while canning, be careful while following the different steps involved in the process. You will also be introduced to different tips and suggestions that can be used to improve the quality or chances of success you achieve while canning.

Before you decide to start canning, it's important to test the pressure canner. Whether you are testing the accuracy, the sealing ring, or the pressure that can develop, check everything. Once you know the appliance is working as intended, obtaining better results while canning becomes probable.

If you want to get good results, you must follow the recipe and USDA guidelines carefully. There's room for experimentation. That said, always learn the basics fast. It's also important to focus on the basics and USDA guidelines because food safety is crucial.

Ensure that you are handling the jars with care. When removing them from the pressure canner, use a jar lifter. Ensure the jars are always placed in an upright position. Another thing that you must check for is to ensure the jars are sealed properly.

Whenever you are canning, make sure that you are using sufficient water. Water starts evaporating from the pot in the form of steam. Water is the barrier between the jars and the bottom of the pot. If there is no water, the jars will be in direct contact with high heat.

Canning is a simple process, but it is usually quite messy. To reduce the mess, use aluminum foil to cover the work surface. Even cover the countertop with one or two layouts of aluminum foil. Once done, you simply need to wad the foil up and throw it in the bin.

The role played by heat and pressure cannot be ignored when it comes to pressure canning. Depending on the altitude, the temperature needs to be adjusted. Go through the information given in the previous section about pressure, altitude, and acidity while canning. Another important aspect you must remember when it comes to temperature is to ensure the jars are warm when you fill them up. Also, don't forget to immediately place the jars in the canner as soon as they are filled.

Before you decide to open the lid of the pressure canner, ensure the pressure has dissipated. It simply means turning off with heat and waiting for a couple of minutes until the pressure reduces. If you notice even a little resistance while trying to open the lid, let it cool down for a while longer.

Make sure everything is thoroughly cleaned before getting started. It means, you must not only clean the jars and lids but the canner and the countertops too. Ensure all items and surfaces you come in contact with while canning is clean. This reduces the risk of cross-contamination.

Chapter 3:
Lentils and Beans

Dried Beans

Makes: 7 pint jars (500 ml) or 14 ½ pint jars (250 ml)

Ingredients:

- 2 pounds (907 g) dried beans like pinto beans, black-eyed peas, black beans, peas, kidney beans, etc.

- Boiling water, as required

- ¼ teaspoon (1.4 g) salt per half pint jar or ½ teaspoon (2.8 g) salt per pint size jar (optional)

Directions:

1. To start off, pick the beans for any dirt, stones, discolored beans etc. Rinse the beans with fresh water and soak in a large pot of water. Soak them for at least 12 hours. Discard the soaked water.

2. If you do not want to soak the beans for 12 hours, there is another way you can do it: Place beans in a saucepan and cover with water. The water should be at least 2 to 3 inches over the beans. Place the saucepan over high heat and wait for it to start boiling. Let it boil for two minutes and turn off the heat. Let the beans soak in the hot water for an hour.

3. Transfer the beans into a large stock pot. Cover the beans with fresh water and place the stock pot over high heat. When water begins to boil, lower the heat slightly and cook for about 30 minutes or until the beans are tender.

4. Now the next thing to do is to arrange the pressure canner, canning lids and

jars. You need seven 1 pint jars (500 ml) or fourteen ½ pint jars (250 ml).

5. Pour enough water into the pressure canner following the manufacturer's instructions such that it is about 3 inches (8 cm) in height from the bottom of the canner. Place the canner on your stovetop over low heat. Place the jars in the canner so that the jars remain warm. The temperature of the water in the canner should be maintained at 180°F (82°C). Place the lids in a small saucepan of water over low heat on another burner.

6. Boil a kettle of water. Lift the jars from the canner and place over the towel. Sprinkle salt in each jar if using.

7. Carefully ladle the beans into the jars along with the cooked liquid. Make sure the beans are equally distributed among the jars. If the beans are not covered in water, pour enough boiling water to cover the beans to get headspace of 1 inch (2.5 cm) and make sure to remove bubbles using a bubble removing tool. Reassess the headspace and pour more water if required.

8. Take a clean damp cloth and wipe the rim of the jars. Place the canning lid on each jar using the lid lifter. Place the canning ring on each jar and tighten it as suggested.

9. Place the jars in the canner and process the jars following the manufacturer's instruction manual at 10 psi (69 kPa). Set the timer for 75 minutes adjusting for altitude if required. Once the timer goes off, turn off the burner.

10. Once you are done with the processing, let the pressure release naturally before opening the canner and taking out the jars. Let the jars cool completely on your countertop for no less than 12 hours. Wipe the jars with a dry kitchen cloth or paper towel. Make sure to check for the seals. Use the beans within a year.

11. **Serving suggestion**: You can use these beans to serve with meat or add it into soups or salads. Warm them up before serving.

Lentils with Vegetables

Makes: 4 pint jars (500 ml)

Ingredients:

- 1 ½ pounds (680 g) dried lentils
- 1-2 fresh celery stalks
- Five cloves garlic
- One large onion
- A large handful chopped greens like kale, Swiss chard, green cabbage or any other greens of your choice
- Two basil leaves, minced
- ¼ teaspoon (14 g) dried oregano
- 3 cups (710 ml) low-fat, low-sodium organic beef broth
- ¼ teaspoon ground black pepper
- 1/8 teaspoon (0.4 g) red pepper flakes or to taste
- ½ tablespoon (7.2 g) salt

Serving instructions per 1 pint jar (500 ml):

1. Grated parmesan cheese to garnish
2. Salt and pepper to taste
3. Any seasoning to taste (optional)

4. Chopped parsley to garnish

5. Some cooked noodles or browned ground beef crumbles (optional)

6. Squeeze of lemon or lime juice (optional)

Directions:

1. Place lentils in a large pot and cover with enough water such that the water is about 2 to 3 inches over the lentils. Let the lentils soak overnight. If you are short of time and are not able to soak them overnight, then place the pot over high heat and wait for the water to start boiling. Once the water starts boiling, let the lentils cook for two minutes. Turn off the heat and let them soak for an hour.

2. The following morning (after soaking the lentils overnight), have your other ingredients ready. Finely chop the celery stalks, garlic, and onion. Check the greens for any wild plants and discard them. Rinse the greens well and discard the stems. Chop the leaves into smaller pieces if desired.

3. Now the next thing to do is to arrange the pressure canner, canning lids and jars. You need four 1 pint jars (500 ml).

4. Pour enough water into the pressure canner following the manufacturer's instructions such that it is about 3 inches (8 cm) in height from the bottom of the canner. Place the canner on your stovetop over low heat. Place the jars in the canner so that the jars remain warm. The temperature of the water in the canner should be maintained at 180°F (82°C). Place the lids in a small saucepan of water over low heat on another burner.

5. Now add celery, garlic, onion, greens, herbs, broth, salt, and spices into a stock pot and place the pot over high heat on your stovetop. When the mixture starts boiling, lower the heat and cook for 15 minutes. Turn off the heat.

6. Lift the jars from the canner with a jar lifting tongs and place over the towel. Place funnel over the rim of the jars and carefully add lentils and vegetables into the jars using the slotted spoon. Fill the lentils up to 2/3 of the jars. Make sure the lentils and vegetables are equally distributed among the jars.

7. Now pour the hot stock into the jars until you get a headspace of 1 inch (2.5 cm). If the stock is not sufficient, boil some hot water in a kettle and pour into the jars. Make sure to remove bubbles using a bubble removing tool. Reassess the headspace and pour more boiling water or hot stock if required.

8. Take a clean damp cloth and wipe the rim of the jars. Place the canning lid on each jar using the lid lifter. Place the canning ring on each jar and tighten it as suggested.

9. Place the jars in the canner and process the jars following the manufacturer's instruction manual at 10 psi (69 kPa). Set the timer for 75 minutes adjusting for altitude if required. Once the timer goes off, turn off the burner.

10. Once you are done with the processing, let the pressure release naturally before opening the canner and taking out the jars. Let the jars cool completely on your countertop for no less than 12 hours. Wipe the jars with a dry kitchen cloth or paper towel. Make sure to check for the seals. Use the lentils within a year.

11. **Serving suggestion**: Empty the contents of a jar into a saucepan. Heat the lentils over medium heat on your stovetop. Add cooked noodles or beef if desired. Add salt and pepper to taste. If you like to dilute the lentils, add some water or stock while heating the lentils. Ladle into bowls. Garnish with parsley and parmesan cheese and serve.

Baked Beans

Makes: 6 pint jars (500 ml)

Ingredients:

- 2.2 pounds (1 kg) dried navy beans
- 12 ounces (340 g) tomato paste
- 3 teaspoons (15 g) mustard powder
- 3 teaspoons (15 g) ground black pepper
- 2 tablespoons (30 g) kitchen bouquet (optional)
- 6 cups (1.5 L) cooked bean water
- Two medium onions, chopped
- 3 tablespoons (30 g) Worcestershire sauce
- 3 teaspoons (15 g) salt
- 6 tablespoons (90 g) brown sugar
- Four bay leaves

Serving instructions per 1 pint jar (500 ml):

- Sweet chili sauce to taste
- Chopped cooked sausages
- Salad or cooked pasta

Directions:

1. Place beans in a stock pot and cover with water. The water should be at least

2 to 3 inches (5 to 7.5 cm) over the beans. Place the pot over high heat and wait for it to start boiling. Let it boil for two minutes and turn off the heat. Let the beans soak in the hot water for an hour. Make sure to cover the pot while the beans are soaking.

2. Meanwhile combine onions, Worcestershire sauce, salt, brown sugar, tomato paste, mustard, pepper, and kitchen bouquet in a large microwave safe bowl. Keep it aside as of now.

3. Drain off the water and put the beans in a large pot. Add bay leaves and cover with water. The water should be at least 2 to 3 inches (5 to 7.5 cm) over the beans. Place the pot over high heat and wait for it to start boiling. Let it boil for 1-2 minutes and turn off the heat. Do not boil the beans longer than two minutes or else you will end up with mashed beans.

4. You also need to arrange the pressure canner, canning lids and jars. You need six 1 pint jars (500 ml). Pour enough water into the pressure canner following the manufacturer's instructions such that it is about 3 inches (8 centimeters) in height from the bottom of the canner. Place the canner on your stovetop over low heat. Place the jars in the canner so that the jars remain warm. The temperature of the water in the canner should be maintained at 180°F (82°C). Place the lids in a small saucepan of water over low heat on another burner.

5. Now place a colander over a large bowl and drain the beans into the colander. Do not discard the cooked liquid. You need some of it to make the sauce. The bay leaves are no longer needed.

6. Pour 6 cups (1.5 L) of the drained liquid into the microwave safe bowl with the sauce ingredients and stir. Cover the bowl and place it in the microwave. Cook on high power for about seven minutes. Or until you get a nice sauce. Take out the bowl and stir the sauce.

7. Distribute the beans among the jars. You should be able to fill each jar up to about ¾ the jar. Pour the sauce mixture into the jars until you get a headspace of 1 inch (2.5 cm). It is better to use a funnel while pouring sauce into the jars.

8. Make sure to remove bubbles using a bubble removing tool. Reassess the headspace and add more of the mixture into the jar.

9. Take a clean damp cloth and wipe the rim of the jars. Place the canning lid on each jar using the lid lifter. Place the canning ring on each jar and tighten it as suggested.

10. Place the jars in the canner and process the jars following the manufacturer's instruction manual at 10 psi (69 kPa). Set the timer for 65 minutes adjusting for altitude if required. Once the timer goes off, turn off the burner.

11. Once you are done with the processing, let the pressure release naturally before opening the canner and taking out the jars. Let the jars cool completely on your countertop for no less than 12 hours. Wipe the jars with a dry kitchen cloth or paper towel. Make sure to check for the seals. These jars will last you for 12 to 15 months.

12. **Serving suggestion**: There are numerous ways of serving baked beans. You can serve it over toasted bread. You can serve eggs over beans. You can serve it as a side dish along with meat. You can mash up the beans and serve as a bean mash. You can also make muffins or frittatas using the baked beans.

Here is one favorite way I use the baked beans: Empty the contents of a baked beans can into a saucepan. Add sweet chili sauce and sausages and heat it over medium heat until very nice and hot. Serve it over hot cooked pasta or along with a salad.

Chili Con Carne

Makes: 11 pint jars (500 ml)

Ingredients:

- 1 ½ pounds (680 g) dried kidney beans
- 1 ½ pounds (680 g) lean ground beef
- Three cloves garlic, minced
- 1 ½ tablespoons (22 ml) oil
- 1 ½ large onions, chopped
- 3 tablespoons (42 g) chili powder
- 1 tablespoon (15 g) salt
- 1 ½ tablespoons (21 g) beef bouillon granules powder
- ½ tablespoon (7.5 g) onion powder

- 1 ½ cans {14.5 ounces (400 g) each} diced tomatoes
- 1 ½ cups (350 ml) water
- ½ tablespoon (7.5 g) sugar
- 1 tablespoon (15 g) ground cumin
- ½ teaspoon (2.8 g) freshly ground black pepper
- ½ teaspoon (2.8 g) garlic powder
- ½ can {from a 14.5 ounces (400 g) can} tomato sauce

<u>Serving instructions per 1 pint jar (500 ml):</u>

- Salt and pepper to taste
- Chopped parsley to garnish

Directions:

1. To start off, pick the beans for any dirt, stones, discolored beans etc. Rinse the beans with fresh water and soak in a large pot of water. Soak them for at least 12 hours. Discard the soaked water.

2. If you do not want to soak the beans for 12 hours, there is another way you can do it: Place beans in a saucepan and cover with water. The water should be at least 2 to 3 inches over the beans. Place the saucepan over high heat and wait for it to start boiling. Let it boil for two minutes and turn off the heat. Let the beans soak in the hot water for an hour. Drain off the water.

3. Transfer the beans into a large stock pot. Cover the beans with fresh water and place the stock pot over high heat. When water begins to boil, lower the heat slightly (i.e. medium heat) and cook for about 30 minutes or until the beans are tender. Turn off the heat and drain off the liquid. Rinse the beans well and

put it aside for the time being.

4. Now the next thing to do is to arrange the pressure canner, canning lids and jars. You need eleven 1 pint jars (500 ml).

5. Pour enough water into the pressure canner following the manufacturer's instructions such that it is about 3 inches (8 centimeters) in height from the bottom of the canner. Place the canner on your stovetop over low heat. Place the jars in the canner so that the jars remain warm. The temperature of the water in the canner should be maintained at 180°F (82°C). Place the lids in a small saucepan of water over low heat on another burner.

6. While the canner is slowly heating, pour oil into a large stock pot and let the oil heat over high heat. Once the oil is hot, add ground beef and cook until brown. As you stir, break the beef into crumbles. Stir in the onions and garlic and cook until the onions turn tender. This should take around 7-8 minutes. Discard as much fat as you can from the pot.

7. Now add pepper, onion powder, garlic powder, cumin, beef bouillon powder, and chili powder, and keep stirring for about a minute or until you get a nice aroma. Add beans, tomato sauce, diced tomatoes, salt, and sugar and mix well. When the mixture starts boiling, bring down the heat to low heat and let the mixture cook for about 3-4 minutes. Make sure to stir often. Turn off the heat.

8. Lift the jars from the canner with a jar lifting tongs and place over the towel. Place funnel over the rim of the jars and carefully spoon the mixture into the jars until you get headspace of 1 inch (2.5 cm). It is better to use a funnel while spooning into the jars.

9. Make sure to remove bubbles using a bubble removing tool. Reassess the headspace and add more of the mixture into the jar.

10. Take a clean damp cloth and wipe the rim of the jars. Place the canning lid on

each jar using the lid lifter. Place the canning ring on each jar and tighten it as suggested.

11. Place the jars in the canner and process the jars following the manufacturer's instruction manual at 10 psi (69 kPa). Set the timer for 75 minutes adjusting for altitude if required. Once the timer goes off, turn off the burner.

12. Once you are done with the processing, let the pressure release naturally before opening the canner and taking out the jars. Let the jars cool completely on your countertop for no less than 12 hours. Wipe the jars with a dry kitchen cloth or paper towel. Make sure to check for the seals. These jars will last you for 12 to 15 months.

13. **Serving suggestion**: Empty the contents of a jar into a saucepan. Heat the chili over medium heat on your stovetop. Ladle into bowls. Add some salt and pepper to taste if desired. Garnish with parsley or any other fresh herbs of your choice and serve.

Pork and Beans

Makes: 6 pint jars (500 ml) or 3 quart jars (1 L)

Ingredients:

- 1 ½ pounds (680 g) dried navy beans or white beans
- 2 tablespoons (30 ml) apple cider vinegar
- 1 tablespoon (15 g) ground dry mustard
- 2-3 tablespoons (30–45 g) brown sugar or to taste
- 1 tablespoon (15 ml) Worcestershire sauce

- ¾ pound (340 g) bacon, diced
- Three cloves garlic, peeled, minced
- 2-3 tablespoons (30–45 ml) molasses (optional)
- 1 ½ tablespoons (22.5 g) kosher salt
- ¼ cup (120 ml) ketchup
- Two medium onions, chopped
- ½ teaspoon (2.5 g) ground black pepper
- Two bay leaves
- ¼ teaspoon (1.25 g) ground cloves

Serving instructions per 1 pint jar (500 ml):

- Grated parmesan cheese
- Chopped fresh herbs of your choice

Directions:

1. Place beans in a stock pot and cover with water. The water should be at least 2 to 3 inches (5 to 7.5 cm) over the beans. Place the pot over high heat and wait for it to start boiling. Let it boil for two minutes and turn off the heat. Let the beans soak in the hot water for an hour. Make sure to cover the pot while the beans are soaking.

2. Drain off the water and put the beans in a large stock pot. Pour 3.5 quarts (4.5 L) into the pot. Place the pot over high heat and wait for it to start boiling. Let it boil for two minutes and turn off the heat.

3. Now place a colander over a large bowl and drain the beans into the colander. Do not discard the cooked liquid.

4. Now put the bacon into a large stock pot and cook over medium heat on your stovetop until bacon turns crisp. Discard all the cooked fat from the pot. Next, put the onions into the pot and stir-fry for a few minutes until the onions turn pink. Stir in the garlic and cook for about a minute or until you get a nice aroma. Add beans, vinegar, mustard, brown sugar, Worcestershire sauce, molasses if using, salt, ketchup, pepper, bay leaves, and ground cloves.

5. Pour the drained liquid into the stock pot and stir the ingredients until well combined. When the mixture starts boiling, lower the heat and cook covered, until the beans are slightly tender. Make sure the beans are not overcooked as they have to be processed in the canner as well. If you find the liquid less in the pot at any time, feel free to add more

6. You also need to arrange the pressure canner, canning lids and jars. You can do this after about 30 minutes after you start cooking the beans. You need seven 1 pint jars (500 ml) or three quart size (1 L) jars. Pour enough water into the pressure canner following the manufacturer's instructions such that it is about 3 inches (8 centimeters) in height from the bottom of the canner. Place the canner on your stovetop over low heat. Place the jars in the canner so that the jars remain warm. The temperature of the water in the canner should be maintained at 180°F (82°C). Place the lids in a small saucepan of water over low heat on another burner.

7. Place the jars over a towel on your countertop. It is better to use a funnel while pouring the beans into the jars. Remove beans with a slotted spoon and place them in the jars. Make sure to distribute the beans equally among the jars. Pour enough cooked liquid from the pot into the jars until you get headspace of 1 inch (2.5 cm).

8. Make sure to remove bubbles using a bubble removing tool. Reassess the

headspace and add more of the liquid into jars if required. In case you run short of liquid, you can compensate by pouring boiling water to fill up to the required headspace.

9. Take a clean damp cloth and wipe the rim of the jars. Place the canning lid on each jar using the lid lifter. Place the canning ring on each jar and tighten it as suggested.

10. Place the jars in the canner and process the jars following the manufacturer's instruction manual at 10 psi (69 kPa). Set the timer for 65 minutes if you are using pint size jars or 75 minutes if you are using quart size jars, adjusting for altitude if required. Once the timer goes off, turn off the burner.

11. Once you are done with the processing, let the pressure release naturally before opening the canner and taking out the jars. Let the jars cool completely on your countertop for no less than 12 hours. Wipe the jars with a dry kitchen cloth or paper towel. Make sure to check for the seals. These jars will last you for about 12 months.

12. **Serving suggestion**: Empty the contents of a jar into a saucepan. Heat over medium heat on your stovetop. Ladle into bowls. Add some salt and pepper to taste if desired. Garnish with cheese and any other fresh herbs of your choice and serve.

Chapter 4:
Tomatoes

Canning Tomatoes

Makes: 4 pint jars (500 ml) or 2 quart jars (1 L)

Ingredients:

- 6 pounds (2.7 kg) fresh, ripe plum tomatoes
- Boiling water, as required
- ½ teaspoon salt per pint size jar or 1 teaspoon salt per quart size jar (optional)

<u>**Use any one of these acidic ingredients:**</u> **(This is important)**

- 1 tablespoon lemon juice per pint size jar or 2 tablespoons lemon juice per quart size jar (preferably bottled lemon juice)
- 2 tablespoons 5% acidic vinegar per pint size jar or 4 tablespoons 5% acidic vinegar per quart size jar
- ¼ teaspoon citric acid per pint size jar or ½ teaspoon citric acid per quart size jar

Directions:

1. Boil a pot of water over high heat. While the water is boiling, rinse the tomatoes well. Remove any stem or leaves from the tomatoes. Make an 'X' on the top of each tomato using a paring knife.
2. Have a bowl of ice water ready on your countertop near the stovetop. Drop the tomatoes carefully into the pot with boiling water. Let the tomatoes cook for a minute. Soon you can see a bit of loose skin around the area of the 'X'

on the tomatoes.

3. Pick the tomatoes with a slotted spoon and drop them into the bowl of ice water. In a few minutes the tomatoes would have cooled down. Peel off the skin from the tomatoes.

4. Put the peeled tomatoes into a large bowl.

5. While you are peeling the tomatoes, arrange the pressure canner, canning lids, and jars. You need two quart (1 L) size jars or four 1 pint jars (500 ml). Pour enough water into the pressure canner following the manufacturer's instructions such that it is about 3 inches (8 centimeters) in height from the bottom of the canner. Place the canner on your stovetop over low heat. Place the jars in the canner so that the jars remain warm. The temperature of the water in the canner should be maintained at 180°F (82°C). Place the lids in a small saucepan of water over low heat on another burner.

6. Place a kitchen towel on your countertop and spread it. Lift the jars from the canner and place over the towel. Add the chosen acidic ingredient in each jar. Add the salt if using. Place the tomatoes in the jars until you get a headspace of ¼ inch (1.25 cm). It is better to use a funnel while adding the sauce into the jars.

7. Make sure to remove bubbles using a bubble removing tool. Reassess the headspace. On reassessing, if the headspace increases, pour some liquid of the tomatoes that has been collected in the bowl. If there is no liquid in the tomatoes, add some boiling water.

8. Take a clean damp cloth and wipe the rim of the jars. Place the canning lid on each jar using the lid lifter. Place the canning ring on each jar and tighten it as suggested.

9. Place the jars in the canner and process the jars following the manufacturer's instruction manual at 10 psi (69 kPa). Set the timer for 65 minutes adjusting for altitude if required. Once the timer goes off, turn off the burner.

10. Once you are done with the processing, let the pressure release naturally before opening the canner and taking out the jars. Let the jars cool completely on your countertop for no less than 12 hours. Wipe the jars with a dry kitchen cloth or paper towel. Make sure to check for the seals. These jars will last you for 12 to 15 months.

11. **Serving suggestion**: You can use tomatoes in just almost anything like curries, sauces, etc. Use as much as required and store the remaining in the refrigerator.

Spaghetti Sauce

Makes: 4 pints

Ingredients:

- 15 pounds (6.8 kg) Roma tomatoes or any fresh tomatoes
- 1 large onion, chopped
- 1 tablespoon salt
- 2 – 3 cloves garlic, peeled, minced
- ½ pound (227 g) mushrooms, sliced (optional)
- 1 tablespoon dried oregano flakes
- 2 tablespoons (25 g) brown sugar or unrefined cane sugar
- 2 tablespoons (28.4 g) butter or olive oil
- 1 stalk celery or 1 small green bell pepper, chopped
- 1 teaspoon ground black pepper
- A handful fresh parsley, minced

Directions:

1. Rinse the tomatoes well. Remove any stem or leaves from the tomatoes. Cut tomatoes into 4 quarters each and place them in a large saucepan. Place the saucepan over medium-high heat.
2. Wait for it to come to a boil. Make sure to stir often.
3. Lower the heat and cook for about 15 – 18 minutes. As it cooks, stir periodically so that the tomatoes do not get stuck on the bottom of the saucepan. Turn off the heat and spoon the tomatoes into a food mill or strainer in batches and strain the tomatoes. Discard the solids remaining in the food

mill.

4. Pour the strained tomatoes into the saucepan. Place the saucepan over medium heat and cook until it is reduced to about half its original quantity or to the thickness you desire.

5. Meanwhile, place a pan over medium heat. Add butter or oil. When butter melts, add onion, celery, garlic, and mushrooms and cook for 5 – 6 minutes until vegetables are slightly tender.

6. Turn off the heat and transfer the sautéed vegetables into the saucepan containing tomato sauce.

7. Stir in pepper, oregano, salt, sugar, and parsley. Stir often until sugar dissolves completely.

8. Lower the heat and let it simmer on low heat to keep warm.

9. While the sauce is cooking, during the last 30 minutes, arrange the pressure canner, canning lids, and jars. You need about three to four 1 pint jars (500 ml). Pour enough water into the pressure canner following the manufacturer's instructions such that it is about 3 inches (8 centimeters) in height from the bottom of the canner. Place the canner on your stovetop over low heat. Place the jars in the canner so that the jars remain warm. The temperature of the water in the canner should be maintained at 180°F (82°C). Place the lids in a small saucepan of water over low heat on another burner.

10. Take out the jars from the canner with the help of the canning tongs. Place the funnel on top of the jar. Spoon the tomato sauce into the jars until you get a headspace of 1 inch (2.5 cm).

11. Make sure to remove bubbles using a bubble removing tool. Reassess the headspace. On reassessing, if the headspace increases, add some more sauce.

12. Take a clean damp cloth and wipe the rim of the jars. Place the canning lid on each jar using the lid lifter. Place the canning ring on each jar and tighten it as suggested.

13. Place the jars in the canner and process the jars following the manufacturer's instruction manual at 5 psi (36 kPa). Set the timer for 20 minutes for sea level. The timing will be 50 minutes at 6 psi (41 kPa) between 1,001 to 3,000 feet. The timing will be 55 minutes at 7 psi (48 kPa) between 3,001 to 6,000 feet. The timing will be 60 minutes at 8 psi (55 kPa) for above 6,001 feet. Once the timer goes off, turn off the burner.

14. Once you are done with the processing, let the pressure release naturally before opening the canner and taking out the jars. Let the jars cool completely on your countertop for no less than 12 hours. Wipe the jars with a dry kitchen cloth or paper towel. Make sure to check for the seals. These jars will last you for 12 to 18 months.

15. **Serving suggestion**: You can use spaghetti sauce in numerous dishes like curries, pasta, pizzas, soups, braised meat etc. to make it more flavorful.

Tomato Sauce

Makes: 4 – 5 pint jars (500 ml) or 2 – 3 quart jars (1 L)

Ingredients:

For thick tomato sauce:

- 14 pounds whole tomatoes for pint size jars or 23 pounds tomatoes for quart size jars
- ½ teaspoon salt per pint size jar or 1 teaspoon salt per quart size jar (optional)
- Seasoning blend to taste

For thin tomato sauce:

- 10.5 pounds whole tomatoes for pint size jars or 17.5 pounds tomatoes for quart size jars
- ½ teaspoon salt per pint size jar or 1 teaspoon salt per quart size jar (optional)
- Seasoning blend to taste

Use any one of these acidic ingredients: This is important, whether for thick sauce or thin sauce.

- 1 tablespoon lemon juice per pint size jar or 2 tablespoons lemon juice per quart size jar (bottled lemon juice)
- ¼ teaspoon citric acid per pint size jar or ½ teaspoon citric acid per quart size jar

Seasoning blend variations:

Creole seasoning blend:

- 2 tablespoons hot paprika
- 2 tablespoons dried oregano

- 4 teaspoons onion powder
- 4 teaspoons dried thyme
- 2 teaspoons ground white pepper
- 2 tablespoons sweet paprika
- 2 tablespoons ground red pepper
- 4 teaspoons garlic powder
- 4 teaspoons ground black pepper
- 2 teaspoons celery seeds

<u>Mexican seasoning blend:</u>

- 4 teaspoons garlic powder
- 4 teaspoons dried oregano
- 8 teaspoons chili powder
- 8 teaspoons ground chipotle pepper
- 4 teaspoons coriander seeds
- 4 teaspoons cumin seeds

<u>Italian seasoning blend:</u>

- 4 teaspoons dried crushed red pepper
- 2 tablespoons garlic powder
- 4 tablespoons dried oregano
- 4 teaspoons dried thyme
- 4 teaspoons dried basil

Directions:

1. To make seasoning blend: You will need to add more seasoning blend to make thin sauce and lesser seasoning blend for thick sauce. You can always add enough to suit your taste.

2. To make creole seasoning blend and Italian seasoning blend, simply gather the ingredients and mix them together in a bowl.

3. To make Mexican seasoning blend, add coriander and cumin seeds into a dry pan and place the pan over medium-low heat. Toast the spices until you get a nice aroma. Turn off the heat and let it cool for a few minutes. Powder the spices in a spice grinder or in a mortar using a pestle.

4. Add the ground spices into a bowl along with the rest of the ingredients and mix well. Rinse the tomatoes well. Remove any stem or leaves from the tomatoes.

5. Cut about a pound of tomatoes, each into four quarters, and place them in a large saucepan.

6. Place the saucepan over high heat. Continue quartering the tomatoes about a pound at a time and keep adding them to the pot. Be quick while cutting and adding.

7. Stir as you add tomatoes and mash the tomatoes with the back of a large stirring spoon or potato masher. When all the tomatoes are added, wait for it to come to a boil. Make sure to stir often. Lower the heat and cook for about five minutes. As it cooks, stir often so that the tomatoes do not get stuck on the bottom of the saucepan.

8. Turn off the heat and spoon the tomatoes into a food mill or strainer in batches and strain the tomatoes. Discard the solids remaining in the food mill. Pour the strained tomatoes into the saucepan. Add the seasoning blend now and

stir.

9. Place the saucepan over medium heat and cook until the sauce reduces to 2/3 of the strained mixture for thin sauce. Cook until the sauce reduces to ½ the strained mixture for thick sauce.

10. While the tomato sauce is cooking, arrange the pressure canner, canning lids, and jars. You need four to five 1 pint jars (500 ml) or two to three quart size jars (1 L). Pour enough water into the pressure canner following the manufacturer's instructions such that it is about 3 inches (8 centimeters) in height from the bottom of the canner. Place the canner on your stovetop over low heat. Place the jars in the canner so that the jars remain warm. The temperature of the water in the canner should be maintained at 180°F (82°C). Place the lids in a small saucepan of water over low heat on another burner.

11. Place the jars on a towel on your countertop. Add citric acid and lemon juice into each jar. Place a funnel over the jars. Spoon the tomato sauce into the jars until you get a headspace of ¼ inch (0.6 cm).

12. Make sure to remove bubbles using a bubble removing tool. Reassess the headspace. On reassessing, if the headspace increases, add some more tomato sauce.

13. Take a clean damp cloth and wipe the rim of the jars. Place the canning lid on each jar using the lid lifter. Place the canning ring on each jar and tighten it as suggested.

14. Place the jars in the canner and process the jars following the manufacturer's instruction manual at 5 psi (36 kPa). Set the timer for 20 minutes for sea level. The timing will be 50 minutes at 6 psi (41 kPa) between 1,001 to 3,000 feet. The timing will be 55 minutes at 7 psi (48 kPa) between 3,001 to 6,000 feet. The timing will be 60 minutes at 8 psi (55 kPa) for above 6,001 feet. Once the

timer goes off, turn off the burner.

15. Once you are done with the processing, let the pressure release naturally before opening the canner and taking out the jars. Let the jars cool completely on your countertop for no less than 12 hours. Wipe the jars with a dry kitchen cloth or paper towel. Make sure to check for the seals. These jars will last you for 12 to 18 months.

16. **Serving suggestion**: You can use tomato paste in numerous dishes like curries, pasta sauce, soups, braised meat etc. to make it more flavorful.

Chapter 5:
Meat

Pork

Makes: 6 pint jars (500 ml)

Ingredients:

- 4.4 pounds (2 kg) pork butt
- 3 teaspoons (15 g) kosher salt
- 1 teaspoon (5 g) Cure #1
- 1 teaspoon (5 g) ground allspice
- Two cloves garlic, minced
- 1 tablespoon (15 g) caramelized onion per jar
- 1 teaspoon (5 g) ground black pepper
- One bay leaf per jar

Serving instructions per 1 pint jar (500 ml):

- Grated cheese
- Chopped fresh herbs of your choice
- Butter

Directions:

1. Trim the pork of extra fat and chop into 1 inch chunks and place in a large bowl.

2. To cure the meat: Combine salt and cure #1 in a bowl and sprinkle the salt mixture over the meat. Toss well. Cover the bowl with cling wrap and place it in the refrigerator for a minimum of 24 hours and a maximum of 48 hours.

3. Once you are done with curing, arrange the pressure canner, canning lids, and jars. You need six 1 pint jars (500 ml). Pour enough water into the pressure canner following the manufacturer's instructions such that it is about 3 inches (8 centimeters) in height from the bottom of the canner. Place the canner on your stovetop over low heat. Place the jars in the canner so that the jars remain warm. The temperature of the water in the canner should be maintained at 180°F (82°C). Place the lids in a small saucepan of water over low heat on another burner.

4. Add pepper, allspice, and garlic into the bowl of pork and stir until well combined. Place the jars over a towel on your countertop. It is better to use a funnel while pouring the meat into the jars. Add meat into the jars until you get a headspace of 1 inch (2.5 cm). Pack the meat in the jars but do not pack very tightly. Place a bay leaf in each jar. Place a tablespoon of caramelized onion in each jar.

5. No water or broth is to be added to the jars and the meat will leave its liquid on pressure canning.

6. Make sure to remove bubbles using a bubble removing tool. Reassess the headspace and add more meat if required to fill up to the required headspace.

7. Take a clean damp cloth and wipe the rim of the jars. Place the canning lid on each jar using the lid lifter. Place the canning ring on each jar and tighten it as

suggested.

8. Place the jars in the canner and process the jars following the manufacturer's instruction manual at 15 psi (103 kPa). Set the timer for 65 to 70 minutes depending on how you like the meat cooked, adjusting for altitude if required. Once the timer goes off, turn off the burner. I prefer to cook it for 70 minutes.

9. Once you are done with the processing, let the pressure release naturally before opening the canner and taking out the jars. Let the jars cool completely on your countertop for no less than 12 hours. Wipe the jars with a dry kitchen cloth or paper towel. Make sure to check for the seals. These jars will last you for about 12 months.

10. **Serving suggestion**: Empty the contents of a jar into a saucepan. Heat over medium heat on your stovetop. Discard the bay leaf. Ladle into bowls. Add some salt and pepper to taste if desired. Add a blob of butter in each bowl. Garnish with cheese and any other fresh herbs of your choice and serve.

Pulled Pork Barbecue

Makes: 6 pint jars (500 ml)

Ingredients:

- 7 pounds (3.2 kg) pork butt (barbequed or cooked in a slow cooker)
- 2 quarts (2 L) beef stock or water
- 2 pints (4 L) BBQ or more to taste

For BBQ sauce:

- 3 ¾ cups (830 ml) ketchup

- ½ cup (110 g) brown sugar
- ½ cup (110 g) prepared mustard
- ½ cup (125 ml) apple cider vinegar
- 2 teaspoons (10 g) ground black pepper
- 2 tablespoons (30 ml) Worcestershire sauce
- 1 tablespoon (15 ml) lemon juice
- 1 tablespoon (15 g) garlic powder
- 1 tablespoon (15 ml) liquid smoke
- 2 tablespoons (30 ml) hot sauce

Serving instructions per 1 pint jar (500 ml):

- Burger buns or tortillas
- Toppings of your choice
- Grated cheese
- Chopped fresh herbs of your choice

Directions:

1. You can cook the pork in a BBQ or in a slow cooker or as you normally cook. In case you have cooked the pork in a BBQ, use only ½ tablespoon (7.5 ml) of the liquid smoke. Now pull the pork with a pair of forks and add into a large stock pot.

2. Arrange the pressure canner, canning lids, and jars. You need about six 1 pint (500 ml) size jars. Pour enough water into the pressure canner following the manufacturer's instructions such that it is about 3 inches (8 centimeters) in height from the bottom of the canner. Place the canner on your stovetop over

low heat. Place the jars in the canner so that the jars remain warm. The temperature of the water in the canner should be maintained at 180°F (82°C). Place the lids in a small saucepan of water over low heat on another burner.

3. Boil water or stock in a pot.

4. Combine all the BBQ sauce ingredients in a large stock pot. Stir until well combined. Add the pulled pork and place the pot over high heat. Bring to a boil, stirring often. If the sauce is not coating well over the pork, you can add some water.

5. Distribute the meat among the jars. Pour enough boiling water into the jars until you get headspace of 1 inch (2.5 cm)

6. Make sure to remove bubbles using a bubble removing tool. Reassess the headspace and add more water if required to fill up to the required headspace.

7. Take a clean damp cloth and wipe the rim of the jars. Place the canning lid on each jar using the lid lifter. Place the canning ring on each jar and tighten it as suggested.

8. Place the jars in the canner and process the jars following the manufacturer's instruction manual at 10 psi (69 kPa). Set the timer for 65 minutes adjusting for altitude if required. Once the timer goes off, turn off the burner.

9. Once you are done with the processing, let the pressure release naturally before opening the canner and taking out the jars. Let the jars cool completely on your countertop for no less than 12 hours. Wipe the jars with a dry kitchen cloth or paper towel. Make sure to check for the seals. These jars will last you for about 12 months.

10. **Serving suggestion**: Empty the contents of the jar into a pan and heat thoroughly. Serve over burger buns or over tortillas or over lettuce leaves with

cheese and toppings of your choice.

Pork Meatballs

Makes: 8 – 9 pint jars (500 ml) or 4 – 5 quart jars (1 L)

Ingredients:

- 4 pounds (1.8 kg) ground pork
- 1 teaspoon (5 g) ground black pepper
- 4 teaspoons (20 g) garlic powder
- 2 teaspoons (10 g) dried thyme
- 2 teaspoons (10 g) ground cumin
- 2 teaspoons (10 g) ground coriander
- 4 teaspoons (20 g) onion powder
- 4 teaspoons (20 g) sweet paprika
- 4 teaspoons (20 g) kosher salt
- Water, stock or tomato juice, as required

Serving instructions per serving of 2 meatballs:

- Pasta sauce of your choice
- Hot cooked pasta or rice

Directions:

1. Combine pork, salt, and spices in a bowl. Make small balls of the mixture of about 3 inches (7.5 cm) each. I suggest you dip your hands often in water and make the meatballs. This way the meat will not stick to your hands. Make sure

you do not add any binders like egg or breadcrumbs.

2. Arrange the pressure canner, canning lids, and jars. You need about eight to nine 1 pint (500 ml) size jars or four to five quart (1 L) size jars. Pour enough water into the pressure canner following the manufacturer's instructions such that it is about 3 inches (8 centimeters) in height from the bottom of the canner. Place the canner on your stovetop over low heat. Place the jars in the canner so that the jars remain warm. The temperature of the water in the canner should be maintained at 180°F (82°C). Place the lids in a small saucepan of water over low heat on another burner.

3. Boil water or stock or tomato stock in a pot.

4. Place a skillet over medium heat. Spray some cooking spray into the skillet. Add a few meatballs into the pan without overcrowding. And cook until brown all over. It should not be cooked through as it will be cooked further while processing. Remove the meatballs from the pan and make sure to keep them warm until the remaining meatballs are browned.

5. Place the jars over a towel on your countertop. Place meatballs in the jar. Pack them loosely. Pour enough boiling liquid into the jars until you get headspace of 1 inch (2.5 cm).

6. Make sure to remove bubbles using a bubble removing tool. Reassess the headspace and add more boiling liquid if required to fill up to the required head pace.

7. Take a clean damp cloth and wipe the rim of the jars. Place the canning lid on each jar using the lid lifter. Place the canning ring on each jar and tighten it as suggested.

8. Place the jars in the canner and process the jars following the manufacturer's

instruction manual at 10 psi (69 kPa). Set the timer for 75 minutes for a pint-sized (500 ml) jar or 90 minutes for a quart-sized (1 L) jars adjusting for altitude if required. Once the timer goes off, turn off the burner.

9. Once you are done with the processing, let the pressure release naturally before opening the canner and taking out the jars. Let the jars cool completely on your countertop for no less than 12 hours. Wipe the jars with a dry kitchen cloth or paper towel. Make sure to check for the seals. These jars will last you for about 12 months.

10. **Serving suggestion**: Add some pasta sauce into a pan and let it heat over medium heat. Add the meatballs and heat thoroughly. Serve over hot cooked pasta or rice.

Hamburger Patties

Makes: 4 quart jars (1 L)

Ingredients:

- 6 pounds (1.8 kg) ground beef or pork
- One bell pepper, diced
- Two onions, diced
- 2 tablespoons (30 g) ranch dressing
- 2 tablespoons (30 g) beef bouillon
- 2 tablespoons (30 g) seasoned salt
- 2 tablespoons (30 ml) Worcestershire sauce
- Boiling water or stock or tomato juice as required

Serving instructions per burger:

- One burger bun
- One lettuce leaf
- One cheese slice (optional)
- Any other toppings of your choice

Directions:

1. Combine meat, onion, bell pepper, Worcestershire sauce, ranch dressing, and seasoned salt in a large bowl. Make sure you do not use any binders like eggs or breadcrumbs.

2. Make patties of the meat mixture such that they are as wide as the mouth of the jar and they fit well into the jars. You can use your hands to shape the patties. You can also use the help of the canning rings to shape the burgers. You should use a wide mouth jar to can the burgers. You cook the patties in a pan or oven. They only need to be browned and not cooked through inside.

3. To cook them in an oven, place the patties on a baking sheet and bake them in an oven preheated to 375°F for about 15 minutes on each side.

4. If you are cooking them in batches, make sure the burgers are kept warm until you place them in the jars.

5. While the burgers are cooking, arrange the pressure canner, canning lids, and jars. You need about four quart (1 L) size jars. Pour enough water into the pressure canner following the manufacturer's instructions such that it is about 3 inches (8 centimeters) in height from the bottom of the canner. Place the canner on your stovetop over low heat. Place the jars in the canner so that the jars remain warm. The temperature of the water in the canner should be

maintained at 180°F (82°C). Place the lids in a small saucepan of water over low heat on another burner.

6. Place a kitchen towel on your countertop and spread it. Lift the jars from the canner and place over the towel. Place the burgers in the jars. Pour the chosen boiling liquid into the jars to cover the burgers leaving headspace of 1 inch (2.5 cm).

7. Make sure to remove bubbles using a bubble removing tool. Reassess the headspace and add more liquid if required to fill up to the required headspace.

8. Take a clean damp cloth and wipe the rim of the jars. Place the canning lid on each jar using the lid lifter. Place the canning ring on each jar and tighten it as suggested.

9. Place the jars in the canner and process the jars following the manufacturer's instruction manual at 10 psi (69 kPa). Set the timer for 90 minutes, adjusting for altitude if required. Once the timer goes off, turn off the burner.

10. Once you are done with the processing, let the pressure release naturally before opening the canner and taking out the jars. Let the jars cool completely on your countertop for no less than 12 hours. Wipe the jars with a dry kitchen cloth or paper towel. Make sure to check for the seals. These jars will last you for about 12 months.

11. **Serving suggestion**: Take out a burger from the jar and place on a hot pan over medium heat. You can spray some oil into the pan before placing the burger and cook until crisp on both the sides. Split the bun into two and lightly toast the bun. Place a lettuce leaf over the bottom half of the bun followed by the burger and a slice of cheese. Place any other topping or sauce of your choice. Cover with the top half of the bun and serve.

Venison

Makes: 5 pint jars (500 ml)

Ingredients:

- 5 pounds lean venison, cubed
- 1 ¼ teaspoons ground black pepper
- 20 slices onion
- 5 teaspoons salt
- 5 teaspoons minced garlic
- 5 tablespoons minced green bell pepper (optional)

Serving instructions per 1 pint jar (500 ml):

- Chopped parsley

Directions:

1. Arrange the pressure canner, canning lids, and jars. You need about five 1 pint (500 ml) size jars. Pour enough water into the pressure canner following the manufacturer's instructions such that it is about 3 inches (8 centimeters) in height from the bottom of the canner. Place the canner on your stovetop over low heat. Place the jars in the canner so that the jars remain warm. The temperature of the water in the canner should be maintained at 180°F (82°C). Place the lids in a small saucepan of water over low heat on another burner.

2. Meanwhile, combine meat, salt, garlic, and pepper in a large bowl.

3. Place a kitchen towel on your countertop and spread it. Lift the jars from the canner and place over the towel.

4. Fill the jars with the meat, leaving a headspace of ½ inch (1.25 cm). Do not pack the meat very tightly. Add five slices of onion and 1 tablespoon of green bell pepper into each jar. No water or broth needs to be added to the jars as the meat will leave enough liquid on pressure canning.

5. Make sure to remove bubbles using a bubble removing tool. Reassess the headspace and add more meat if required to fill up to the required headspace.

6. Take a clean damp cloth and wipe the rim of the jars. Place the canning lid on each jar using the lid lifter. Place the canning ring on each jar and tighten it as suggested.

7. Place the jars in the canner and process the jars following the manufacturer's instruction manual at 10 psi (69 kPa). Set the timer for 75 minutes, adjusting for altitude if required. Once the timer goes off, turn off the burner.

8. Once you are done with the processing, let the pressure release naturally before opening the canner and taking out the jars. Let the jars cool completely on your countertop for no less than 12 hours. Wipe the jars with a dry kitchen cloth or paper towel. Make sure to check for the seals. These jars will last you for about 12 months.

9. **Serving suggestion**: Empty the contents of the jar into a pan and heat thoroughly. Transfer into a bowl. Garnish with parsley and serve. You can serve this as it is or serve it as a filling for sandwiches. You can also add the meat to stews or chilies.

Sausage

Makes: 6 pint jars (500 ml)

Ingredients:

- 4 pounds sausage links, cut into desired size
- Boiling stock or water or tomato juice

Serving instructions per 1 pint jar (500 ml):

- Two eggs
- Salt and pepper to taste
- Grated cheese to taste (optional)

Directions:

1. Arrange the pressure canner, canning lids, and jars. You need six 1 pint (500 ml) size jars. Pour enough water into the pressure canner following the

manufacturer's instructions such that it is about 3 inches (8 centimeters) in height from the bottom of the canner. Place the canner on your stovetop over low heat. Place the jars in the canner so that the jars remain warm. The temperature of the water in the canner should be maintained at 180°F (82°C). Place the lids in a small saucepan of water over low heat on another burner.

2. Place a pan over high heat. When the pan is hot, add sausage links and cook until brown. Place a kitchen towel on your countertop and spread it. Lift the jars from the canner and place over the towel.

3. Fill the jars with the sausage pieces making sure to divide them equally. Pour boiling liquid into the jars to cover the sausages leaving headspace of 1 inch (2.5 cm).

4. Make sure to remove bubbles using a bubble removing tool. Reassess the headspace and add more liquid if required to fill up to the required headspace.

5. Take a clean damp cloth and wipe the rim of the jars. Place the canning lid on each jar using the lid lifter. Place the canning ring on each jar and tighten it as suggested.

6. Place the jars in the canner and process the jars following the manufacturer's instruction manual at 10 psi (69 kPa). Set the timer for 90 minutes, adjusting for altitude if required. Once the timer goes off, turn off the burner.

7. Once you are done with the processing, let the pressure release naturally before opening the canner and taking out the jars. Let the jars cool completely on your countertop for no less than 12 hours. Wipe the jars with a dry kitchen cloth or paper towel. Make sure to check for the seals. These jars will last you for about 12 months.

8. **Serving suggestion**: Grease a microwave bowl with some oil. Add sausage and heat for a couple of minutes. Add beaten eggs, salt, and pepper and stir.

Cook for about a minute in the microwave until the eggs are cooked. Make sure to stir the mixture every 15 to 17 seconds. Serve hot. You can use the sausages in different ways like in making egg muffins, adding to breakfast hash, frittatas, soups, stews, etc.

Beef Stew

Makes: 6 pint jars (500 ml)

Ingredients:

- 2.5 pounds (1.1 kg) beef stew meat, cut into 1 ½ inch (3.8 cm) cubes
- Three medium carrots, peeled, sliced
- 3 teaspoons (15 g) sea salt
- Boiling water or broth, as required

- Five medium-large potatoes, peeled, cut into cubes
- 1 ½ large onions, diced
- Pepper to taste (optional)

<u>Serving instructions per 1 pint jar (500 ml):</u>
- Hot cooked rice or noodles
- Side dish of your choice

Directions:

1. Arrange the pressure canner, canning lids, and jars. You need six 1 pint (500 ml) size jars. Pour enough water into the pressure canner following the manufacturer's instructions such that it is about 3 inches (8 centimeters) in height from the bottom of the canner. Place the canner on your stovetop over low heat. Place the jars in the canner so that the jars remain warm. The temperature of the water in the canner should be maintained at 180°F (82°C). Place the lids in a small saucepan of water over low heat on another burner.

2. Boil a pot of water or broth.

3. Place a kitchen towel on your countertop and spread it. Lift the jars from the canner and place over the towel.

4. Fill the jars with meat, potatoes, carrots, and onions. Make sure they are equally distributed. Add ½ teaspoon salt into each jar. Add pepper to taste if desired. Pour boiling liquid into the jars to cover the meat and vegetables leaving headspace of 1 inch (2.5 cm).

5. Make sure to remove bubbles using a bubble removing tool. Reassess the headspace and add more liquid if required to fill up to the required headspace.

6. Take a clean damp cloth and wipe the rim of the jars. Place the canning lid on

each jar using the lid lifter. Place the canning ring on each jar and tighten it as suggested.

7. Place the jars in the canner and process the jars following the manufacturer's instruction manual at 10 psi (69 kPa). Set the timer for 75 minutes, adjusting for altitude if required. Once the timer goes off, turn off the burner.

8. Once you are done with the processing, let the pressure release naturally before opening the canner and taking out the jars. Let the jars cool completely on your countertop for no less than 12 hours. Wipe the jars with a dry kitchen cloth or paper towel. Make sure to check for the seals. These jars will last you for about 12 months.

9. **Serving suggestion**: Empty the contents of a jar into a saucepan and heat it thoroughly. Serve over hot cooked rice or noodles with a side dish like green beans.

Sloppy Joe Filling

Makes: 12 pint jars (500 ml) or 6 quart jars (1 L)

Ingredients:

- 8 pounds (3.6 kg) ground chuck
- Two medium green bell peppers, diced
- 4 tablespoons (60 ml) Worcestershire sauce
- 1 cup (250 ml) water
- ½ cup (125 ml) apple cider vinegar
- 2 teaspoons (10 g) salt

- Three medium onions, diced
- 6-8 large cloves garlic, peeled, minced
- 6 cups (1.5 L) ketchup
- ½ cup (110 g) brown sugar
- 2 tablespoons (30 g) mustard

<u>Serving instructions per 1 pint jar (500 ml):</u>

- Cheese slices
- Burger buns

Directions:

1. Arrange the pressure canner, canning lids, and jars. You need about twelve 1 pint (500 ml) size jars or six quart (1 L) size jars. Pour enough water into the pressure canner following the manufacturer's instructions such that it is about 3 inches (8 centimeters) in height from the bottom of the canner. Place the canner on your stovetop over low heat. Place the jars in the canner so that the jars remain warm. The temperature of the water in the canner should be maintained at 180°F (82°C). Place the lids in a small saucepan of water over low heat on another burner.

2. Put the onions and meat into a large stockpot and cook the mixture over medium-high heat until the meat is brown. Drain off as much fat as possible. Add bell pepper, garlic, water, vinegar, salt, ketchup, brown sugar, and mustard and mix well. When the mixture starts boiling, lower the heat and cook for about 20 minutes, stirring often.

3. Place a kitchen towel on your countertop and spread it. Lift the jars from the canner and place over the towel.

4. Fill the jars with the meat mixture leaving a headspace of 1 inch (2.5 cm).

5. Make sure to remove bubbles using a bubble removing tool. Reassess the headspace and add more meat mixture if required to fill up to the required headspace.

6. Take a clean damp cloth and wipe the rim of the jars. Place the canning lid on each jar using the lid lifter. Place the canning ring on each jar and tighten it as suggested.

7. Place the jars in the canner and process the jars following the manufacturer's instruction manual at 10 psi (69 kPa). Set the timer for 75 minutes for pint size (500 ml) or 90 minutes for quart (1 L) size, adjusting for altitude if required. Once the timer goes off, turn off the burner.

8. Once you are done with the processing, let the pressure release naturally before opening the canner and taking out the jars. Let the jars cool completely on your countertop for no less than 12 hours. Wipe the jars with a dry kitchen cloth or paper towel. Make sure to check for the seals. These jars will last you for about 12 months.

9. **Serving suggestion**: Empty the contents of the jar into a pan and heat thoroughly. Serve over burger buns with a slice or 2 of cheese.

Un-Stuffed Cabbage Rolls

Makes: 12 quart jars (1 L)

Ingredients:

- 4 pounds (1.8 kg) ground chuck

- 4-6 large cloves garlic, minced
- Two medium cabbages, cored, chopped
- 1 pound (454 g) mushrooms, halved or quartered depending on the size
- 2 cups (500 ml) water
- 4 teaspoons (20 g) ground black pepper
- Two large onions, chopped
- 2 cups (256 g) julienne cut carrots
- 4 cups (720 g) chopped tomatoes
- 4 cups (1 L) tomato sauce
- 4 teaspoons (20 g) salt

Serving instructions per 1 quart jar (1 L):

- Cucumber salad or bean salad (optional)
- Roasted potatoes or mashed potatoes

Directions:

1. Arrange the pressure canner, canning lids, and jars. You need about twelve quart (1 L) size jars. Pour enough water into the pressure canner following the manufacturer's instructions such that it is about 3 inches (8 centimeters) in height from the bottom of the canner. Place the canner on your stovetop over low heat. Place the jars in the canner so that the jars remain warm. The temperature of the water in the canner should be maintained at 180°F (82°C). Place the lids in a small saucepan of water over low heat on another burner.

2. Put the onions and meat into a large stockpot and cook the mixture over medium-high heat until the meat is brown. Drain off as much fat as possible.

Add cabbage, carrots, mushrooms, tomatoes, garlic, water, salt, and tomato sauce and mix well. When the mixture starts boiling, lower the heat and cook for 3-4 minutes, until cabbage wilts slightly, stirring often.

3. Place a kitchen towel on your countertop and spread it. Lift the jars from the canner and place over the towel.

4. Fill the jars with the meat mixture leaving a headspace of 1 inch (2.5 cm).

5. Make sure to remove bubbles using a bubble removing tool. Reassess the headspace and add more meat mixture if required to fill up to the required headspace.

6. Take a clean damp cloth and wipe the rim of the jars. Place the canning lid on each jar using the lid lifter. Place the canning ring on each jar and tighten it as suggested.

7. Place the jars in the canner and process the jars following the manufacturer's instruction manual at 10 psi (69 kPa). Set the timer for 90 minutes for quart (1 L) size, adjusting for altitude if required. Once the timer goes off, turn off the burner.

8. Once you are done with the processing, let the pressure release naturally before opening the canner and taking out the jars. Let the jars cool completely on your countertop for no less than 12 hours. Wipe the jars with a dry kitchen cloth or paper towel. Make sure to check for the seals. These jars will last you for about 12 months.

9. **Serving suggestion**: Empty the contents of the jar into a pan and heat thoroughly. Serve along with any one of the suggested side dishes for a complete meal.

Corned Beef and Potatoes

Makes: 4 – 5 quart jars (1 L)

Ingredients:

- 8–10 pounds (3.6–4.5 kg) beef brisket, home cured or pre-cured package
- ¼ teaspoon (1.25 g) pickling spice per quart (1 L) size jar
- 10–12 russet potatoes, scrubbed, peeled, cut into 1 inch cubes
- 4–5 carrots (optional), peeled, cut into 1 inch cubes
- Boiling water as required

Serving instructions per 1 quart jar (1 L):

- Favorite salad of your choice

Directions:

1. Arrange the pressure canner, canning lids, and jars. You need about four to five quart (1 L) size jars. Pour enough water into the pressure canner following the manufacturer's instructions such that it is about 3 inches (8 centimeters) in height from the bottom of the canner. Place the canner on your stovetop over low heat. Place the jars in the canner so that the jars remain warm. The temperature of the water in the canner should be maintained at 180°F (82°C). Place the lids in a small saucepan of water over low heat on another burner.

2. Boil a pot or kettle of water.

3. Trim the fat from the briskets and chop into 1 inch chunks.

4. Place a kitchen towel on your countertop and spread it. Lift the jars from the canner and place over the towel. Add pickling spice into each jar.

5. First divide the meat among the jars. Layer with equal amount of potatoes and carrots in each jar. Fill the jars with the boiling water covering the meat, leaving a headspace of 1 inch (2.5 cm).

6. Make sure to remove bubbles using a bubble removing tool. Reassess the headspace and add more water if required to fill up to the required headspace.

7. Take a clean damp cloth and wipe the rim of the jars. Place the canning lid on each jar using the lid lifter. Place the canning ring on each jar and tighten it as suggested.

8. Place the jars in the canner and process the jars following the manufacturer's instruction manual at 10 psi (69 kPa). Set the timer for 90 minutes for quart (1 L) size, adjusting for altitude if required. Once the timer goes off, turn off the burner.

9. Once you are done with the processing, let the pressure release naturally before opening the canner and taking out the jars. Let the jars cool completely on

your countertop for no less than 12 hours. Wipe the jars with a dry kitchen cloth or paper towel. Make sure to check for the seals. These jars will last you for about 12 months.

10. **Serving suggestion**: Empty the contents of the jar into a pan and heat thoroughly. Serve along with your favorite salad for a complete meal. If there is not particularly a favorite salad of your choice, here are a few suggestions apart from salads that go well like potato gratin, dinner rolls, roasted red potatoes, marinated artichoke hearts etc.

Burrito in a Jar

Makes: 4 quart jars (1 L)

Ingredients:

- 1 cup (171 g) dried pinto beans
- One large green bell pepper, diced

- 2 pounds (907 g) ground beef
- 2 tablespoons (30 g) taco seasoning
- Beef broth, as required
- Two medium onions, diced
- ½ cup (125 g) Rotel tomatoes
- 1 teaspoon (5 g) salt

Serving instructions per 1 quart jar (1 L):

- 1 cup cooked rice
- Tortillas
- Lettuce
- Tomatoes
- Any other favorite toppings of your choice

Directions:

1. Arrange the pressure canner, canning lids, and jars. You need about four quart (1 L) size jars. Pour enough water into the pressure canner following the manufacturer's instructions such that it is about 3 inches (8 centimeters) in height from the bottom of the canner. Place the canner on your stovetop over low heat. Place the jars in the canner so that the jars remain warm. The temperature of the water in the canner should be maintained at 180°F (82°C). Place the lids in a small saucepan of water over low heat on another burner.

2. Put the meat into a large stockpot and cook the mixture over medium-high heat until the meat is brown. Turn off the heat. Drain off as much fat as possible. Boil stock in a pot.

3. Place a kitchen towel on your countertop and spread it. Lift the jars from the canner and place over the towel.

4. You need to place the ingredients in layers. It looks so very nice and tempting. First divide the dried beans among the jars. Layer with equal amount of bell peppers in each jar followed by onions. Next layer with equal quantities of beef in each jar followed by tomatoes. Sprinkle ½ tablespoon taco seasoning and ¼ teaspoon salt in each jar. Fill the jars with the boiling stock to cover the ingredients, leaving a headspace of 1 inch (2.5 cm).

5. Make sure to remove bubbles using a bubble removing tool. Reassess the headspace and add more liquid if required to fill up to the required headspace.

6. Take a clean damp cloth and wipe the rim of the jars. Place the canning lid on each jar using the lid lifter. Place the canning ring on each jar and tighten it as suggested.

7. Place the jars in the canner and process the jars following the manufacturer's instruction manual at 10 psi (69 kPa). Set the timer for 90 minutes for quart (1 L) size, adjusting for altitude if required. Once the timer goes off, turn off the burner.

8. Once you are done with the processing, let the pressure release naturally before opening the canner and taking out the jars. Let the jars cool completely on your countertop for no less than 12 hours. Wipe the jars with a dry kitchen cloth or paper towel. Make sure to check for the seals. These jars will last you for about 12 months.

9. **Serving suggestion**: Empty the contents of the jar into a pan. Add cooked rice and heat thoroughly. Heat up the tortillas following the instructions given on the package. Top the burrito mixture over tortillas. Top with lettuce, tomatoes, and any other favorite burrito toppings of your choice and serve.

Chicken and Gravy

Makes: 8 pint jars (500 ml) or 4 quart jars (1 L)

Ingredients

- 2 cups (350 g) chopped onion
- 2 cups (350 g) peeled, diced potatoes
- 2 cups (250 g) finely chopped celery
- 4 pounds (1.8 kg) boneless chicken, cut into 2 inch (5 cm) chunks
- 4 teaspoons (20 g) poultry seasoning
- 4 teaspoons (20 g) salt
- 2 teaspoons (10 g) ground black pepper
- Boiling chicken stock or water, as required
- 8 tablespoons (118 ml) dry white wine

<u>Serving instructions per 1 pint jar (500 ml):</u>

- Chopped parsley
- 1 tablespoon (15 g) cornstarch mixed with ¼ cup (125 ml) water
- Hot cooked rice

Directions:

1. Arrange the pressure canner, canning lids, and jars. You need eight 1 pint (500 ml) size jars or four quart size (1 L) jars. Pour enough water into the pressure

canner following the manufacturer's instructions such that it is about 3 inches (8 centimeters) in height from the bottom of the canner. Place the canner on your stovetop over low heat. Place the jars in the canner so that the jars remain warm. The temperature of the water in the canner should be maintained at 180°F (82°C). Place the lids in a small saucepan of water over low heat on another burner.

2. Boil a pot of water or broth. Meanwhile, combine chicken, potatoes, celery, and onions in a bowl.

3. Place a kitchen towel on your countertop and spread it. Lift the jars from the canner and place over the towel. Pack the mixture into the jars using a funnel. They should be firmly packed and not tightly packed. Pour boiling liquid into the jars to cover the mixture leaving a headspace of 1 inch (2.5 cm).

4. Make sure to remove bubbles using a bubble removing tool. Reassess the headspace and add more liquid if required to fill up to the required headspace.

5. Take a clean damp cloth and wipe the rim of the jars. Place the canning lid on each jar using the lid lifter. Place the canning ring on each jar and tighten it as suggested.

6. Place the jars in the canner and process the jars following the manufacturer's instruction manual at 10 psi (69 kPa). Set the timer for 75 minutes, adjusting for altitude if required. Once the timer goes off, turn off the burner.

7. Once you are done with the processing, let the pressure release naturally before opening the canner and taking out the jars. Let the jars cool completely on your countertop for no less than 12 hours. Wipe the jars with a dry kitchen cloth or paper towel. Make sure to check for the seals. These jars will last you for about 12 months.

8. **Serving suggestion**: Empty the contents of the jar into a pan and place the

pan over high heat. Add cornstarch mixture and stir constantly until thick. Serve over hot cooked rice. Garnish with parsley and serve.

Chicken Marsala

Makes: 20 pint jars (500 ml) or 10 quart jars (1 L)

Ingredients:

- 10-12 pounds (4.5-5 kg) boneless, skinless chicken, trimmed of fat, cut into bite size pieces
- 4 cups (1 L) dry Marsala wine
- Two medium onions, diced
- Two large cloves garlic, chopped
- Four packages (20 ounces (567 g) each) sliced mushrooms
- 4 quarts (4 L) chicken stock
- 1 teaspoon (1 g) dried oregano
- Salt to taste
- Pepper to taste
- Olive oil to cook chicken, as required

Serving instructions per 1 pint jar (500 ml):

- Chopped parsley
- 1 tablespoon (15 g) cornstarch mixed with ¼ cup (125 ml) water
- 4 tablespoons (60 ml) cream or sour cream

- Cooked angel hair pasta or rice to serve

Directions:

1. Arrange the pressure canner, canning lids, and jars. You need twenty 1 pint (500 ml) size jars or ten quart size (1 L) jars. Pour enough water into the pressure canner following the manufacturer's instructions such that it is about 3 inches (8 centimeters) in height from the bottom of the canner. Place the canner on your stovetop over low heat. Place the jars in the canner so that the jars remain warm. The temperature of the water in the canner should be maintained at 180°F (82°C). Place the lids in a small saucepan of water over low heat on another burner.

2. Pour oil into a large pan and let the oil heat over high heat. Sprinkle salt and pepper over the chicken and cook them in batches until brown on the outside. Place a colander over a bowl. Take out the chicken from the pan and place it in the colander so that excess fat will drain off.

3. Lift the jars from the canner and place over the towel. Divide the chicken equally and pack into the jars. Divide the mushrooms into the jars.

4. Add onion, and oregano into the pan in which you cooked the chicken and cook the onions until pink. Pour wine and let it come to a rolling boil for a minute. Lower the heat and let it cook for about 3-4 minutes.

5. Pour stock and stir. Once the mixture starts boiling, let it cook on low heat for five minutes. Place a funnel over the jars and pour the stock mixture into the jars covering the mixture. Leave headspace of 1 inch (2.5 cm).

6. Make sure to remove bubbles using a bubble removing tool. Reassess the headspace and add more liquid if required to fill up to the required headspace.

7. Take a clean damp cloth and wipe the rim of the jars. Place the canning lid on each jar using the lid lifter. Place the canning ring on each jar and tighten it as

suggested.

8. Place the jars in the canner and process the jars following the manufacturer's instruction manual at 10 psi (69 kPa). Set the timer for 75 minutes, adjusting for altitude if required. Once the timer goes off, turn off the burner.

9. Once you are done with the processing, let the pressure release naturally before opening the canner and taking out the jars. Let the jars cool completely on your countertop for no less than 12 hours. Wipe the jars with a dry kitchen cloth or paper towel. Make sure to check for the seals. These jars will last you for about 12 months.

10. **Serving suggestion**: Empty the contents of the jar into a pan and place the pan over high heat. Add cornstarch mixture and stir constantly until thick. Add sour cream or cream and stir. Turn off the heat. Serve rice or pasta in serving plates or bowls. Ladle the chicken Marsala on top of the rice or pasta and serve garnished with parsley.

Apricot Chicken

Makes: 4 pint jars (500 ml) or 2 quart jars (1 L)

Ingredients:

- 3 pounds (1.4 kg) chicken breast or chicken breast tenderloins
- ½ teaspoon (2.5 g) spice mix of your choice per pint size jar or 1 teaspoon (5 g) spice mix per quart size jar
- 2 packages dried apricots
- 2 cups (500 ml) chicken broth

Serving instructions per 1 pint jar (500 ml):

- Hot cooked rice or egg noodles

Directions:

1. Arrange the pressure canner, canning lids, and jars. You need four 1 pint (500 ml) size jars or two quart size (1 L) jars. Pour enough water into the pressure canner following the manufacturer's instructions such that it is about 3 inches (8 centimeters) in height from the bottom of the canner. Place the canner on your stovetop over low heat. Place the jars in the canner so that the jars remain warm. The temperature of the water in the canner should be maintained at 180°F (82°C). Place the lids in a small saucepan of water over low heat on another burner.

2. Boil broth in a pot.

3. Lift the jars from the canner and place over the towel. Drop 4-5 apricots into each jar. Add spice mix into each jar. Fill chicken up to half of each jar. Drop 2-3 apricots in the jar once again. Divide the remaining chicken among the jars. Place remaining apricots in the jar. Place a funnel over the jars and pour the broth into the jars. Leave headspace of 1 inch (2.5 cm).

4. Make sure to remove bubbles using a bubble removing tool. Reassess the headspace and add more liquid if required to fill up to the required headspace.

5. Take a clean damp cloth and wipe the rim of the jars. Place the canning lid on each jar using the lid lifter. Place the canning ring on each jar and tighten it as suggested.

6. Place the jars in the canner and process the jars following the manufacturer's instruction manual at 10 psi (69 kPa). Set the timer for 75 minutes, adjusting for altitude if required. Once the timer goes off, turn off the burner.

7. Once you are done with the processing, let the pressure release naturally before opening the canner and taking out the jars. Let the jars cool completely on your countertop for no less than 12 hours. Wipe the jars with a dry kitchen cloth or paper towel. Make sure to check for the seals. These jars will last you for about 12 months.

8. **Serving suggestion**: Empty the contents of the jar into a pan and place the pan over high heat and heat thoroughly. Serve apricot chicken over rice or egg noodles.

White Bean and Chicken Chili

Makes: 6 pint jars (500 ml)

Ingredients:

- 1 ¼ cups Great Northern beans, soaked in water overnight
- 3 cups boneless, skinless chicken cubes
- Three cloves garlic, minced
- ½ tablespoon dried oregano
- 5 cups low-fat chicken broth
- ½ tablespoon olive oil
- ½ medium onion, chopped
- 1/8 teaspoon ground cumin
- ½ teaspoon cayenne pepper
- ½ cup diced green chilies

Serving instructions per serving 1 pint (500 ml) jar:

- Diced tomatoes
- Diced avocado
- Chopped cilantro

Directions:

1. Put the soaked beans along with the soaked water into a pot and cook it over medium-high heat for 30 minutes. Drain.

2. Arrange the pressure canner, canning lids, and jars. You need six 1 pint (500 ml) size jars. Pour enough water into the pressure canner following the manufacturer's instructions such that it is about 3 inches (8 centimeters) in height from the bottom of the canner. Place the canner on your stovetop over low heat. Place the jars in the canner so that the jars remain warm. The temperature of the water in the canner should be maintained at 180°F (82°C). Place the lids in a small saucepan of water over low heat on another burner.

3. Meanwhile, pour oil into another pot and place it over medium heat. Stir in the chicken. Stir often and cook for about 8–10 minutes.

4. Stir in garlic, onions, oregano, cumin, and cayenne pepper. Place the beans in the pot.

5. Stir in the green chilies and broth. When the mixture starts boiling, reduce the heat to medium-low and let it cook for 8–9 minutes. Turn off the heat.

6. Place the jars on a towel. Place the funnel over the rim of the jar. Remove beans and chicken with a slotted spoon and add into the jars, making sure each jar has equal amounts of beans and chicken. The jars would be about half filled with the vegetables and meat.

7. Now pour the broth into the jars until you get 1 inch (2.5 cm) headspace.

8. Make sure to remove bubbles using a bubble removing tool. Reassess the headspace and add more boiling liquid if required to fill up to the required headspace.

9. Take a clean damp cloth and wipe the rim of the jars. Place the canning lid on each jar using the lid lifter. Place the canning ring on each jar and tighten it as suggested.

10. Place the jars in the canner and process the jars following the manufacturer's instruction manual at 10 psi (69 kPa). Set the timer for 70 minutes for 1 pint size (500 ml) jars, adjusting for altitude if required. Once the timer goes off, turn off the burner.

11. Once you are done with the processing, let the pressure release naturally before opening the canner and taking out the jars. Let the jars cool completely on your countertop for no less than 12 hours. Wipe the jars with a dry kitchen cloth or paper towel. Make sure to check for the seals. These jars will last you for about 12 months.

12. **Serving suggestion**: Empty the contents of a jar into a saucepan. Place the saucepan over medium heat. Heat the chili thoroughly. Serve garnished with avocado, tomatoes and cilantro.

Bourbon Chicken

Makes: 6 pint jars (500 ml)

Ingredients:

- 4 pounds chicken, cut into bite size pieces
- Two cloves garlic, crushed

- ½ cup apple juice
- 4 tablespoons ketchup
- 1 cup water
- 4 tablespoons oil
- 2 teaspoons crushed red pepper
- 2/3 cup light brown sugar
- 2 tablespoons cider vinegar
- 2/3 cup soy sauce

Serving instructions per serving 1 pint (500 ml) jar:

- Sliced green onion
- 1 teaspoon cornstarch mixed with 2 tablespoons water (optional)

Directions:

1. Arrange the pressure canner, canning lids, and jars. You need six 1 pint (500 ml) size jars. Pour enough water into the pressure canner following the manufacturer's instructions such that it is about 3 inches (8 centimeters) in height from the bottom of the canner. Place the canner on your stovetop over low heat. Place the jars in the canner so that the jars remain warm. The temperature of the water in the canner should be maintained at 180°F (82°C). Place the lids in a small saucepan of water over low heat on another burner.

2. Combine garlic, apple juice, ketchup, water, red pepper, sugar, vinegar, and soy sauce in a saucepan and let it come to a boil. Stir occasionally. Turn off the heat.

3. Meanwhile, heat oil in another pan and add chicken. Cook until the chicken is light brown. Turn off the heat.

4. Place the jars on a towel. Place the funnel over the rim of the jar. Divide the chicken and sauce among the jars, leaving a headspace of 1 inch (2.5 cm).

5. If you do not have this headspace, pour some apple juice or water to get the headspace.

6. Make sure to remove bubbles using a bubble removing tool. Reassess the headspace and add more boiling liquid if required to fill up to the required headspace.

7. Take a clean damp cloth and wipe the rim of the jars. Place the canning lid on each jar using the lid lifter. Place the canning ring on each jar and tighten it as suggested.

8. Place the jars in the canner and process the jars following the manufacturer's instruction manual at 10 psi (69 kPa). Set the timer for 75 minutes for 1 pint size (500 ml) jars, adjusting for altitude if required. Once the timer goes off, turn off the burner.

9. Once you are done with the processing, let the pressure release naturally before opening the canner and taking out the jars. Let the jars cool completely on your countertop for no less than 12 hours. Wipe the jars with a dry kitchen cloth or paper towel. Make sure to check for the seals. These jars will last you for about 12 months.

10. **Serving suggestion**: Empty the contents of a jar into a saucepan. Place the saucepan over medium heat. Heat thoroughly and serve. If the sauce is watery, stir in cornstarch mixture and stir constantly until thick.

Sweet and Sour Chicken

Makes: 10 quart jars (1 L)

Ingredients:

- 5 pounds cooked chicken, cut into cubes or shredded
- Four medium onions, cut into large dice
- Four green bell pepper, deseeded, cut into 1 inch (2.5 cm) squares
- Two red bell peppers, deseeded, cut into 1 inch (2.4 cm) squares
- Six cans {15 ounces (425 g) each} pineapple chunks
- 3 cups (639 g) packed brown sugar
- 6 cups (1.5 L) pineapple juice
- 5 cups (1.25 L) white vinegar
- 1 cup (250 ml) ketchup
- 1 ½ cups (357 ml) soy sauce
- 2 inches (5 cm) fresh ginger, peeled, grated

<u>Serving instructions per 1 pint jar (500 ml):</u> Use any one or two of these

- Hot cooked rice or egg noodles
- Chinese potato salad
- Cucumber salad
- Vegetables tossed in noodles
- Broccoli and garlic stir-fry
- Egg fried rice

Directions:

1. Arrange the pressure canner, canning lids, and jars. You need ten quart size (1 L) jars. Pour enough water into the pressure canner following the manufacturer's instructions such that it is about 3 inches (8 centimeters) in height from the bottom of the canner. Place the canner on your stovetop over low heat. Place the jars in the canner so that the jars remain warm. The temperature of the water in the canner should be maintained at 180°F (82°C). Place the lids in a small saucepan of water over low heat on another burner.

2. Lift the jars from the canner and place over the towel. Open the cans of pineapple. Place a colander over a large bowl and drain the pineapple into the colander. We need the drained pineapple juice as well as the pineapple juice that is mentioned in the ingredients section.

3. You now have to place the ingredients in layers in the jars. Start off layering the jars with chicken followed by onions. Next place bell peppers in the jars followed by pineapple. Make sure you distribute the chicken, onions, bell peppers, and pineapple chunks in the jars.

4. Combine brown sugar, soy sauce, vinegar, pineapple juice and 6 cups of the retained pineapple juice into a large saucepan. Place the saucepan over medium heat and stir often until sugar dissolves completely. When the sauce mixture begins to boil, turn off the heat.

5. Place a funnel over the jars and pour the sauce mixture into the jars. Leave headspace of 1 inch (2.5 cm).

6. Make sure to remove bubbles using a bubble removing tool. Reassess the headspace and add more liquid if required to fill up to the required headspace.

7. Take a clean damp cloth and wipe the rim of the jars. Place the canning lid on each jar using the lid lifter. Place the canning ring on each jar and tighten it as suggested.

8. Place the jars in the canner and process the jars following the manufacturer's instruction manual at 10 psi (69 kPa). Set the timer for 90 minutes, adjusting for altitude if required. Once the timer goes off, turn off the burner.

9. Once you are done with the processing, let the pressure release naturally before opening the canner and taking out the jars. Let the jars cool completely on your countertop for no less than 12 hours. Wipe the jars with a dry kitchen cloth or paper towel. Make sure to check for the seals. These jars will last you for about 12 months.

10. **Serving suggestion**: Empty the contents of the jar into a pan and place the pan over high heat and heat thoroughly. Serve with any one of the suggested serving options.

Venison Stew

Makes: 14 quart jars (1 L)

Ingredients:

- 14 cups (2.1 kg) cubed venison stew meat
- Eight medium carrots, peeled, diced (around 8 cups after dicing)
- Eight stalks celery, chopped
- 20 cups (5 L) beef broth or more if required
- Eight large onions, chopped (about 8 cups after dicing)
- Eight medium potatoes, peeled, diced (about 8 cups after dicing)
- ½ cup seasoning blend of your choice

<u>Serving instructions per 1 quart jar (1 L):</u>

- Hot cooked rice or noodles
- Side dish of your choice
- 1 tablespoon (15 g) cornstarch mixed with 2 tablespoons water

Directions:

1. First of all arrange the pressure canner, canning lids, and jars. You need fourteen quart size (1 L) jars. Pour enough water into the pressure canner following the manufacturer's instructions such that it is about 3 inches (8 centimeters) in height from the bottom of the canner. Place the canner on your stovetop over low heat. Place the jars in the canner so that the jars remain warm. The temperature of the water in the canner should be maintained at 180°F (82°C). Place the lids in a small saucepan of water over low heat on another burner.

2. Boil broth in a pot.

3. Meanwhile, combine meat in a large bowl with seasoning blend. Place a cup of the meat in each jar. Layer with ½ cup of each vegetable over the meat in any manner you please. Make it look colorful and appealing.

4. Place a funnel over the jars and pour boiling broth into the jars. Leave headspace of 1 inch (2.5 cm).

5. Make sure to remove bubbles using a bubble removing tool. Reassess the headspace and add more liquid if required to fill up to the required headspace.

6. Take a clean damp cloth and wipe the rim of the jars. Place the canning lid on each jar using the lid lifter. Place the canning ring on each jar and tighten it as suggested.

7. Place the jars in the canner and process the jars following the manufacturer's

instruction manual at 10 psi (69 kPa). Set the timer for 90 minutes, adjusting for altitude if required. Once the timer goes off, turn off the burner.

8. Once you are done with the processing, let the pressure release naturally before opening the canner and taking out the jars. Let the jars cool completely on your countertop for no less than 12 hours. Wipe the jars with a dry kitchen cloth or paper towel. Make sure to check for the seals. These jars will last you for about 12 months.

9. **Serving suggestion**: Empty the contents of the jar into a pan and place the pan over high heat. Stir in the cornstarch mixture and heat thoroughly, stirring constantly until thick. Serve with a side dish of your choice. If you do not have any particular favorites, I suggest a few side dishes like homemade regular bread or garlic bread, mashed potatoes, green salad, cheddar cheese biscuits, cooked rice, rice pilaf, etc.

Venison Spaghetti Sauce

Makes: 14 quart jars (1 L)

Ingredients:

- ½ cup (125 ml) olive oil
- Two large yellow onions, minced
- Two cans (6 ounces each) tomato paste
- ¼ cup (12 g) dried oregano
- 1 teaspoon (5 g) red pepper flakes
- 2 quarts (2 L) venison stock or beef stock
- Two cans {28 ounces (794 g) each} crushed tomatoes
- Salt to taste
- Sugar to taste
- Pepper to taste
- 5 pounds (2.27 kg) ground venison
- 12 cloves garlic, peeled, minced
- 2 cups (500 ml) red wine
- ½ cup (30.8 g) minced fresh parsley

Serving instructions per 1 quart jar (1 L):

- Hot cooked spaghetti or any other pasta

Directions:

1. Not just venison, you can make this sauce with any kind of ground meat. So you can change ground venison meat to any other meat of your choice.
2. Add venison into a large Dutch oven or a large heavy pot and place the pot

over medium-high heat. If your meat has come with all fat removed from it, only then you need to add all of the olive oil to cook the meat. But if the meat has a little fat, you need to add only a little of the olive oil. You decide on how much oil is to be added.

3. Cook until the meat is brown. As you stir, break the meat into crumbles. Now add onions and cook until onions are soft. Make sure to stir the mixture frequently. Add garlic and cook for a couple of minutes. Next goes in the tomato paste. Stir until well combined. Cook for about 2-3 minutes, making sure to stir often.

4. Add wine, oregano, red pepper flakes, and parsley and stir until well combined. Cook until the wine is half its original quantity. Stir in the stock and tomatoes and let it come to a boil. Now reduce the heat and cook for about 45 minutes. Stir in sugar, salt, and pepper.

5. Once you add the tomatoes into the pot and reduce the heat, it is time for you to arrange the pressure canner, canning lids, and jars. You need fourteen quart size (1 L) jars. Pour enough water into the pressure canner following the manufacturer's instructions such that it is about 3 inches (8 centimeters) in height from the bottom of the canner. Place the canner on your stovetop over low heat. Place the jars in the canner so that the jars remain warm. The temperature of the water in the canner should be maintained at 180°F (82°C). Place the lids in a small saucepan of water over low heat on another burner.

6. Place the jars over a towel. Place a funnel over the jars and pour the sauce mixture into the jars. Leave headspace of 1 inch (2.5 cm).

7. Make sure to remove bubbles using a bubble removing tool. Reassess the headspace and add more liquid if required to fill up to the required headspace.

8. Take a clean damp cloth and wipe the rim of the jars. Place the canning lid on

each jar using the lid lifter. Place the canning ring on each jar and tighten it as suggested.

9. Place the jars in the canner and process the jars following the manufacturer's instruction manual at 10 psi (69 kPa). Set the timer for 70 minutes, adjusting for altitude if required. Once the timer goes off, turn off the burner.

10. Once you are done with the processing, let the pressure release naturally before opening the canner and taking out the jars. Let the jars cool completely on your countertop for no less than 12 hours. Wipe the jars with a dry kitchen cloth or paper towel. Make sure to check for the seals. These jars will last you for about 24 months.

11. **Serving suggestion**: Empty the contents of the jar into a pan and place the pan over medium heat and heat thoroughly. Add pasta and toss well. Serve right away with some cheese if you wish. There are numerous ways you can use the spaghetti sauce. You can use it to make lasagna, shepherd's pie, top it over hot dogs and nachos, fill it up in bell peppers, spread it over crepes, fajitas etc.

Spicy Turkey Burgers

Makes: 3 quart jars (1 L)

Ingredients:

- 4 pounds (1.8 kg) lean ground turkey
- 2 inches (5 cm) fresh ginger root, peeled, minced
- Two medium onions, diced

- 2 teaspoons (10 g) salt
- 2 tablespoons (30 g) freshly ground black pepper
- 2 tablespoons (30 g) ground dry mustard
- 1 tablespoon (15 ml) Worcestershire sauce
- Eight large cloves garlic, minced
- 4 fresh green chili peppers, minced
- ½ cup (30.8 g) finely chopped cilantro
- ½ cup (125 ml) low-sodium soy sauce
- 6 tablespoons (40.8 g) paprika
- 2 tablespoons (30 g) ground cumin
- Boiling water or stock or tomato juice as required

<u>Serving instructions per burger:</u>

- One burger bun
- One lettuce leaf
- One cheese slice (optional)
- Any other toppings of your choice

Directions:

1. Combine turkey meat, onion, chili pepper, Worcestershire sauce, soy sauce, paprika, cilantro, ginger, garlic, pepper, mustard, cumin, and salt in a large bowl. Make sure you do not use any binders like eggs or breadcrumbs.

2. Make patties of the meat mixture such that they are as wide as the mouth of the jar and they fit well into the jars. You can use your hands to shape the

patties. You can also use the help of the canning rings to shape the burgers. You should use a wide mouth jar to can the burgers. You can cook the patties in a pan or in an oven. They only need to be browned and not cooked through inside. Boil water, stock or tomato juice in a pot.

3. To cook them in the oven, place the patties on a baking sheet and bake them in an oven that has been preheated to 375°F for about 15 minutes on each side.

4. If you are cooking them in batches, make sure the burgers are kept warm until you place them in the jars.

5. While the burgers are cooking, arrange the pressure canner, canning lids, and jars. You need about three quart (1L) size jars. Pour enough water into the pressure canner following the manufacturer's instructions such that it is about 3 inches (8 centimeters) in height from the bottom of the canner. Place the canner on your stovetop over low heat. Place the jars in the canner so that the jars remain warm. The temperature of the water in the canner should be maintained at 180°F (82°C). Place the lids in a small saucepan of water over low heat on another burner.

6. Place a kitchen towel on your countertop and spread it. Lift the jars from the canner and place over the towel. Place the burgers in the jars. Pour the chosen boiling liquid into the jars to cover the burgers leaving headspace of 1 inch (2.5 cm).

7. Make sure to remove bubbles using a bubble removing tool. Reassess the headspace and add more liquid if required to fill up to the required headspace.

8. Take a clean damp cloth and wipe the rim of the jars. Place the canning lid on each jar using the lid lifter. Place the canning ring on each jar and tighten it as suggested.

9. Place the jars in the canner and process the jars following the manufacturer's instruction manual at 10 psi (69 kPa). Set the timer for 90 minutes, adjusting for altitude if required. Once the timer goes off, turn off the burner.

10. Once you are done with the processing, let the pressure release naturally before opening the canner and taking out the jars. Let the jars cool completely on your countertop for no less than 12 hours. Wipe the jars with a dry kitchen cloth or paper towel. Make sure to check for the seals. These jars will last you for about 12 months.

11. **Serving instructions**: Take out a burger from the jar and place on a hot pan over medium heat. You can spray some oil into the pan before placing the burger and cook until crisp on both the sides. Split the bun into 2 and lightly toast the bun. Place a lettuce leaf over the bottom half of the bun followed by the burger and a slice of cheese. Place any other topping or sauce of your choice. Cover with the top half of the bun and serve. Make sure to keep the opened jar in the refrigerator and use it as soon as possible.

Turkey and Gravy

Makes: 8 quart jars (1 L)

Ingredients:

- 4 cups (700 g) chopped onion
- 4 cups (500 g) finely chopped celery
- 6 cups (1,050 g) peeled, diced potatoes
- 8 pounds (3.6 kg) boneless turkey cut into 2 inch (5 cm) chunks
- 1 teaspoon (5 g) salt per quart (1 L) size jar

- 1 teaspoon (5 g) poultry seasoning per quart (1 L) size jar
- ½ teaspoon (2.5 g) ground black pepper per quart (1 L) size jar
- 2 tablespoons (30 ml) dry white wine per quart (1 L) size jar (optional)
- Boiling turkey broth or water, as required

Serving instructions per 1 pint jar (500 ml):

- Chopped parsley
- 1 tablespoon (15 g) flour
- Hot cooked rice

Directions:

1. Arrange the pressure canner, canning lids, and jars. You need eight quart size (1 L) jars. Pour enough water into the pressure canner following the manufacturer's instructions such that it is about 3 inches (8 centimeters) in height from the bottom of the canner. Place the canner on your stovetop over low heat. Place the jars in the canner so that the jars remain warm. The temperature of the water in the canner should be maintained at 180°F (82°C). Place the lids in a small saucepan of water over low heat on another burner.

2. Boil a pot of water or broth.

3. Place a kitchen towel on your countertop and spread it. Lift the jars from the canner and place over the towel. Add salt, poultry seasoning, pepper and dry white wine if using, into each jar. Divide the meat into the jars. Next layer with ½ cup celery in each jar followed by ½ cup onions. Finally divide the potatoes among the jars. Pour boiling liquid into the jars to cover the mixture leaving a headspace of 1 inch (2.5 cm).

4. Make sure to remove bubbles using a bubble removing tool. Reassess the

headspace and add more liquid if required to fill up to the required headspace.

5. Take a clean damp cloth and wipe the rim of the jars. Place the canning lid on each jar using the lid lifter. Place the canning ring on each jar and tighten it as suggested.

6. Place the jars in the canner and process the jars following the manufacturer's instruction manual at 10 psi (69 kPa). Set the timer for 75 minutes, adjusting for altitude if required. Once the timer goes off, turn off the burner.

7. Once you are done with the processing, let the pressure release naturally before opening the canner and taking out the jars. Let the jars cool completely on your countertop for no less than 12 hours. Wipe the jars with a dry kitchen cloth or paper towel. Make sure to check for the seals. These jars will last you for about 12 months.

8. **Serving suggestion**: Empty the contents of the jar into a pan and place the pan over high heat. Add flour into a bowl. Add a little of the liquid (before it gets hot) from the can into the bowl and stir well. Add the mixture and stir constantly until thick. Serve over hot cooked rice. Garnish with parsley and serve.

Asian Turkey Meatballs

Makes: 5 pint jars (500 ml)

Ingredients:

- 1 ½ pounds (680g) lean ground turkey
- 1 inch (2.5 cm) fresh ginger, peeled, grated
- ½ teaspoon (2.5 g) garlic powder
- ½ teaspoon (2.5 g) freshly ground pepper
- 1 tablespoon (15 ml) soy sauce
- Two green onions, finely chopped
- Three cloves garlic, peeled, grated
- 1 ½ teaspoons (7.5 g) salt
- 2 ½ tablespoons (37.5 ml) teriyaki ginger sauce
- Red pepper flakes to taste (optional)
- Boiling chicken stock, as required

Serving instructions per serving 1 pint (500 ml) jar:

- Hot cooked egg noodles or rice

Sauce to serve:

- 4 tablespoons (60 ml) light soy sauce
- 2 teaspoons (10 ml) honey
- ½ inch (1.25 cm) fresh ginger, minced
- ½ teaspoon (2.5 ml) sesame oil
- 1 tablespoon (15 g) cornstarch
- Hot sauce to taste
- Two cloves garlic, minced

Directions:

1. Combine turkey, salt, ginger, soy sauce, teriyaki sauce, green onion, garlic, and spices in a bowl. Make 30 equal portions of the mixture and shape them into small balls. The balls may be about 1.5 inches (3.75 cm) each. I suggest you dip your hands often in water and make the meatballs. This way the meat will not stick to your hands. Make sure you do not add any binders like egg or breadcrumbs.

2. Next thing to be done is to arrange the pressure canner, canning lids, and jars. You need about five 1 pint (500 ml) size jars. Pour enough water into the pressure canner following the manufacturer's instructions such that it is about 3 inches (8 centimeters) in height from the bottom of the canner. Place the canner on your stovetop over low heat. Place the jars in the canner so that the jars remain warm. The temperature of the water in the canner should be maintained at 180°F (82°C). Place the lids in a small saucepan of water over low heat on another burner.

3. Boil chicken stock in a pot.

4. Place a skillet over medium heat. Spray some cooking spray into the skillet. Add a few meatballs into the pan without overcrowding. And cook until brown all over, turning the meatballs occasionally. It should not be cooked through as it will be cooked further while processing. Remove the meatballs from the pan and make sure to keep them warm until the remaining meatballs are browned. You can also bake the meatballs in an oven for about 45 minutes in a preheated oven at a temperature of 350°F. Turn the meatballs every 15 minutes in the oven.

5. Place the jars over a towel on your countertop. Place six meatballs in each jar. Pour enough boiling stock into the jars until you get headspace of 1 inch (2.5 cm)

6. Make sure to remove bubbles using a bubble removing tool. Reassess the headspace and add more boiling liquid if required to fill up to the required headspace.

7. Take a clean damp cloth and wipe the rim of the jars. Place the canning lid on each jar using the lid lifter. Place the canning ring on each jar and tighten it as suggested.

8. Place the jars in the canner and process the jars following the manufacturer's instruction manual at 10 psi (69 kPa). Set the timer for 75 minutes for a pint (500 ml) size jar, adjusting for altitude if required. Once the timer goes off, turn off the burner.

9. Once you are done with the processing, let the pressure release naturally before opening the canner and taking out the jars. Let the jars cool completely on your countertop for no less than 12 hours. Wipe the jars with a dry kitchen cloth or paper towel. Make sure to check for the seals. These jars will last you

for about 12 months.

10. **Serving suggestion**: Empty the broth from the jar into a saucepan. Take out some liquid from the jar and add it into a bowl. Add the sauce ingredients into the bowl and whisk well. Place the saucepan over medium heat. Pour the sauce mixture into the saucepan and keep stirring until the sauce thickens. Add meatballs and stir until the meatballs are well coated with the sauce. Let the meatballs heat through. Serve over egg noodles or hot cooked rice.

Chapter 6:
Vegetables

Green Beans

Makes: 16 pint jars (500 ml)

Ingredients:

- 10 pounds (4.8 kg) green beans, trimmed (make sure they are fresh and tender)
- Boiling water, as required
- ½ teaspoon (2.5 g) salt per pint size jar (optional)
- 10 large cloves garlic, peeled

Serving instructions per serving 1 pint (500 ml) jar:

- One onion, thinly sliced
- Salt and pepper to taste
- Red pepper flakes to taste
- Any spices of your choice to taste
- Oil to cook, as required

Directions:

1. Firstly arrange the pressure canner, canning lids, and jars. You need about sixteen 1 pint (500 ml) size jars. Pour enough water into the pressure canner following the manufacturer's instructions such that it is about 3 inches (8 centimeters) in height from the bottom of the canner. Place the canner on your stovetop over low heat. Place the jars in the canner so that the jars remain

warm. The temperature of the water in the canner should be maintained at 180°F (82°C). Place the lids in a small saucepan of water over low heat on another burner.

2. Meanwhile, wash the green beans well. Cut the beans into pieces of about 2 inches or as per your choice.

3. Place a clove of garlic in each jar. Sprinkle salt in each jar if using.

4. Meanwhile, boil a pot of water to fill the jars and another pot of water if you want to cook the green beans.

5. If you want to can the green beans raw, simply fill it into the canning jars. Make sure you pack them tightly. If you want to can cooked green beans, drop them in one of the pots of boiling water and cook for five minutes. Drain the green beans in a colander. Pack the cooked beans lightly in the jars.

6. Place a kitchen towel on your countertop and spread it. Lift the jars from the canner and place over the towel.

7. Place the funnel on the rim of the jar and pour boiling water from the other pot into the jar to cover the green beans leaving headspace of 1 inch (2.5 cm).

8. Make sure to remove bubbles using a bubble removing tool. Reassess the headspace and add more boiling liquid if required to fill up to the required headspace.

9. Take a clean damp cloth and wipe the rim of the jars. Place the canning lid on each jar using the lid lifter. Place the canning ring on each jar and tighten it as suggested.

10. Place the jars in the canner and process the jars following the manufacturer's instruction manual at 10 psi (69 kPa). Set the timer for 20 minutes for a pint (500 ml) size jar, adjusting for altitude if required. Once the timer goes off,

turn off the burner.

11. Once you are done with the processing, let the pressure release naturally before opening the canner and taking out the jars. Let the jars cool completely on your countertop for no less than 12 hours. Wipe the jars with a dry kitchen cloth or paper towel. Make sure to check for the seals. These jars will last you for about 12 months.

12. **Serving suggestion**: Drain the contents of the jar into a colander. Place a pan over high heat. Add a splash of oil and let the oil heat. Add onion slices and cook until translucent. Add the green beans, salt, pepper, red pepper flakes and any other spices of your choice and mix well. Heat thoroughly and serve.

Ratatouille

Makes: 10 – 11 pint jars (500 ml)

Ingredients:

- 10 tablespoons (150 ml) extra-virgin olive oil, divided
- 2 pounds (907 g) zucchini or summer squash, discard stems and cut into 1 inch cubes
- Six large whole tomatoes
- Eight cloves garlic, peeled, minced
- 2 teaspoons (2.3 g) minced fresh thyme leaves
- Freshly ground black pepper to taste
- 2 pounds (907 g) eggplant, cut into 1 inch chunks
- Six medium onions, cut into thick slices
- Four large red bell peppers, cut into 1 inch (2.5 cm) squares
- ½ cup (27.2 g) torn fresh basil leaves
- Salt to taste

Serving instructions per serving 1 pint (500 ml) jar:

- Chopped fresh basil and thyme

Directions:

1. Set up your oven to broil mode and preheat it to high heat.
2. Place eggplants, onion, zucchini, onion, and bell pepper in a large bowl. Drizzle 8 tablespoons of oil over the vegetables and toss them up well. The vegetables should be coated in oil.
3. Take two large baking sheets and line them with parchment paper. Scatter the vegetables on the baking sheets, spreading it evenly. Place the tomatoes in between the vegetables and place the baking sheets in the oven in batches and

broil for a few minutes until visibly brown at a few places. Make doubly sure they do not burn. Take out the tomatoes from the baking sheet and keep them aside on a plate. These will be used later.

4. Arrange the pressure canner, canning lids, and jars. You need about ten to eleven pint (500 ml) size jars. Pour enough water into the pressure canner following the manufacturer's instructions such that it is about 3 inches (8 centimeters) in height from the bottom of the canner. Place the canner on your stovetop over low heat. Place the jars in the canner so that the jars remain warm. The temperature of the water in the canner should be maintained at 180°F (82°C). Place the lids in a small saucepan of water over low heat on another burner.

5. Pour 2 tablespoons (30 ml) oil into a large pot and place the pot over medium-low heat.

6. Add garlic and cook for a few seconds until you get a nice aroma in the air. Stir in thyme. Add the broiled vegetables from the baking sheet and mix well. Let the vegetables cook for about five minutes. Stir occasionally.

7. Meanwhile, take out the stems and peel from the tomatoes. Try to take out the seed part as well and keep the pulp on your cutting board. Chop pulp into coarse pieces and add into the pot along with vegetables. Mix well and turn off the heat. Add basil, pepper, and salt and mix well.

8. Place a kitchen towel on your countertop and spread it. Lift the jars from the canner and place over the towel.

9. Pack the hot vegetables into the jars leaving headspace of 1 ½ inches (3.75 cm). Make sure to remove bubbles using a bubble removing tool. Reassess the headspace and add more vegetables if required to fill up to the required headspace.

10. Take a clean damp cloth and wipe the rim of the jars. Place the canning lid on each jar using the lid lifter. Place the canning ring on each jar and tighten it as suggested.

11. Place the jars in the canner and process the jars following the manufacturer's instruction manual at 10 psi (69 kPa). Set the timer for 30 minutes for a pint (500 ml) size jar, adjusting for altitude if required. The time for altitudes 1,001 to 6,000 feet is 20 minutes though and beyond 6,001 feet is 25 minutes. Once the timer goes off, turn off the burner.

12. Once you are done with the processing, let the pressure release naturally before opening the canner and taking out the jars. Let the jars cool completely on your countertop for no less than 12 hours. Wipe the jars with a dry kitchen cloth or paper towel. Make sure to check for the seals. These jars will last you for about 12 months.

13. **Serving suggestion**: Empty the contents of a jar into a pan. Heat thoroughly and serve garnished with basil and thyme.

Herbed Potatoes

Makes: 8 pint jars (500 ml) or 4 quart jars (1 L)

Ingredients:

- 5 pounds (2.3 kg) white potatoes, halved or quartered, depending on the size but no more than 2 inches (5 cm)
- Boiling chicken broth or vegetable broth or water as required
- 4 teaspoons (20 g) salt

- 2 teaspoons (2 g) dried rosemary
- 2 teaspoon (10 g) ground black pepper
- 2 teaspoons (2 g) dried thyme

Serving instructions per serving 1 pint (500 ml) jar or quart (1 L) jar:

- Blob of butter
- Milk

Directions:

1. As you start chopping potatoes, add them to a pot of cold water. This way some starch will be released from the potatoes also it will prevent the potatoes from browning.

2. Arrange the pressure canner, canning lids, and jars. You need eight 1 pint (500 ml) size jars or four quart size (1 L) jars. Pour enough water into the pressure canner following the manufacturer's instructions such that it is about 3 inches (8 centimeters) in height from the bottom of the canner. Place the canner on your stovetop over low heat. Place the jars in the canner so that the jars remain warm. The temperature of the water in the canner should be maintained at 180°F (82°C). Place the lids in a small saucepan of water over low heat on another burner.

3. Boil broth in a pot.

4. Lift the jars from the canner and place over the towel. Combine salt, oregano, thyme, and pepper in a bowl. Divide equally the spices among the jars. Pack the potatoes into the jars leaving headspace of 1 inch (2.5 cm). Pour boiling liquid into the jars to get the required headspace.

5. Make sure to remove bubbles using a bubble removing tool. Reassess the headspace and add more boiling liquid if required to fill up to the required

headspace.

6. Take a clean damp cloth and wipe the rim of the jars. Place the canning lid on each jar using the lid lifter. Place the canning ring on each jar and tighten it as suggested.

7. Place the jars in the canner and process the jars following the manufacturer's instruction manual at 10 psi (69 kPa). Set the timer for 35 minutes for a pint (500 ml) size jar or 40 minutes for quart (1L) size jars, adjusting for altitude if required. Once the timer goes off, turn off the burner.

8. Once you are done with the processing, let the pressure release naturally before opening the canner and taking out the jars. Let the jars cool completely on your countertop for no less than 12 hours. Wipe the jars with a dry kitchen cloth or paper towel. Make sure to check for the seals. These jars will last you for about 12 months.

9. **Serving instructions**: Empty the contents of a jar into a pan. Heat thoroughly. Drain off the liquid and transfer the potatoes into a bowl. Mash them adding some butter and milk. Add salt and pepper to taste and you now have mashed potatoes. You can add some fresh herbs as well. You can also use the drained potatoes in many ways like in salads, stir-fry the potatoes in oil with some spices if desired, etc.

Roasted Root Vegetables

Makes: 12 pint jars (500 ml) or 6 quart jars (1 L)

Ingredients:

- 2 pounds (907 g) large beets, cut into 1 inch chunks

- 2 pounds (907 g) parsnips cut into 1 inch chunks
- 2 pounds (907 g) turnips cut into 1 inch chunks
- Four medium carrots, peeled, cut into 1 inch pieces
- 16 cups (4 L) chicken broth
- 1 cup (250 ml) orange juice
- 2 teaspoons (10 g) salt
- ½ cup (125 ml) olive oil
- 2 teaspoons (10 g) finely shredded orange peel
- 2 tablespoons (30 ml) bottled lemon juice
- 1 teaspoon (5 g) freshly ground black pepper
- 16 cups (4 L) chicken broth
- 1 cup (250 ml) orange juice
- 2 teaspoons (10 g) salt

<u>Serving instructions per 1 quart jar (1 L):</u>

- Grated parmesan cheese
- Two cloves garlic, minced
- A dash of oil
- Salt and pepper to taste

Directions:

1. Set up your oven and preheat it to 425°F. Place beets, parsnips, turnips and carrots in a bowl and toss well. Drizzle oil over the vegetables and toss well. Take two large baking sheets and line them with parchment paper. Scatter the

vegetables on the baking sheets, spreading it evenly. Place the baking sheets in the oven together in the oven on 2 racks and bake for about 20 to 25 minutes. Make sure to exchange the baking sheets to ensure even cooking. The vegetables should be tender and brown at the edges.

2. While the vegetables are roasting, arrange the pressure canner, canning lids, and jars. You need twelve 1 pint (500 ml) size jars or six quart size (1 L) jars. Pour enough water into the pressure canner following the manufacturer's instructions such that it is about 3 inches (8 centimeters) in height from the bottom of the canner. Place the canner on your stovetop over low heat. Place the jars in the canner so that the jars remain warm. The temperature of the water in the canner should be maintained at 180°F (82°C). Place the lids in a small saucepan of water over low heat on another burner.

3. Boil broth, orange juice, orange peel, salt, pepper, and lemon juice in a pot. Place the jars on a towel. Distribute the vegetables among the jars. Pour boiling liquid into the jars to get the required headspace.

4. Make sure to remove bubbles using a bubble removing tool. Reassess the headspace and add more boiling liquid if required to fill up to the required headspace.

5. Take a clean damp cloth and wipe the rim of the jars. Place the canning lid on each jar using the lid lifter. Place the canning ring on each jar and tighten it as suggested.

6. Place the jars in the canner and process the jars following the manufacturer's instruction manual at 10 psi (69 kPa). Set the timer for 75 minutes for quart (1L) size jars, adjusting for altitude if required. Once the timer goes off, turn off the burner.

7. Once you are done with the processing, let the pressure release naturally before

opening the canner and taking out the jars. Let the jars cool completely on your countertop for no less than 12 hours. Wipe the jars with a dry kitchen cloth or paper towel. Make sure to check for the seals. These jars will last you for about 12 months.

8. **Serving suggestion**: You can make soup of the vegetables. For this, empty the contents of the jar into a blender and blend until smooth. Add salt and pepper to taste. Pour into a saucepan. Heat thoroughly and serve with grated cheese. To serve it as a side dish, drain off the liquid from the can. Pour oil into a pan and let it heat over high heat. Add garlic and cook for a few seconds until you get a nice aroma. Add roasted vegetables and stir-fry for a few minutes, until thoroughly heated. Add salt and pepper to taste. Transfer into a bowl. Garnish with cheese and serve.

Chapter 7: Bonus Chapter -
Soups

Sweet Potato Soup

Makes: 8 pint jars (500 ml) or 4 quart jars (1 L)

Ingredients:

- Four large sweet potatoes, peeled, rinsed, cut into cubes
- 1 teaspoon (5 g) salt
- Two carrots, chopped
- Four cloves garlic, minced
- Ground pepper to taste
- 4 tablespoons oil
- 2 tablespoons red wine vinegar
- Two small onions, chopped
- Two stalks celery, chopped
- 2 teaspoons (5 g) chopped fresh rosemary
- 12 cups (1.5 L) chicken broth

Serving instructions per serving 1 pint (500 ml) jar or quart (1 L) jar:

- Grated cheese
- Chopped parsley

Directions:

1. Place sweet potatoes in a bowl. Add half of each-the oil, garlic, salt, and rosemary and toss well. Drizzle vinegar and toss well. Transfer the mixture onto a baking sheet and roast the sweet potatoes in a preheated oven at 450°F for 20 minutes.

2. Next arrange the pressure canner, canning lids, and jars. You need eight 1 pint (500 ml) size jars or four quart size (1 L) jars. Pour enough water into the pressure canner following the manufacturer's instructions such that it is about 3 inches (8 centimeters) in height from the bottom of the canner. Place the canner on your stovetop over low heat. Place the jars in the canner so that the jars remain warm. The temperature of the water in the canner should be maintained at 180°F (82°C). Place the lids in a small saucepan of water over low heat on another burner.

3. While the sweet potatoes are roasting, pour remaining oil into a stock pot. Place the stock pot over medium-high heat. Add onion, garlic, carrot, rosemary, and pepper and sauté for 4-5 minutes. Pour broth and let it come to a boil. Add salt and stir. Turn off the heat.

4. Place the jars on a towel. Distribute the sweet potatoes among the jars. Remove the vegetables from the stock pot with a slotted spoon and distribute them among the jars. Pour boiling broth into the jars to get 1 inch (2.5 cm) headspace.

5. Make sure to remove bubbles using a bubble removing tool. Reassess the headspace and add more boiling liquid if required to fill up to the required headspace.

6. Take a clean damp cloth and wipe the rim of the jars. Place the canning lid on each jar using the lid lifter. Place the canning ring on each jar and tighten it as suggested.

7. Place the jars in the canner and process the jars following the manufacturer's instruction manual at 10 psi (69 kPa). Set the timer for 60 minutes for 1 pint size (500 ml) jars or 75 minutes for quart (1L) size jars, adjusting for altitude if required. Once the timer goes off, turn off the burner.

8. Once you are done with the processing, let the pressure release naturally before opening the canner and taking out the jars. Let the jars cool completely on your countertop for no less than 12 hours. Wipe the jars with a dry kitchen cloth or paper towel. Make sure to check for the seals. These jars will last you for about 12 months.

9. **Serving suggestion**: Empty the contents of a can into a blender and blend until smooth. Pour the soup into a saucepan and heat thoroughly. Ladle into soup bowls and serve with cheese and parsley.

Carrot and Fennel Soup

Makes: 6 pint jars (500 ml) or 3 quart jars (1 L)

Ingredients:

- 2.2 pounds (1 kg) carrots, peeled, sliced
- ½ tablespoon (7.5 ml) olive oil
- 1 tablespoon (15 g) salt
- ½ teaspoon (½ g) dried thyme
- ½ teaspoon (2.5 g) ground coriander
- ¼ teaspoon (1.25 g) ground cumin
- ½ tablespoon (7.5 ml) olive oil
- 1 teaspoon (5 g) onion powder
- ½ teaspoon (2.5 g) ground dried ginger
- ½ teaspoon (2.5 g) ground black pepper
- 1 ½ tablespoons (7.5 ml) bottled lemon juice

Serving instructions per serving 1 pint (500 ml) jar or quart (1 L) jar:

- Crème fraiche
- Maple syrup

Directions:

1. Arrange the pressure canner, canning lids, and jars. You need six 1 pint (500 ml) size jars or three quart size (1 L) jars. Pour enough water into the pressure canner following the manufacturer's instructions such that it is about 3 inches (8 centimeters) in height from the bottom of the canner. Place the canner on your stovetop over low heat. Place the jars in the canner so that the jars remain warm. The temperature of the water in the canner should be maintained at 180°F (82°C). Place the lids in a small saucepan of water over low heat on another burner.

2. Pour oil into a stock pot and heat the oil over high heat. Add fennel and carrot and sauté for a couple of minutes. Add the spices and salt and stir for about a minute. You will get a nice fragrance. Pour broth and let it start boiling. Lower the heat and let it simmer for a few minutes until tender. The vegetables are not to be fully cooked as they will cook further in the canning process. Turn off the heat.

3. Place the jars on a towel. Remove the vegetables from the stock pot with a slotted spoon and distribute them among the jars. Make sure the vegetables are equally distributed in the jars. Pour boiling broth into the jars to get 1 inch (2.5 cm) headspace.

4. Make sure to remove bubbles using a bubble removing tool. Reassess the headspace and add more boiling liquid if required to fill up to the required headspace.

5. Take a clean damp cloth and wipe the rim of the jars. Place the canning lid on each jar using the lid lifter. Place the canning ring on each jar and tighten it as suggested.

6. Place the jars in the canner and process the jars following the manufacturer's instruction manual at 10 psi (69 kPa). Set the timer for 40 minutes for 1 pint size (500 ml) jars or 50 minutes for quart (1L) size jars, adjusting for altitude if required. Once the timer goes off, turn off the burner.

7. Once you are done with the processing, let the pressure release naturally before opening the canner and taking out the jars. Let the jars cool completely on your countertop for no less than 12 hours. Wipe the jars with a dry kitchen cloth or paper towel. Make sure to check for the seals. These jars will last you for about 12 months.

8. **Serving instructions**: Empty the contents of a can into a blender and blend

until smooth. Pour the soup into a saucepan and heat thoroughly. Combine some crème fraiche and maple syrup in a bowl. Ladle into soup bowls. Drizzle crème fraiche mixture on top and serve.

Asparagus Soup

Makes: 8 pint jars (500 ml)

Ingredients:

- 6 pounds (2.7 kg) fresh asparagus
- 2 cups (320 g) minced shallots

- 1 teaspoon (5 g) salt
- 16 cups (4 L) chicken broth or stock
- Six large cloves garlic, minced
- ½ teaspoon (2.5 g) ground white pepper
- 1 tablespoon (15 ml) olive oil

<u>Serving instructions per serving 1 pint (500 ml) jar:</u>

- ¼ cup (62.5 ml) heavy cream
- Grated parmesan cheese to taste
- Salt and pepper to taste

Directions:

1. Trim the hard part of the stems from the asparagus and discard. Cut the asparagus into ½ inch (1.25 cm) pieces.

2. Pour oil into a pan and allow the oil to heat over medium heat. Add shallots and garlic and cook for a few minutes until soft, being careful not to cook them for too long. Boil broth in a pot.

3. Next arrange the pressure canner, canning lids, and jars. You need eight 1 pint (500 ml) size jars. Pour enough water into the pressure canner following the manufacturer's instructions such that it is about 3 inches (8 centimeters) in height from the bottom of the canner. Place the canner on your stovetop over low heat. Place the jars in the canner so that the jars remain warm. The temperature of the water in the canner should be maintained at 180°F (82°C). Place the lids in a small saucepan of water over low heat on another burner.

4. Place the jars on a towel. Place the funnel over the rim of the jar. Add asparagus

pieces into the jars, filling up to ¾ the jars. Divide the shallot mixture among jars. Divide the salt and pepper among the jars.

5. Pour boiling broth into the jars until you get 1 inch (2.5 cm) headspace.

6. Make sure to remove bubbles using a bubble removing tool. Reassess the headspace and add more boiling liquid if required to fill up to the required headspace.

7. Take a clean damp cloth and wipe the rim of the jars. Place the canning lid on each jar using the lid lifter. Place the canning ring on each jar and tighten it as suggested.

8. Place the jars in the canner and process the jars following the manufacturer's instruction manual at 10 psi (69 kPa). Set the timer for 75 minutes for 1 pint size (500 ml) jars, adjusting for altitude if required. Once the timer goes off, turn off the burner.

9. Once you are done with the processing, let the pressure release naturally before opening the canner and taking out the jars. Let the jars cool completely on your countertop for no less than 12 hours. Wipe the jars with a dry kitchen cloth or paper towel. Make sure to check for the seals. These jars will last you for about 12 months.

10. **Serving suggestion**: Empty the contents of a jar into a saucepan. Place the saucepan over medium heat. Remove a few pieces of asparagus from the saucepan and keep it aside. Blend the asparagus in the saucepan with an immersion blender until pureed well. Add salt and pepper to taste. Add cream and let the cream blend well into the soup. When the soup is nice and hot, turn off the heat. Ladle the soup into bowls. Top with retained asparagus pieces and cheese and serve.

Vegetable Soup

Makes: 6 pint jars (500 ml)

Ingredients:

- 2 ½ quarts (2.5 L) vegetable broth or chicken broth
- Four ears corn, use the kernels
- 12–15 green beans, cut into 1 inch pieces
- 1 cup (125 g) sliced celery
- Two cloves garlic, peeled, minced
- 2 cups (400 g) peeled, chopped tomatoes
- ½ pound (227 g) potatoes, peeled, cut into cubes
- One large carrot, sliced
- One medium onion, chopped
- ½ teaspoon (½ g) dried thyme, crushed
- ½ teaspoon (½ g) dried marjoram, crushed
- ½ teaspoon (½ g) dried parsley, crushed
- ½ teaspoon (½ g) dried rosemary, crushed
- Ground black pepper to taste

<u>Serving instructions per serving 1 pint (500 ml) jar:</u>

- 1 tablespoon cornstarch
- Chopped fresh herbs of your choice

- Grated cheese

Directions:

1. Arrange the pressure canner, canning lids, and jars. You need six 1 pint (500 ml) size jars. Pour enough water into the pressure canner following the manufacturer's instructions such that it is about 3 inches (8 centimeters) in height from the bottom of the canner. Place the canner on your stovetop over low heat. Place the jars in the canner so that the jars remain warm. The temperature of the water in the canner should be maintained at 180°F (82°C). Place the lids in a small saucepan of water over low heat on another burner.

2. Put the vegetables into a stock pot along with the stock, dried herbs and pepper. Place the pot over high heat. When the mixture starts boiling, reduce the heat and cover the pot. Cook for 3-4 minutes. Turn off the heat. The vegetables should be crisp but not tender so do not cook for longer than 3 to 4 minutes. Turn off the heat.

3. Place the jars on a towel. Place the funnel over the rim of the jar. Remove vegetables with a slotted spoon and add into the jars, making sure each jar has an equal amount of vegetables.

4. Now pour the broth into the jars until you get 1 inch (2.5 cm) headspace.

5. Make sure to remove bubbles using a bubble removing tool. Reassess the headspace and add more boiling liquid if required to fill up to the required headspace.

6. Take a clean damp cloth and wipe the rim of the jars. Place the canning lid on each jar using the lid lifter. Place the canning ring on each jar and tighten it as suggested.

7. Place the jars in the canner and process the jars following the manufacturer's instruction manual at 10 psi (69 kPa). Set the timer for 60 minutes for 1 pint

size (500 ml) jars, adjusting for altitude if required. Once the timer goes off, turn off the burner.

8. Once you are done with the processing, let the pressure release naturally before opening the canner and taking out the jars. Let the jars cool completely on your countertop for no less than 12 hours. Wipe the jars with a dry kitchen cloth or paper towel. Make sure to check for the seals. These jars will last you for about 12 months.

9. **Serving suggestion:** Take out a little of the broth from the jar and add into a bowl. Add cornstarch and whisk well. Empty the contents of a jar into a saucepan. Place the saucepan over medium heat. Add cornstarch mixture and keep stirring until the soup is thickened. Heat thoroughly. Ladle the soup into soup bowls. Garnish with herbs and parsley and serve.

Tomato Soup

Makes: 8 pint jars (500 ml)

Ingredients:

- 16 pounds (7.3 kg) tomatoes
- Four medium onions, diced
- 12 bay leaves
- 1 teaspoon (5 g) ground black pepper
- ½ cup (100 g) sugar (optional)
- 2 cups (250 g) sliced celery
- 2 cups (110 g) chopped fresh parsley
- 1 ½ cups (375 ml) Clear Gel canning starch
- 5 tablespoons (75 g) salt or to taste (optional)

<u>Serving instructions per serving 1 pint (500 ml) jar:</u>

- 2 cups milk or water or broth
- Light cream
- Grated cheese

Directions:

1. Add tomatoes, onion, parsley, bay leaves, and parsley into a large stainless steel pot and place the pot over medium heat.
2. As it cooks, stir periodically so that the tomatoes do not get stuck on the bottom of the saucepan. Turn off the heat and spoon the mixture into a food mill or strainer in batches and strain the tomatoes. Discard the solids remaining in the food mill. Pour 4 cups of the strained mixture into a bowl and keep it aside to cool. Pour remaining soup into the pot.

3. Arrange the pressure canner, canning lids, and jars. You need eight 1 pint (500 ml) size jars. Pour enough water into the pressure canner following the manufacturer's instructions such that it is about 3 inches (8 centimeters) in height from the bottom of the canner. Place the canner on your stovetop over low heat. Place the jars in the canner so that the jars remain warm. The temperature of the water in the canner should be maintained at 180°F (82°C). Place the lids in a small saucepan of water over low heat on another burner.

4. Place the pot over medium-high heat. Let the soup start boiling. Once the puree cools, add clear gel and whisk well. Add into the pot. Stir constantly until the soup is thick. Add salt, pepper, and sugar and mix well. Keep stirring until sugar dissolves completely. Turn off the heat.

5. Place the jars on a towel. Place the funnel over the rim of the jar. Now pour the soup into the jars until you get 1 inch (2.5 cm) headspace.

6. Make sure to remove bubbles using a bubble removing tool. Reassess the headspace and add more boiling liquid if required to fill up to the required headspace.

7. Take a clean damp cloth and wipe the rim of the jars. Place the canning lid on each jar using the lid lifter. Place the canning ring on each jar and tighten it as suggested.

8. Place the jars in the canner and process the jars following the manufacturer's instruction manual at 10 psi (69 kPa). Set the timer for 25 minutes for 1 pint size (500 ml) jars, adjusting for altitude if required. Once the timer goes off, turn off the burner.

9. Once you are done with the processing, let the pressure release naturally before opening the canner and taking out the jars. Let the jars cool completely on your countertop for no less than 12 hours. Wipe the jars with a dry kitchen

cloth or paper towel. Make sure to check for the seals. These jars will last you for about 12 months.

10. **Serving suggestion**: Empty the contents of a jar into a saucepan. Add the chosen liquid and place the saucepan over medium heat. Stir often and bring the soup to a boil. Turn

11. off the heat. Ladle the soup into bowls. Drizzle some cream on top. Garnish with cheese and serve.

Mexican Beef Garden Soup

Makes: 9 pint jars (500 ml)

Ingredients:

- 1 tablespoon (15 ml) vegetable oil
- 2.5 quarts (2.5 L) low-sodium beef broth
- Four carrots about 1 inch (2.5 cm) diameter, cut into ¼ inch (0.6 cm) round slices
- 1 cup (174 g) fresh or frozen corn kernels
- Two Poblano chili pepper, discard stem and seeds, chopped
- Six cloves garlic, mined
- ½ tablespoon (7.5 g) chili powder
- 2.5 pounds (1.1 kg) beef chuck roast, trimmed of fat, cut into 1 inch (2.5 cm) chunks
- Four Roma tomatoes, deseeded, chopped

- One medium sweet potato, peeled, chopped
- 1 ½ medium onions, chopped
- 2 jalapeño peppers, deseeded, finely chopped
- 1 tablespoon (15 g) salt
- ½ tablespoon (7.5 g) ground black pepper

Serving instructions per serving 1 pint (500 ml) jar:

- Chopped avocado
- Chopped fresh cilantro
- Chopped red onions
- Tortilla chips, crumbled
- Squeeze of lemon juice

Directions:

1. Pour oil into a large stock pot and let the pot heat over medium-high heat. When oil is hot, add beef and cook until brown all over.

2. Pour broth and scrape the bottom of the pot to remove any browned bits that may be stuck. When the soup starts boiling, lower the heat and cover with a lid. Let the meat cook until tender.

3. Meanwhile, arrange the pressure canner, canning lids, and jars. You need nine 1 pint (500 ml) size jars. Pour enough water into the pressure canner following the manufacturer's instructions such that it is about 3 inches (8 centimeters) in height from the bottom of the canner. Place the canner on your stovetop over low heat. Place the jars in the canner so that the jars remain warm. The temperature of the water in the canner should be maintained at 180°F (82°C).

Place the lids in a small saucepan of water over low heat on another burner.

4. Once meat is tender, add all the spices and vegetables into the pot. When the mixture starts boiling, cover the pot with a lid and let it cook for five minutes. Turn off the heat.

5. Place the jars on a towel. Place the funnel over the rim of the jar. Remove vegetables and meat with a slotted spoon and add into the jars, making sure each jar has equal amounts of vegetables and meat. The jars would be about half filled with the vegetables and meat.

6. Now pour the broth into the jars until you get 1 inch (2.5 cm) headspace.

7. Make sure to remove bubbles using a bubble removing tool. Reassess the headspace and add more boiling liquid if required to fill up to the required headspace.

8. Take a clean damp cloth and wipe the rim of the jars. Place the canning lid on each jar using the lid lifter. Place the canning ring on each jar and tighten it as suggested.

9. Place the jars in the canner and process the jars following the manufacturer's instruction manual at 10 psi (69 kPa). Set the timer for 60 minutes for 1 pint size (500 ml) jars, adjusting for altitude if required. Once the timer goes off, turn off the burner.

10. Once you are done with the processing, let the pressure release naturally before opening the canner and taking out the jars. Let the jars cool completely on your countertop for no less than 12 hours. Wipe the jars with a dry kitchen cloth or paper towel. Make sure to check for the seals. These jars will last you for about 12 months.

11. **Serving suggestion**: Empty the contents of a jar into a saucepan. Place the saucepan over medium heat. Heat the soup thoroughly. Ladle the soup into

soup bowls. Drizzle lemon juice on top. Top with avocado, onion, and cilantro. Finally top with tortilla chips and serve.

Colorful Soup

Makes: 5 quart jars (1 L)

Ingredients:

- Five medium potatoes, peeled, cut into cubes (about 5 cups)
- 4 cups (696 g) corn kernels
- 2 ½ cups (370 g) cooked chicken, retain the broth in which chicken was cooked
- 2-3 fresh Roma tomatoes, chopped
- Five medium carrots, sliced (about 5 cups)
- 4 cups (696 g) sliced green beans
- One large onion, chopped
- 1 2/3 cups (242 g) green peas
- 2 ½ chicken bouillon cubes

<u>Serving instructions per serving 1 quart (1 L) jar:</u>

- Squeeze of lemon juice
- Chopped fresh herbs of your choice

Directions:

1. Arrange the pressure canner, canning lids, and jars. You need five quart size (1 L) jars. Pour enough water into the pressure canner following the

manufacturer's instructions such that it is about 3 inches (8 centimeters) in height from the bottom of the canner. Place the canner on your stovetop over low heat. Place the jars in the canner so that the jars remain warm. The temperature of the water in the canner should be maintained at 180°F (82°C). Place the lids in a small saucepan of water over low heat on another burner.

2. Boil the chicken broth in a pot.

3. Place the jars on a towel. Place the funnel over the rim of the jar. Place the vegetables and chicken in the jars in layers, making sure to distribute the ingredients equally. Make it colorful. You can place alternate layers of dark and light colored vegetables and chicken and make it look colorful.

4. Now pour the broth into the jars until you get 1 inch (2.5 cm) headspace.

5. Make sure to remove bubbles using a bubble removing tool. Reassess the headspace and add more boiling liquid if required to fill up to the required headspace.

6. Take a clean damp cloth and wipe the rim of the jars. Place the canning lid on each jar using the lid lifter. Place the canning ring on each jar and tighten it as suggested.

7. Place the jars in the canner and process the jars following the manufacturer's instruction manual at 10 psi (69 kPa). Set the timer for 90 minutes for quart size (1 L) jars, adjusting for altitude if required. Once the timer goes off, turn off the burner.

8. Once you are done with the processing, let the pressure release naturally before opening the canner and taking out the jars. Let the jars cool completely on your countertop for no less than 12 hours. Wipe the jars with a dry kitchen cloth or paper towel. Make sure to check for the seals. These jars will last you for about 12 months.

9. **Serving suggestion**: Empty the contents of a jar into a saucepan. Place the saucepan over medium heat. Heat the soup thoroughly. Ladle the soup into bowls. Drizzle some lemon juice on top. Garnish with fresh herbs on top and serve.

Chile, Corn, and Chicken Chowder

Makes: 10 quart jars (1 L)

Ingredients:

- 4 tablespoons (60 ml) vegetable oil
- 2 cups (250 g) sliced celery
- 4 teaspoons ground Ancho chili pepper or mild chili powder
- 10 cups (1.74 kg) fresh corn kernels
- Freshly ground black pepper to taste
- Six medium onions, chopped
- Four Poblano chili peppers, deseeded, chopped
- 6 quarts (6 L) low-sodium chicken broth

Serving instructions per serving 1 quart (1 L) jar:

- ½ cup instant mashed potato flakes
- American cheese slices

Directions:

1. Arrange the pressure canner, canning lids, and jars. You need 10 quart size (1 L) jars. Pour enough water into the pressure canner following the

manufacturer's instructions such that it is about 3 inches (8 centimeters) in height from the bottom of the canner. Place the canner on your stovetop over low heat. Place the jars in the canner so that the jars remain warm. The temperature of the water in the canner should be maintained at 180°F (82°C). Place the lids in a small saucepan of water over low heat on another burner.

2. Pour oil into a large stock pot and let the pot heat over medium-high heat. When oil is hot, drop the onions, chilies, and celery into the pot and cook for a few minutes until onions are pink. Add chili powder and mix well.

3. Stir in chicken, broth, black pepper, and corn. When the mixture starts boiling, turn off the heat.

4. Place the jars on a towel. Place the funnel over the rim of the jar. Remove the vegetables and chicken with a slotted spoon and place in the jars.

5. Now pour the broth into the jars until you get 1 inch (2.5 cm) headspace. In case you are short of broth, boil some more broth or water and add.

6. Make sure to remove bubbles using a bubble removing tool. Reassess the headspace and add more boiling liquid if required to fill up to the required headspace.

7. Take a clean damp cloth and wipe the rim of the jars. Place the canning lid on each jar using the lid lifter. Place the canning ring on each jar and tighten it as suggested.

8. Place the jars in the canner and process the jars following the manufacturer's instruction manual at 10 psi (69 kPa). Set the timer for 75 minutes for quart size (1 L) jars, adjusting for altitude if required. Once the timer goes off, turn off the burner.

9. Once you are done with the processing, let the pressure release naturally before opening the canner and taking out the jars. Let the jars cool completely on

your countertop for no less than 12 hours. Wipe the jars with a dry kitchen cloth or paper towel. Make sure to check for the seals. These jars will last you for about 12 months.

10. **Serving suggestion**: Empty the contents of a jar into a saucepan. Place the saucepan over medium heat. Cover the saucepan and let it heat for about 10 minutes. Turn off the heat. Stir in instant mashed potato flakes. Tear up a couple of slices of cheese and add into the soup. Mix well. Once cheese melts, ladle into soup bowls and serve.

Appendix 1 – Altitude in USA Cities & Canadian Cities

Chart of the 20 largest cities in the U.S. and their Altitudes

City	State	Altitude	Rank by population
Phoenix	Arizona	1086 ft	5
Denver	Colorado	948 ft	19
Columbus	Ohio	902 ft	15
Charlotte	North Carolina	761 ft	16
Indianapolis	Indiana	719 ft	17
Fort Worth	Texas	653 ft	13
San Antonio	Texas	650 ft	7
Chicago	Illinois	597 ft	3
Dallas	Texas	430 ft	9
Austin	Texas	425 ft	11
Washington	D.C.	409 ft	20

Los Angeles	California	305 ft	2
Seattle	Washington	174 ft	18
Houston	Texas	105 ft	4
San Jose	California	82 ft	10
San Diego	California	62 ft	8
San Francisco	California	52 ft	14
Philadelphia	Pennsylvania	39 ft	6
New York City	New York	33 ft	1
Jacksonville	Florida	16 ft	12

5 cities with the highest altitudes in the U.S.

City	State	Altitude
Alma	Colorado	10,361 ft
Leadville	Colorado	10,150 ft

Blue River	Colorado	10,020 ft
Breckenridge	Colorado	9,600 ft
Flagstaff	Arizona	6,910 ft

Altitude of the 10 largest cities in Canada

City	Province	Altitude	Rank by population
Vancouver,	British Columbia	6,562 ft	8
Calgary	Alberta	3,428 ft	3
Edmonton	Alberta	2,116 ft	5
Hamilton	Ontario	1083 ft	10
Winnipeg	Manitoba	784 ft	7
Montreal	Quebec	764 ft	2
Brampton	Ontario	715 ft	9
Mississauga	Ontario	512 ft	6

| Toronto | Ontario | 251 ft | 1 |
| Ottawa | Ontario | 230 ft | 4 |

Appendix 2 - Measurement Conversion

Cups	Tablespoons	Teaspoons	Milliliters
		1 tsp	5 ml
1/16 cups	1 tbsp	3 tsp	15 ml
⅛ cups	2 tbsp	6 tsp	30 ml
¼ cups	4 tbsp	12 tsp	60 ml
⅓ cups	5 ⅓ tbsp	16 tsp	80 ml
½ cups	8 tbsp	24 tsp	120 ml
⅔ cups	10 ⅔ tbsp	32 tsp	160ml
¾ cups	12 tbsp	36 tsp	180 ml
1 cup	16 tbsp	48 tsp	240 ml

1 Gallon = 4 quarts = 8 pints =16 cups= 120 oz = 3.8 liters

1 Quart = 2 pints= 4 cups = 32 oz = 950 ml

1 Pint = 2 cups= 16 oz = 480 ml

1 cup = 8oz= 240ml

Cooking Temperatures

Fahrenheit = (Celsius x 1.8) +32

Celsius = (Fahrenheit - 32) x 0.5556

Pounds to Kilograms

1 lb = 0.45 kg	1 kg= 2.22 lbs
2 lbs = 0.90 kg	2 kg= 4.44 lbs
3 lbs = 1.35 kg	3 kg= 6.67 lbs
4 lbs = 1.80 kg	4 kg= 8.89 lbs
5 lbs = 2.25 kg	5 kg= 11.11 lbs
6 lbs = 2.70 kg	6 kg= 13.33 lbs
7 lbs = 3.15 kg	7 kg= 15.56 lbs
8 lbs = 3.60 kg	8 kg= 17.78 lbs
9 lbs = 4.05 kg	9 kg= 20.00 lbs
10 lbs = 4.50 kg	10 kg= 22.22 lbs

Conclusion

"Laughter is brightest where food is best."

In this book, you were introduced to all the information you need about canning. Before you start, it is important that you take time to learn about the USDA guidelines for safe canning and how your pressure canner works. Learning about the different parts of the pressure canner will give you a better understanding of pressure canning. Knowing this makes a lot of difference when it comes to the results obtained while using a specific recipe. By now, you might have realized that pressure canning is easier than you believed. Once you start following the step-by-step process described, you can get brilliant results every single time.

You should also make it a point to develop a few practices to ensure high-quality results. Whether it is strictly following a recipe, cleanliness protocols while canning, or handling the pressure canner, best practices for safety and so on. Also, these practices ensure you get high-quality results. When it comes to food safety, it is always better to err on the side of caution. Always listen to the recipe, but first make sure it aligns with the USDA's food protocols. Do not forget to adjust the temperature and pressure according to altitude. Also make it a point that you always focus on the acidity of the ingredients used too.

You were also introduced to different recipes you can use to start canning at home. The sky's the limit when it comes to canning. Once you've become comfortable with your pressure canner, feel free to be creative. Don't forget to try different vegetarian and vegan-friendly food options as well. Canning is easy once you have all the tools and equipment needed along with the correct ingredients. After this, you simply need to follow the instructions given in the recipe and start canning! Once you get the hang of it, you can enjoy your favorite food with your loved ones all year long. Thank you and all the best!

References

Andress, E. (2014). *Preserving food: Using pressure canners.* National Center for Home Food Preservation | UGA Publications. https://nchfp.uga.edu/publications/uga/using_press_canners.html

Chihaak, S. (2020, April 6). *Master pressure canning at home in 9 simple steps.* Better Homes & Gardens. https://www.bhg.com/recipes/how-to/preserving-canning/pressure-canning-basics/

HGIC 3030. (2011, August 20). *Canning foods—the pH factor.* Home & Garden Information Center | Clemson University, South Carolina. Https://hgic.clemson.edu/factsheet/canning-foods-the-pH factor/#:~:text=The%20acidity%2C%20or%20pH%2C%20of,processed%20in%20a%20pressure%20canner.

Homestead Dreamer. (2016, October 10). *Unraveling the mystery: Water bath vs pressure canning.* Homestead Dreamer. Http://www.homesteaddreamer.com/2016/10/10/water-bath-vs-pressure-canning/

Kring, L. (2016, July 23). *13 top tips for successful pressure canning.* Foodal. https://foodal.com/knowledge/things-that-preserve/tips-home-canning/

Meredith, L. (2020, September 17). *Boiling water bath and pressure canning - When to use which.* The Spruce Eats. https://www.thespruceeats.com/boiling-water-bath-versus-pressure-canning-1327438

Mountain Feed & Farm Supply. (n.d.). *Our must-have list of canning equipment & supplies.* Mountain Feed & Farm Supply. Https://www.mountainfeed.com/blogs/learn/15522713-our-must-have-list-of-canning-equipment-supplies

Penn State Extension. (n.d.). *Time, temperature, pressure in canning foods.* Penn State Extension. Https://extension.psu.edu/time-temperature-pressure-in-canning-foods

Peterson, S. (2020, April 11). *What is botulism?* SimplyCanning. Https://www.simplycanning.com/botulism/

Peterson, S. (2021, October 7). *Pressure canners: The brands, features, and how they work!* SimplyCanning. Https://www.simplycanning.com/pressure-canner/#pressurecanner3

Images References

Anshu. (n.d.). *Tomato sauce* [Unsplash].https://unsplash.com/photos/mVUs_adTiX8

Brown, M. (n.d.). *Pressure dial gauge* [Pixabay]. https://pixabay.com/photos/pressure-gauge-gauge-pressure-5156070/

Cala. (n.d.). *Carrot soup* [Unsplash]. https://unsplash.com/photos/w6ftFbPCs9I

Castrejon, E. (n.d.). *Canned dried beans* [Unsplash]. **https://unsplash.com/photos/1SPu0KT-Ejg**

Didier. (n.d.). *Tomato sauce* [Pixabay]. https://pixabay.com/users/mrdidg-11821588/

Dmitriy. (n.d.). *Canned baked beans* [Pixabay]. https://pixabay.com/photos/vegetarian-white-canned-bean-5029296/

Doan, V. (n.d.). *Green beans* [Pixabay]. https://pixabay.com/photos/green-bean-food-green-healthy-1443290/

Kalhh. (n.d.). *Chili con carne* [Pixabay]. https://pixabay.com/photos/chili-con-carne-chili-cook-378952/

Licht-aus. (n.d.). *Food strainer* [Pixabay]. https://pixabay.com/photos/sock-strainer-banana-chopsticks-6316925/

Mona. (n.d.). *Asparagus soup* [Pixabay]. https://pixabay.com/photos/soup-asparagus-green-colour-2649392/

Merkman, K. (n.d.). *Tin can vessel* [Pixabay]. https://pixabay.com/vectors/tin-can-vessel-disposal-metal-3778762/

Myriam. (n.d.). *Ratatouille* [Pixabay]. https://pixabay.com/photos/ratatouille-dish-food-vegetables-6498448/

Owen-Wahl, R. (n.d.). *Corned beef and potatoes* [Pixabay]. https://pixabay.com/photos/beef-food-peas-plate-snack-lunch-1238623/

Rivas, H. (n.d.). *Canned food* [Unsplash]. https://unsplash.com/photos/N7M7mSgUgwo

Schwarzenberger, M. (n.d.). *Pressure regulator* [Pixabay]. https://pixabay.com/photos/oxygen-pressure-regulator 502887/

Shaw, C. (n.d.). *Canned sausages* [Unsplash]. https://unsplash.com/photos/

Shrewberry, R. (n.d.). *Canned food* [Unsplash]. https://unsplash.com/photos/bhni1zsPiio

Tant, P. (n.d.). *Tomato soup* [Pixabay]. https://pixabay.com/photos/pepper-soup-tomato-soup-soup-food-1234763/

Thrainer, R. (n.d.). *Herbed potatoes* [Pixabay]. https://pixabay.com/photos/roasted-potatoes-rosemary-herbs-6568342/

Vittoriosi, E. (n.d.). *Asian turkey meatballs* [Unsplash]. https://unsplash.com/photos/OFismyezPnY

A

acidic, 255, 257, 311, 400, 401

air bubbles, 267, 298, 301

alkaline, 257

allspice, 286, 287, 352, 370, 375, 383

Apple Butter on Toast, 374

apple cider vinegar, 286, 287, 323, 336, 354, 375, 378, 379, 380

Apple-Solutely Delicious Jam, 274, 306

Apricots, 320, 408

Asparagus, 390

Awesomesauce Applesauce, 306, 307

B

Baby Sauce, 339

Barbecue Sauce, 354, 408

basil, 340, 341, 343, 381

bay leaves, 340, 342

Be Grape-Ful Jelly, 288

beets, unpeeled, 382

berries, 273, 305, 363, 366, 391

berry, 252, 273, 330, 414

black peppercorns, 314, 356

Blasting Blueberries, 296, 297, 305, 365

Bloody Mary, 348, 350, 410

blueberries, 365

Blueberry Syrup Around, 365

boiling water, 255, 257, 268, 272, 291,

301, 393, 400, 401

bourbon, 354

Broccoli, 390

C

Cabbages, 390

Cantaloupes, 391

Cauliflower, 390

cauliflower florets, 316

cayenne pepper, 354, 370

celery seed, 325, 379, 380

celery,, 346, 349, 359

Cherry Bomb Pie Filling, 303, 305

cherry tomatoes, 331

Chicken Wing Sauce, 369

chili powder, 336

Chili Sauce, 358, 413

chopped onion, 284, 325, 338

chutney, 261, 284, 285, 286, 287, 288, 293, 395, 409, 412

Chutney Recipes, 284

cider vinegar, 311, 325, 326, 361

cinnamon, 301, 304, 307, 308, 319, 320, 321, 352, 353, 358, 359, 367, 370, 375, 383, 413

Cinnamon Pear Sauce, 307, 309, 413

clove, 284, 287, 314

Cocktail, 321

Condiments, 352, 358, 396

Cowboy Candy Over Salmon, 379

cranberries, 366, 367, 410

Cranberry Sauce, 366, 410

crystallized ginger, 284

cucumber, 323

cumin, 336, 338

cups of sugar, 275, 280, 281, 284, 291,

292, 298, 299, 301, 304, 375

cups of white sugar, 289

cups sugar, 276

D

dandelion petals, 291

Dandy Dandelion Jelly, 290

Diced Tomatoes, 329, 411

dried rosemary, 341

E

ears of corn, 316

F

fennel seeds, 342

flakes, 284, 340, 343, 354, 380

fresh blueberries, 297, 305

G

garlic, 284, 287, 314, 317, 335, 336, 337, 338, 340, 341, 343, 344, 349, 354, 355, 356, 357, 370, 378, 379, 380, 381, 399

Glad Marmalade, 278

golden raisins, 284, 286

Granny's Apple Pie Filling, 300

granulated sugar, 273, 278, 305, 364, 367, 378, 381

Greek Yogurt with Mango, 376

green bell pepper, 381

Grigio, 356, 357

ground black pepper, 286, 287, 336, 342

ground cloves, 375

ground coriander, 286, 287

H

habanero pepper, 378

Harmony, 359

honey, 273, 274, 284, 320, 343, 361, 362, 408

Honeycrisp apples, 274

Honeydew melons, 391

Horseradish, 359, 409, 411

hot chili pepper, 286

Hot Sauce, 368, 410

J

jalapeño peppers, 378

jalapeños, 379

jam, 261, 273, 274, 275, 276, 277, 293, 296, 362, 364, 391, 396, 408, 411, 413,

414

Jam Recipes, 273

jams, 257, 274, 400

Jellies, 250, 273

jelly, 261, 273, 289, 290, 291, 292, 293, 296, 364, 366, 396, 411, 413

K

Krazy Kiwi, 299, 300

L

large pears, 308

lemon juice, 257, 275, 276, 277, 278, 279, 280, 291, 300, 301, 302, 304, 305, 308, 329, 330, 331, 332, 333, 340, 342, 343, 346, 347, 349, 364, 365, 366, 375, 376, 377, 381, 382

Lemon Zest Blueberry Sauce, 305, 306

light brown sugar, 286, 287

lime juice, 378

low-acid foods, 258

M

mangoes, 284, 376

Marinara Sauce, 341, 411

marmalade, 261, 278, 279, 280, 281, 282, 293, 305, 408, 410, 413, 414

Marmalade Recipes, 278

Marmalades, 273

Marry Me Mustard, 356

Meat, 257, 339

Mild Salsa, 334

minced, 284, 338, 340, 341, 343, 349, 370, 378, 381

Mushrooms, 391

mustard seed, 325, 356, 357, 358, 361

mustard seeds, whole, 284

O

oranges, 278, 279, 367, 413

oregano, 341, 343, 381

P

paprika, 338, 354

parsley, 340, 347, 349, 381

Pasta La Vista, 339

Peach Salsa Tacos, 377

peaches, 285, 286, 296, 318, 319, 320,

321, 374, 378, 391, 409, 412

Peachy Keen Chutney, 285, 319

Pear-Fect Chutney, 287, 308

Pectin, 273, 274, 400

peel, 278, 279, 286, 345, 364, 375, 400

peeled, 281, 284, 286, 287, 288, 300, 319, 334, 335, 346, 354, 358, 370, 376, 378, 381

Persian limes, 281

Pesticides, 393, 400

Pickled Beets Salad, 382

Pickled Onions, 315

Pickled Peaches, 318, 409

pickles, 257, 311, 312, 313, 315, 323, 392, 397, 413, 414

Pickling, 311, 313, 328, 401

pickling cucumbers, 314

pickling spice, 368

Piña Coladas Jam, 276

Pinot, 356, 357

Pizza Sauce, 343, 411

Puns Jelly, 292

pureed pineapple, 276

R

raspberries, 298, 411

red chili pepper, 284

red pepper flake, 340

Relish, 323, 324, 326, 408, 410, 412

Rhubarb Pie Filling, 302, 409

ripe plums, 292

Rockin Raspberries, 297, 299

Roma tomatoes, 332, 350

rosemary, 356, 357

S

sage, 342

Salsa Verde, 337, 408

salt, 286, 287, 312, 314, 315, 317, 322, 323, 324, 325, 326, 331, 332, 335, 336, 338, 340, 341, 343, 345, 346, 347, 349, 352, 353, 354, 356, 357, 358, 359, 360,

367, 368, 370, 375, 378, 381, 399

Spaghetti, 380, 411

Spicy Salsa, 336

strawberries, 251, 263, 271, 273, 274, 321, 362, 363, 364, 414

Straw-Berry Good Jam, 273

Strawberry Vinaigrette, 362, 413

Sub-Lime Marmalade, 281

T

thyme, 315, 342, 343

Tomato Juice, 345, 408

tomato puree, 344, 352

turmeric, 323, 324, 379, 380

U

unsalted butter, 292

unsweetened fruit juice, 273

V

vegetables, 257, 311, 312, 316, 317, 325, 327, 328, 339, 346, 353, 355, 358, 393, 397, 399, 400, 401, 408

vermouth, 320

vinegar, 257

W

Water Bath Canning, 250, 255, 259, 385, 391, 392, 410, 412, 413

white balsamic vinegar, 320

white onions, diced, 336

white rum, 276

white vinegar, 284, 314, 315, 317, 319, 323, 335, 338, 358, 360, 362, 368, 370, 383

whole eggs, 361

Whole Lotta Whole Tomato, 332

Worcestershire sauce, 340, 349, 381

Y

yellow mustard seeds, 356

Z

zest, 281, 305, 308, 367, 375

Zest Lemon Marmalade, 279

zested, 367

Zoodles, 380, 381

Water Bath Canning

for

Beginners and Beyond

The Essential Guide to Safe Water Bath Canning at Home. Easy and Delicious Recipes for Jams, Jellies, Salsas, Pickled Vegetables, and More!

By
Linda C. Johnson

Introduction

"Be the change you want to see in the world."

- Gandhi

Every year, over a billion pounds of food is sent to landfills. According to the United States Department of Agriculture (USDA), this is the tragic fate of 30-40% of the entire food supply in the United States (USDA, 2010). This wastes many of the country's resources such as land, water, money, and labor. One of the main contributors to food waste is spoilage. As a consumer, you don't have much power over spoilage that occurs during transit or any other time before the goods reach the market.

This food waste is astronomically bad for both the environment and the economy. With all of this in mind, we should ask ourselves how much food leaves our kitchens in garbage bags.

We owe it to ourselves, our children, and the world around us to try our best as individuals to make a difference. The best place to start is preventing spoilage, and lucky for you this book will tell you exactly how to do that in great detail and deliciousness.

Now you may be thinking, wow, this is really serious stuff. I just picked up this book because I have extra strawberries in my garden and want to save them for a pie I'll make later. Well congratulations, that pie is going to help to save the world. That might be a lot of pressure to put on a pie, but with the delicious recipes offered in this book, you don't have to worry about living up to any expectations. As long as your jar is sealed properly, spoilage will be put off indefinitely; but that isn't the only perk to water bath canning your food. For many canners, the biggest reward to using a water bath canner is the preservation of flavor. What is tastier than a berry out of season? That flavor can only be made better with the knowledge that you're helping eliminate unnecessary food waste.

Saving the world is great, but why else should you start home canning? There are numerous health benefits to this practice. The most important of which is actually knowing every single ingredient that goes into your food. Food companies are only required to list ingredients that make up 5% or more of their product. The only instances where this 5% rule doesn't apply is with additives or allergens. These must be listed no matter how small the percentage is. However, the ingredients that fall under the U.S. Food and Drug Administration (FDA)'s category of major food allergens only account for around 90% of all food allergies. Those who suffer from the other 10% are just kind of out of luck when it comes to buying food. With home canning, you can decide exactly what you put in your jars and you never have to worry about the 4% of mystery ingredients you may be consuming.

Preparing your own meals is also a great way to stay in shape, and home canning is a reliable and more sustainable way to do that. With basic meal preparation techniques, you are preparing your food for a week. This can free up several hours of your week that can then be devoted to family time, or other meaningful activities. With home canning, all you need is a day or two out of the entire *year* and you've got fresh and healthy food whenever you need. When you have a family to feed, you don't always have the time to prepare something. This is when easy and unhealthy options like fast food feel like the only choice. Home canning is the opportunity to prepare a healthy meal for days like these that just can't be scheduled.

Also, eating out is expensive. Buying groceries is expensive. Consuming food because you have to live is expensive. Another way that home canning can make your life easier is by saving you a bit of money. Fresh fruit will only last a couple of days before it starts to rot. If you can't eat it in time, that is as good as throwing your money down the drain. Water bath canning will elongate the life span of your fruit so you don't have to worry about wasting it anymore. Save yourself the frustration of replacing food you've already bought. Having healthy food available will also help during those weeks when payday just isn't coming fast enough. Start canning, and your wallet will thank you.

This all said, water bath canning is not a magical cure-all. The benefits aren't given, they are earned. For example, the equipment isn't hard to use, but it will take some time to get used to the process. It's okay if your first jars don't come out perfectly. It can take several tries before you get the results you want. Don't be afraid to experiment with different ingredient and flavor combinations. The more you put into it, the more you'll get out of it. Think of canning as an investment. With a little bit of time and work, you'll be canning like a professional. So if you want to get healthy, save a little money, and maybe even help the world, then get ready to start your personal canning journey.

Chapter 1
Water Bath Canning 101

"Without a solid foundation, you have trouble creating anything of value."

- Ericka Oppenheimer

What is Water Bath Canning?

Water bath canning is an easy method to safely preserve food with high acidic levels. Water bath canning is also referred to as "boiling water canning" or "hot water canning." It is the simple process of boiling jars in a large pot of water for a specified amount of time. Within the pot, the jars are boiled evenly on all sides to ensure the food is thoroughly cooked. After the jars have been boiled and properly sealed, they no longer have to be refrigerated. They will be safely preserved until the jar is opened again as long as they are stored in a cool and dry place.

Produce that is canned in a water bath canner will theoretically last forever. As long as the seal is intact, then the food is still edible. This doesn't mean that the food will be delicious forever, though. After a year, the flavor will start to go downhill and the overall quality will diminish. That's why it's recommended to eat home canned goods within the following 12 months after its processing. I always recommend labeling the jar with the date and having an organized storage system where the oldest products are the easiest to get to and use.

You should also label your jars with the ingredients that you used, and not just what the final product is. Sometimes, it's hard to remember what you put in a jar several months ago, and this way you don't have to rely on your memory. Most of the ingredients used in the recipes in this book will lean more towards healthier options, but that doesn't account for allergens. If you will have to substitute any ingredients, make sure to double-check boiling times as they may differ depending on what you are using. The wrong boiling time could result in under-processed food which will not be safe to eat.

If you choose to substitute an ingredient, it might change whether or not you'll have to raw pack or hot pack. Raw packing is when the food is not cooked before it's packed into the jars. Raw packing is sometimes called cold packing in certain recipes. Hot packing is the opposite, when the food is partially cooked beforehand. After either method, liquid is added to the contents to help preservation. This liquid is usually either boiling water, juice, or syrup. With either method, there should always be around an inch of headspace between the lid and the food or it could seal improperly.

When to Use a Water Bath Canner

Water bath canning isn't the only method of canning. The other method is called pressure canning, and requires a pressure canner that can reach temperatures that the water bath process can't. Also, water bath canners require more water than pressure canners. The food in water bath canning is heated by the boiling water that surrounds it. This means it can only reach the temperature of boiling water, which is 212 °F. Fruits, jams, and pickles are some of the many foods that are safe to process at this temperature. Jars in a pressure canner are heated up by steam that can reach 240 °F. Meat and unpickled vegetables need this higher temperature to process.

So why does some food need higher temperatures to can? It's all about acidity. The acidity of food is measured by its pH level. The pH scale ranges from 0 to 14. Seven is considered neutral since it is in the middle. If something is lower than 7 on the pH scale it is considered acidic. If it is higher, it is considered alkaline. To put this in perspective, lemon juice or vinegar has a pH level of about 2. This makes it acidic and safe to put in a water bath canner. Meat and vegetables are closer to neutral than alkaline but are still considered to be low-acid ranging from 4—7 pH. These levels are used to determine if drinking water has been contaminated or not.

So what will happen if you put low-acid food in a water bath canner? Without exaggerating, you could die. Acidity helps kill dangerous bacteria, but low-acid foods can't do this on their own without reaching certain temperatures.

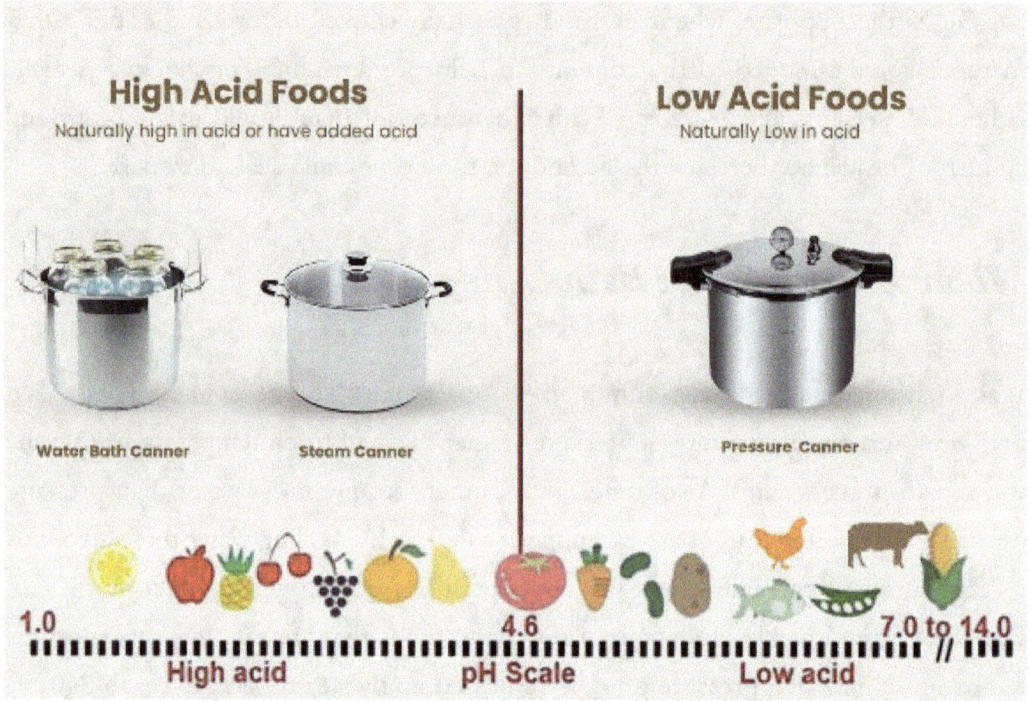

Every canner's biggest fear is catching botulism, the spores of which are mostly found in low-acid foods. So what will happen if you put high-acid food in a pressure canner? It might taste bad. There's not any life-changing risk to it. The worst that could happen is you overcook the food and have to throw it away. (If you're curious about certain foods and their pH levels, you can always contact your local extension service. This is a state agency with the USDA that can provide research and other information.)

Now that you know the difference between the two methods of canning, you may be wondering which one is better in general. Seeing as this is a water bath canning book, we're going to go with that one. In actuality, they are both wonderful methods that have their own pros and cons. Pressure canning is easier to plan meals with while water bath canning is easier to do. Water bath canning is also a cheaper method and a lot less of an investment. You could even call it "no pressure" canning. It is also less dangerous. Modern pressure canners might be incredibly safe but they can still cause a lot of damage if the ventilation becomes clogged. You don't have to worry about your lid possibly flying off into the ceiling if you own a water bath canner.

Water Bath Canning Equipment

You'll never be able to successfully can anything without special canning equipment. While water bath canning is the least expensive option, these purchases are still a must. The first thing you'll need to invest in is a water bath canner. There are specially-made pots for this but all you need is a large pot that can fit jars in it for canning. It's important that the water can cover the jar by 2 inches otherwise the water won't be able to boil. The canner should also have a fitted lid. If you want to go out and buy a special canner then by all means go ahead, it just isn't necessary.

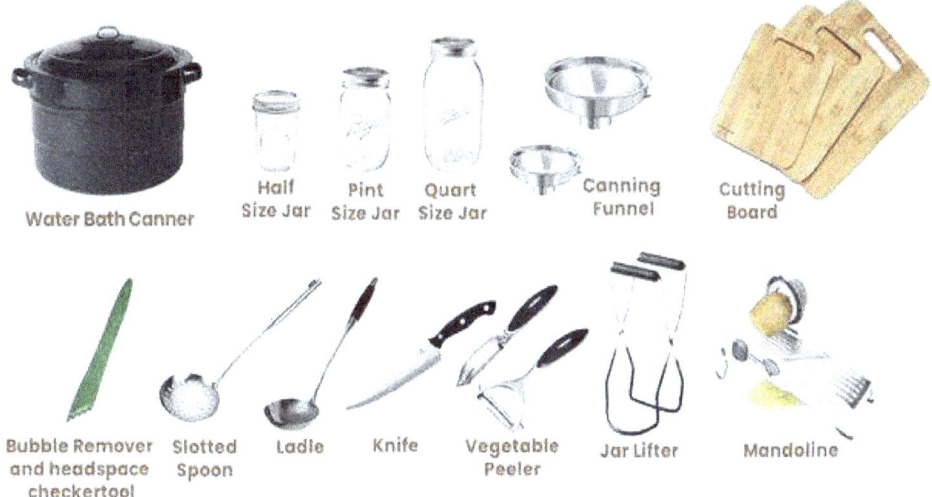

Next you will need a rack to accompany your canner. Racks sit at the bottom of the pot. Their purpose is to make sure the jars aren't touching the bottom of the canner or each other. If jars are put at the bottom of the pot with no rack, the jar's bottom won't heat as evenly as the other sides. If the jars are touching each other they could shake and break, causing glass fragments to go into your food. Water bath canners usually come with racks, but if you're just using a big pot you'll need to make sure the one you buy can fit racks.

You will also need jars to put the food in. Pick mason jars that have a two-piece closure. (The closure should consist of a reusable band and lid.) The lid should be discarded after every use because it can't reseal a jar effectively. If the food doesn't seal right, it may become home to dangerous bacteria. Since mason jars are glass, you should make sure to always inspect them before use. Any slight crack can let in harmful bacteria or break and contaminate the food with glass. Neither is going to be fun to digest. Most canners will suggest using Ball or Kerr brands as they are sturdy and tend to last the longest.

Lastly, you'll be needing a jar lifter. You may feel like this is unnecessary but trust me, after a couple of burns you'll learn your lesson. Jar lifters are just large tongs that can take the jars in and out of the canner. Remember, the water bath canner reaches temperatures of 212 °F. You do not want your hand anywhere near that even after it's cooled. Some other helpful, but not as mandatory, utensils you might need are a ladle and funnel. Ladles are great for spooning ingredients into the jars, while funnels help do the same thing and limit any spilling that might occur.

Choosing a Canning Recipe

This book contains 60 canning recipes for you to use. The easiest place to start is with a simple canned fruit recipe. There are a couple to choose from in Chapter 4's "Fruit" section. You don't have to start there, though. If you're a talented cook, you might be interested in checking out Chapter 3, where I've compiled several jelly, jam, marmalade, and chutney recipes. When it comes to water bath canning, these types of recipes are the most used. If you want to show off your work as a beginner, or even a canning veteran, this is definitely the way to go. Another easy way to leave an impression is by making a pie filling. The dessert is an American classic and with so many options it's a delicious start to your canning pantry.

Before you choose a recipe, you should know what you're looking for. A recipe may sound fun to make but are you actually going to eat it? If you plan on selling your canned goods, do you know what types are most popular on the market right now? Don't get excited and start canning everything you can. It's worse to can things and end up throwing them away than to just throw something away from the start. You waste time and energy by canning them first. (You get experience, too, but it's not really worth it if you can't enjoy your progress.) If you want to start with big loads, you can just make sure to use it all.

While I have spent a great deal of time finding these recipes, I'm not going to take it personally if you decide you want to try a recipe not found within this book. Finding and choosing your own recipes is an important part of your canning journey. Everyone has their own preferred diet and nutritional needs. Your recipes should reflect that. For example, many of the recipes in this book contain sugar because it's an important part of the water bath canning process. If you're more focused on a lower-calorie diet, you'll need to find recipes that use sugar alternatives. Canners with more experience usually end up substituting their own preferred ingredients into recipes to make it their own.

If you're going to find your own recipes, choose wisely. The internet is a limitless place to start but there are a lot of unreliable sources out there. It's up to you to find safe canning practices. Always double check that what is being canned can be safely processed in your water bath canner. The best way to do this is to research the USDA's canning guidelines. If a recipe is directly contradicting these guidelines then it's definitely not safe. You can always contact your local extension service to find safe recipes that match your chosen diet as well. It's also important to find recipes that work for the amount you want to make. Some processing times change depending on whether you have pints or quarts. You don't want to end up with an under or over-processed product.

Other Helpful Tips

Canning should be fun. If you're not having fun then you're probably not doing it correctly. The best way in my opinion to do this is to not can alone. A canning partner can help you find fun new recipes, challenge you to try something new, and just add a level of excitement you might not have alone. Canning can even be a friendly competition; see whose apple pie filling comes out better, learn from each other, and evolve faster in your canning journey. It can also just be a great bonding experience with siblings, a parent, a child, or a friend. Canning is a fulfilling experience and what could be better than sharing that achievement with a loved one.

Another tip is to only use the freshest of ingredients. Frozen food isn't going to result in high-quality canned goods. The flavor will certainly never match its fresh counterparts. Will it taste unbearably bad? No, but it's just a watered-down version now. If you are putting all of this work into learning, preparing, planning and creating, don't you want the best possible outcome? There isn't any need to preserve frozen fruit. The whole point of canning fruit is to keep it fresh so you can enjoy it in seasons it's not available. Frozen fruit can be found in the grocery aisle whenever. At that point, opening a jar of something that you can just go to the grocery and get loses its magic.

My favorite way to get fresh fruits is to go out and pick them myself. You can get perfectly healthy fruit at a farmer's market for a fair price and there's nothing wrong with that; I do this all the time. However, the experience of apple picking is unmatched. Maybe it's just the giddiness of the season, but the smell of fresh apples and the abundance of choices just makes my heart melt. There's also an unspoken beauty in picking blueberries from a wild bush. Orchard picking isn't something I get to do a lot of, but I certainly suggest trying it, just for the experience, at least once on your canning journey.

Another way to make sure you have fresh ingredients is to grow them yourself. Starting a garden for your canned goods is a whole other journey, one that is just as fulfilling and a little more aesthetic. Not everyone has the space or the time for a home garden and that's okay. There are plenty of other ways to get fresh produce. If you are lucky enough to have the space and time, start off small with some strawberries. Just grow a little batch and use them for canning. It's a great way to test the waters without diving in.

Key Chapter 1 Takeaways

- Water bath canning is a canning method for food with high acid.
- Low-acid food should only be preserved in a pressure canner.
- Make sure you have clean and working equipment before you start canning.

- Make sure your recipe is USDA approved and follows their health and safety protocols.
- For the best results when canning, use the freshest ingredients.

Chapter 2
How to Water Bath Can in 4 Easy Steps

"Every journey begins with a single step."

-Maya Angelou

Step 1: Preparation

The first thing you should always do before starting to can is clean. Clean absolutely everything from the jars to the canner itself. This may seem like overkill and it absolutely is. A good philosophy to have when it comes to canning is that it's better to be safe than sorry. If your utensils have been sitting in storage for half a year, it's likely to have accumulated some dust. You won't want to pour food into dusty jars. Not only could it be dangerous for bacterial reasons but it's not very appetizing either. When you are done washing all of your equipment make sure to thoroughly dry it off.

While a canner's worst fear is botulism, a canner's worst enemy is rust. Cleaning your equipment before use is a great time to check it over for any possible rust. Rust can ruin the integrity of the canner and cause holes where you don't want them. Canners are supposed to last decades if they are properly maintained. The last thing you'll want to do is have to replace your expensive equipment because it's faulty. This is why canners need to be stored in a similar location to the canned goods. The right conditions will keep it safe from any possible rust or even mold.

If the process time for your goods is less than 10 minutes you'll need to sterilize the jars. To do this, place the empty jars in the water bath canner right side up and fill the canner with water. This should come to about 1 inch above the jars. Boil the water for

10 minutes. (Add one minute every 1,000 feet above sea level where you are located.) When this is done, remove the jars from the canner using a jar lifter. Drain the hot water from the jars and dry them off before adding food. You can leave the water in the canner and use it to process the food.

If you don't need to sterilize the jars, you still need to make sure they are warm before the food goes in them. In this case you can fill the water bath canner ⅓ of the way. Place the jars upside down and let the steam keep them warm. (You can also just wash them in a dishwasher and keep them in there until you're ready to use them.) The lids and screw bands should also be warm. An easy way to do this is to put them in a warm bowl of water.

Step 2: Heating

After you have filled the jars and checked them for air bubbles, it's time to put them in the canner. Using a jar lifter, slowly place the jars of food into the water bath canner. Evenly space them out on the rack so they aren't touching. The rack should assist with this. If you have a water bath canner, your rack should be able to rest on the sides of your canner. Once your rack is loaded, you can lower it down so the water is now covering the jar lids. Add water until there are 2 inches of water above the jars. It's important for the process that the water can freely move around the jars.

The time doesn't start until the canner is at a boil. When this starts to happen place the lid over the canner and have it come to a full rolling boil. It's best to measure the cooking time exactly so use an app on your phone or an actual kitchen timer. You'll definitely want an alarm if the process is going to take more than half an hour. If you choose to just pay attention to the clock you may accidentally over-process the food. The canner is going to reach temperatures of 212 °F, so make sure you don't accidentally burn yourself on the canister.

BOILING WATER BATH CANNING
Altitude Adjustment Chart

ALTITUDE	IF YOUR PROCESSING TIME IS LESS THAN 20 MINUTES	IF YOUR PROCESSING TIME IS MORE THAN 20 MINUTES
1,001 - 3,000 ft (305 - 914 m)	add 5 minutes to processing time	add 5 minutes to processing time
3,001 - 6,000 ft (915 - 1828 m)	add 10 minutes to processing time	
6,001 ft and up (1829 m +)	add 15 minutes to processing time	add 10 minutes to processing time

Processing times can change depending on your altitude. Most recipes only provide the processing times for locations under 1,000 feet above sea level. If you live in high altitude places like Colorado, this could be a problem. The reason why altitude can affect processing times is because of the change in atmospheric pressure. By every 1,000 feet, the atmospheric pressure is reduced. This will make water boil at a lower temperature than 212 °F. Since water is boiling at a lower temperature, it's going to take longer to cook. It's important to research your altitude before you begin canning and change the processing times accordingly.

If you have a long processing time, it is vital for the canner to keep up the boiling. Every once in a while lift up the lid and look inside to make sure the canner is doing its job. The pot is supposed to be full of boiling water though, so be very careful. If you've noticed that the water is no longer at a full rolling boil, add some more boiling water to the canner to help it maintain its process. Be careful when adding in the boiling water, as you don't want to spill any and end up with any serious burns.

Step 3: Cooling

Once your timer goes off you can turn the heat off. The water bath canner will still be hot so be careful as you lift up the rack. Always wear protective gear around a heated water bath canner. You don't need goggles or anything dramatic like that, but oven mitts are a must have. Make sure not to shake the jars too much when you are lifting up the rack. The sealing process is still relatively fragile at this stage and you could mess it up. Before you take the jars out, give them a minute or two to cool down.

Grab your trusty jar lifters and slowly take the jars out one by one. The jars are still going to be very hot so make sure to put them on a wooden board or thick towel. You don't want to end up with any scorch marks on your counter. The jars should be in an upright position, as putting them in any other position will mess with the sealing process. There also needs to be a couple of inches between the jars so that air can freely circulate around them. Make sure they aren't located in a spot with a draft; cold air could break the hot glass of the jars and ruin all of your hard work.

In the next couple of minutes the jars will start to cool. As they do this the sealing process begins. You'll most likely hear a pop. This comes from the seal of the inner lid being pulled down and resulting in a satisfying "ping" sound. Make sure not to touch the jars during this cooling process. The worst thing you can do at this point is to press down on the lid. It will mess up the seal and make all of your hard work for nothing. The jars should be left alone for about 24 hours.

After the 24 hours of waiting comes the moment of truth. Press down on the lid to see if the sealing process was a success. If you find that the lid is sucked down and does not pop back up when you press down, congratulations—you did it! If it does pop up, it's not that big of a deal. The seal may not have worked but the food is still good. Just put it in the refrigerator and eat it in the next few days. You could also try to re-process it, but that might result in an overcooked taste and texture.

Step 4: Storing

Before you start canning you should already know where you are going to put your canned goods. Canned food needs a cool and dry environment to stay preserved. This can be a cellar or a temperature-controlled garage. It can also be a regular pantry; just make sure there is no direct sunlight. Another huge issue is using a location with any sort of humidity. If you're storing your canned goods in a cellar, there can't be any hot pipes around. This can result in steam that will pop the sealed lid straight off. Your location should also have enough room for your cans to stay organized. If you make more cans than your space allows, you could end up having to store them in a place that isn't ideal, and lose produce.

Once you have a location, it's time to store your first batch. Make sure to take off the screw band. This won't affect the actual seal and the lid will stay put. The problem with keeping the screw band on is that it could rust over and ruin your jar. It can also make it impossible to open the container safely. If you're having trouble removing a screw band, it's not the end of the world. Just keep it on and check on it every once in a while to make sure no rust is forming. If you try to force it, it can ruin the seal.

After removing the screw bands you're not yet done. The jars need to be labeled. I suggest adding the date that they were canned, the type of food in them, and any ingredients that went into them. The ingredient list might only seem necessary if you're planning on selling the goods, but it can come in handy even if you're not; when you're trying out different recipes, you want to know which ingredients worked best for you. When you are putting on the date, the year is just as important. You don't want to accidentally eat something that's seven years old. It won't kill you but it probably won't taste good.

The USDA recommends eating your canned goods within a year. After this point, the food quality will go down. You'll end up missing out on the nutritional value along with the taste. (However, in the case of an apocalypse, you may be happy you saved strawberries from 30 years ago.) So ultimately the decision whether to throw the food away after it has peaked is up to you. When you're done with a jar, make sure to discard the lid, wash the jar, and store it somewhere safe for the next harvest season.

Key Chapter 2 Takeaways

12. Always wash all equipment between uses.
13. Always use a jar lifter to prevent injury when removing and placing jars.

14. The water in a boiling water bath canner should rise 2 inches above the jars.
15. After canning, let the jars sit for 24 hours; messing with the lids before this time can result in an unsealed jar.
16. Store jars in a cool and dry location for best results.

Chapter 3
Jams, Marmalades, Chutneys, and Jellies

"If life gives you the wobbles, make jelly."

- Magdalena VandenBerg

Jam Recipes

Straw-Berry Good Jam

Straw-Berry Good jam is a healthier alternative to sugar-packed store options. This jam uses honey instead of granulated sugar to sweeten, which infuses it with the honey's antioxidants and anti-inflammatory properties. Honey is also less processed than granulated sugar. The best time to prepare Straw-berry Good Jam is in June, when the berries are in peak season, depending on where you live: for example, strawberry season starts earlier in southern states.

Amount: Two 8 oz jars.

Ingredients: *(See page 172 for Measurement Conversion)*

- 1 ⅓ cups crushed strawberries
- ⅓ cup unsweetened fruit juice
- 1 ½ tablespoons No-Sugar Needed Pectin
- ⅓ cup honey

Directions:

7. Prepare all of the equipment. Wash the jars and sterilize them if necessary. Add water to the canner but wait to boil.
8. In a large saucepan, mix the strawberries and fruit juice at a low setting.
9. Then gradually add and stir in the Pectin to the mix.
10. After this, add the honey and raise the heat to high. Once it reaches a boil, maintain stirring for one minute before removing the pan from the heat source.
11. Funnel the hot jam into a heated jar leaving a ¼ inch of space before wiping the jar's rim and putting on the lid.
12. Using a jar lifter, gently place the jars in the canner, making sure there are 1-2 inches of water above them.
13. Bring the canner to a boil and let it process for 10 minutes. (Adjust time for altitude differences.)
14. After the time is up, turn off the heat and remove the canner's lid. Let it stand for five minutes before removal.
15. To remove the jars, use your jar lifter and let them cool for 24 hours before checking the seal.
16. Enjoy your Straw-Berry Good jam!

Apple-Solutely Delicious Jam

In regards to what type of apples to use for this jam, remember that jams are a lot like pies. You'll want an apple that won't crumble but will still have its sweet flavor. I recommend Granny Smith, Pink Ladies, or Honeycrisp apples. No matter what apple or combination of apples you use, you'll want the freshest ingredients. Apple-picking season is typically from August to October. Trust me, there is no better way to spend a beautiful fall day than in an apple orchard. While Apple-Solutely Delicious Jam isn't sugar-free, it is still a great addition to your breakfast toast.

Amount: Two half-pint jars.

Ingredients: *(See page 172 for Measurement Conversion)*

- 8 cups of diced apples
- 2 cups of sugar
- ¼ cup of lemon juice

Directions:

- Before your jam can be prepared, all of the ingredients must be mixed together in a covered container and be left in the refrigerator for 12 hours to marinate. This will help the jam keep its texture.
- After this waiting period, prepare all of the equipment. Wash the jars and sterilize them if necessary. Add water to the canner but wait to boil.
- In a large saucepan, heat the mixture to a boil on high.
- Stir for 20-30 minutes until the mixture has gelled. At sea level, the mixture will gel at 220 °F. Every 500 feet above sea level the temperature will be 1 degree lower than this. (For instance, at 1,000 feet, the jam will gel at 218 °F.)
- When the mixture has gelled, remove the saucepan from the heat source.
- Funnel the hot jam into a heated jar leaving a ¼ inch of space before wiping the jar's rim and putting on the lid.
- Using a jar lifter, gently place the jars in the canner, making sure there are 1-2 inches of water above them.
  Bring the canner to a boil and let it process for 10 minutes. Adjust time for altitude differences. After the time is up, turn off the heat and remove the canner's lid. Let it stand for five minutes before removal.

- To remove the jars, use your jar lifter and let them cool for 24 hours before checking the seal.

Enjoy your Apple-Solutely Delicious jam!

If You Like Piña Coladas Jam

This is a grown-up alternative to the previous jam recipes. With the special ingredient of rum, it will make a nice addition to brunch with your friends. While you can still find whole pineapples available at your local grocery store throughout the year, the fruit is more often imported to the U.S. than grown here. Even the United States' largest distributor, Hawaii, isn't on the mainland. Since the majority of the pineapples sold in the U.S. are from the West Indies or the Bahamas, finding the freshest ingredients just isn't possible. This jam is more of a fun treat than a dietary staple.

Amount: Five half pint jars

Ingredients: *(See page 172 for Measurement Conversion)*

- 2 cups fresh pureed pineapple
- ⅝ cup cream of coconut
- ¼ cup white rum
- ¼ cup lemon juice
- 3 cups sugar
- 1 ⅔ ounces of liquid pectin

Directions:

- Prepare all of the equipment. Wash the jars and sterilize them if necessary. Add water to the canner but wait to boil.

- In a large saucepan, mix the pineapple, cream of coconut, rum, and lemon juice together. Stir in the sugar.

- Bring the mixture to a boil on high heat and stir it for three minutes.

- Remove the saucepan from the heat source and add in the pectin. Make sure to skim off any foam that may form.

- Funnel the hot jam into a heated jar leaving a ¼ inch of space before wiping the jar's rim and putting on the lid.

- Using a jar lifter, gently place the jars in the canner, making sure there are 1-2 inches of water above them.

- Bring the canner to a boil and let it process for five minutes. Adjust time for altitude differences.

- After the time is up, turn off the heat and remove the canner's lid. Let it stand for five minutes before removal.

- To remove the jars, use your jar lifter and let them cool for 24 hours before checking the seal.

- Enjoy your If You Like Piña Coladas jam!

Marmalade Recipes

Orange You Glad Marmalade

With any orange-based recipe, we must ask ourselves the inevitable question: Florida or California. It all depends on what you are looking for. Florida oranges may have the sweeter taste, but California has a thicker peel. Interestingly, the oranges that are typically used in marmalade, Seville oranges, are not even mass produced in the United States. The most popular oranges are Navel and Valencia. It all comes down to preference, and most kinds of oranges will hold up. The best time to make this marmalade is from November to May, during peak harvest season.

Amount: Six half pint jars

Ingredients: *(See page 172 for Measurement Conversion)*

- 3 oranges
- 3 cups water
- ¼ cup of lemon juice
- 4 ¾ cups of granulated sugar
- 2 tablespoons of pectin

Directions:

- Thinly slice the oranges with the skin on, cutting off the bottom and top stems. Cut the slices again into four pieces.
- In a large stockpot, mix the lemon juice, oranges, and water, and bring to a boil before letting it simmer for one hour. Stir when needed.
- Prepare all of the equipment. Wash the jars and sterilize them if necessary. Add water to the canner but wait to boil.
- Once the peel is tender, mix in the pectin and bring the pot to a rolling boil again. Then stir in all of the sugar at once and return to a boil, this time for four minutes, before removing the pot from the heat source and skimming off any excess foam.
- Funnel the marmalade into a heated jar leaving $\frac{1}{8}$ inch of space before wiping the jar's rim and putting on the lid.
- Using a jar lifter, gently place the jars in the canner, making sure there are 1-2 inches of water above them.
- Bring the canner to a boil and let it process for 10 minutes. Adjust time for altitude differences.
- After the time is up, turn off the heat and remove the canner's lid. Let it stand for five minutes before removal.
- To remove the jars, use your jar lifter and let them cool for 24 hours before checking the seal.
- Enjoy your Orange You Glad marmalade!

Simply the Zest Lemon Marmalade

Simply the Zest marmalade is an easy two-ingredient recipe perfect for marmalade on a budget. While most recipes won't actually call for a specific lemon, Bearss lemons are the most common to find in the U.S., growing in places like California and Arizona. The best thing about Simply the Zest lemon marmalade is that you don't have to wait to make it. Lemons are unique in the fact that the trees can bloom all year round. The only lemon with a peak season is the Meyer lemon that is harvested from November to April.

Amount: Five half pint jars

Ingredients: *(See page 172 for Measurement Conversion)*

13. 3 lbs of fresh lemons
14. 2 cups of sugar

Directions:

- Cut the lemon in half and juice the halves. Save the juice for later use. Next, thinly slice the lemon halves.
- Prepare all of the equipment. Wash the jars and sterilize them if necessary. Add water to the canner but wait to boil.
- In a large stockpot, boil the lemon slices for 10-15 minutes. Once the peels are tender, drain and rinse the lemons.
- In a clean pot, add water to the lemons and bring to a boil. Stir in the sugar and let simmer for an hour.
- Add ½ cup of lemon juice from the squeezed lemons before removing the mixture from the heat source.
- Remove the lemon pits before funneling the marmalade into a heated jar, leaving ¼ inch of space. Wipe the jar's rim and put on the lid.
- Using a jar lifter, gently place the jars in the canner, making sure there are 1-2 inches of water above them.

- Bring the canner to a boil and let it process for 15 minutes. Adjust time for altitude differences.
- After the time is up, turn off the heat and remove the canner's lid. Let it stand for five minutes before removal. To remove the jars, use your jar lifter and let them cool for 24 hours before checking the seal.
- Enjoy your Simply the Zest lemon marmalade!

Sub-Lime Marmalade

While Sub-Lime marmalade is another easy-to-make recipe, garden-fresh ingredients might not be on the table. The United States' climate is not suitable for lime production, so the majority of our commercially sold limes are imported from Mexico. However, you can grow your own in an indoor container. Peak season for limes is usually from May to October, but homegrown limes aren't affected by the climate and can be harvested anytime. Sub-Lime marmalade is certainly worth the investment.

Amount: Five half pint jars

Ingredients: *(See page 172 for Measurement Conversion)*

- 5 peeled Persian limes, zest should be cut into 2 inch strips
- 3 ½ cups of sugar
- 2 ¼ cups of water

Directions:

- To start, cut the lime in half and juice the halves. Save the juice to use later. Next, scrape out the pulp and seeds from the lime halves and place them in a cheese bag.
- In a large saucepan, cover and soak the cheese bag, zest, and juice for eight

hours.
- Prepare all of the equipment. Wash the jars and sterilize them if necessary. Add water to the canner but wait to boil.
- Cook the mixture for 30 minutes or until the peels have softened.
- Remove the cheese bag and add the sugar. Once the sugar has dissolved, boil the mixture until 220 °F.
- Funnel the marmalade into a heated jar, leaving ¼ inch of space. Wipe the jar's rim and put on the lid. Using a jar lifter, gently place the jars in the canner, making sure there are 1-2 inches of water above them.
- Bring the canner to a boil and let it process for 10 minutes. Adjust time for altitude differences.
- After the time is up, turn off the heat and remove the canner's lid. Let it stand for five minutes before removal.
- To remove the jars, use your jar lifter and let them cool for 24 hours before checking the seal.
- Enjoy your Sub-Lime marmalade!

Chutney Recipes

It Takes Two to Mango Chutney

Mango chutney is a traditional Indian dish. Once again I'm substituting honey for sugar here, but if you want a more customary result, you can always use 2 cups of sugar instead. While the mango, similar to the recipe, may have originated from India, mangoes are grown in the United States in the warm climate of Florida. Peak harvest season is from May through September. Imported mangoes from Asia are available all year round.

Amount: Six half pint jars

Ingredients: *(See page 172 for Measurement Conversion)*

- 1 ½ cups of honey
- 1 cup of distilled white vinegar
- 6 cups of mangoes, peeled and cut in ¾ -inch pieces
- 1 cup of chopped onion
- ½ cup of golden raisins
- ¼ cup of crystallized ginger, finely chopped
- 1 garlic clove, minced
- 1 teaspoon mustard seeds, whole
- ¼ teaspoon red chili pepper flakes

Directions:

14. Prepare all of the equipment and ingredients. Wash the jars and sterilize them if necessary. Add water to the canner but wait to boil.
15. In a large pot, mix the honey and vinegar together and set to boil.
16. Add all of the remaining ingredients into the mixture and set to simmer for

45 minutes to an hour. Stir when needed.
17. Once the chutney has slightly thickened and reached its syrupy texture, remove the mixture from the heat source.
18. Funnel the chutney into a heated jar, leaving ½ inch of space. Wipe the jar's rim and put on the lid.
19. Using a jar lifter, gently place the jars in the canner, making sure there are 1-2 inches of water above them.
20. Bring the canner to a boil and let it process for 15 minutes. Adjust time for altitude differences.
21. After the time is up, turn off the heat and remove the canner's lid. Let it stand for five minutes before removal.
22. To remove the jars, use your jar lifter and let them cool for 24 hours before checking the seal.
23. Enjoy your chutney!

Peachy Keen Chutney

Peach chutneys are generally a more Western-style version of a traditional Indian dish. Despite the fact that the state of Georgia is nicknamed the "Peach State," California is the largest contributor of the fruit in the United States. Attaining fresh and local peaches for your chutney will be easy since more than 20 states commercially produce them. The peak harvest season for peaches is usually from May to September, but since the fruit is so widely grown in the U.S. it's available multiple times throughout the year.

Amount: Five half pint jars

Ingredients: *(See page 172 for Measurement Conversion)*

- 3 pounds of peaches

- 1 ¼ cups of light brown sugar
- 1 ½ cups of apple cider vinegar
- 1 cup of golden raisins
- 1 small lemon, seeded and finely chopped, including peel
- ¼ cup fresh ginger, finely chopped
- 1 medium onion, peeled and finely chopped
- 1 small hot chili pepper, finely chopped
- ½ teaspoon salt
- ¼ teaspoon ground allspice
- ¼ teaspoon freshly ground black pepper
- ¼ teaspoon ground coriander

Directions:

- Blanch the peaches for easy skin removal and then chop them up into ½ inch chunks.
- Prepare all of the equipment. Wash the jars and sterilize them if necessary. Add water to the canner but wait to boil.
- In a large pot, combine all of the ingredients and cook over high heat until the peaches are soft.
- If the chutney seems too liquidy, raise the heat to thicken it. Once you've reached an ideal texture remove the mixture from the heat source.
- Funnel the chutney into a heated jar, leaving ½ inch of space. Wipe the jar's rim and put on the lid.
- Using a jar lifter, gently place the jars in the canner, making sure there are 1-2 inches of water above them.
- Bring the canner to a boil and let it process for 10 minutes. Adjust time for altitude differences.

- After the time is up, turn off the heat and remove the canner's lid. Let it stand for five minutes before removal.
- To remove the jars, use your jar lifter and let them cool for 24 hours before checking the seal.
- Enjoy your Peachy Keen chutney!

Pear-Fect Chutney

Pear chutney is another traditional Indian dish. The majority of commercially sold pears are grown on the west coast in states such as California, Oregon, or Washington. Similarly to apples, pears can be harvested in orchards from August to October, and make great plans for a lovely fall day. While planting your own pear tree won't take a lot of maintenance, the crop can take years to yield any results.

Amount: Five half pint jars

Ingredients: *(See page 172 for Measurement Conversion)*

- 3 pounds pears, peeled, cored, and chopped
- 1 ¼ cups of light brown sugar
- 1 ½ cups of apple cider vinegar
- 1 1/2 cups of raisins
- 1 lemon, seeded and finely chopped
- 1/4 cup fresh ginger, peeled and finely chopped
- 1 clove garlic, peeled and finely chopped
- 1 small hot chile pepper, finely chopped
- 1/2 teaspoon kosher salt
- 1/4 teaspoon allspice
- 1/4 teaspoon ground black pepper
- 1/4 teaspoon ground coriander

- Pinch ground cloves

Directions:

- Prepare the pears by washing them before they are cored, peeled, and chopped.
- Prepare all the equipment. Wash the jars and sterilize them if necessary. Add water to the canner but wait to boil.
- In a large pot, combine all of the ingredients and cook over high heat until the pears are soft. Stir regularly.
- If the chutney seems too liquidy, raise the heat to thicken it. Once you've reached an ideal texture remove the mixture from the heat source.
- Funnel the chutney into a heated jar, leaving ½ inch of space. Wipe the jar's rim and put on the lid.
- Using a jar lifter, gently place the jars in the canner, making sure there are 1-2 inches of water above them.
- Bring the canner to a boil and let it process for 10 minutes. Adjust time for altitude differences.
- After the time is up, turn off the heat and remove the canner's lid. Let it stand for five minutes before removal.
- To remove the jars, use your jar lifter and let them cool for 24 hours before checking the seal.
- Enjoy your Pear-Fect chutney!

Jelly Recipes

Be Grape-Ful Jelly

Grapes are popularly grown throughout the United States, but once again California takes the cake for the biggest commercial producer of this fruit. When it comes to choosing what grape to use in your jelly, I would suggest Concord for their sweet taste and aroma. If you grow your own grapes, make sure not to use wine grapes as they have a rather bitter flavor that doesn't really work for jelly. Grape harvest season peaks from August to October.

Amount: Eight pint jars

Ingredients: *(See page 172 for Measurement Conversion)*

- 3 ½ of pounds Concord grapes
- ½ cup of water
- 7 cups of white sugar
- 6 ounces of liquid pectin

Directions:

13. Wash and remove stems from the grapes before crushing them. In a large pot, bring the grapes to a boil. Let the mixture simmer for 10 minutes before removing the heat source and straining the juice. Refrigerate the juice for 12 hours.

14. Prepare all of the canning equipment. Wash the jars and sterilize them if necessary. Add water to the canner but wait to boil.

15. After the juice has cooled, strain it again through a double-thickness damp cheesecloth. This should result in four cups of juice.

16. Mix juice and sugar in a large pot before bringing it to a rolling boil.

17. Stir in the pectin and boil it for one minute before removing the jelly from the heat source. Skim off foam.

18. Funnel the jelly into a heated jar, leaving ¼ inch of space. Wipe the jar's rim and put on the lid. Using a jar lifter, gently place the jars in the canner, making sure there are 1-2 inches of water above them.

19. Bring the canner to a boil and let it process for five minutes. Adjust time for altitude differences.

20. After the time is up, turn off the heat and remove the canner's lid. Let it stand for five minutes before removal.

21. To remove the jars, use your jar lifter and let them cool for 24 hours before checking the seal.

Dandy Dandelion Jelly

Whether or not you consider dandelions a weed or a flower, they sure do make good jelly. One of my favorite things about dandelions is that they grow just about anywhere there is grass. They are also cost-effective since they are so abundant. The best time to find dandelions is in the spring, but they do bloom in the fall as well. Dandelion picking can be a fun activity for the family. Just remember you only need the flowers, not the stems.

Amount: Five half pint jars

Ingredients: *(See page 172 for Measurement Conversion)*

- 2 cups of dandelion petals, lightly packed
- 4 cups of water
- 4 cups of sugar
- 2 tablespoons of lemon juice
- 1 box powdered pectin

Directions:

- Remove all of the green parts from the dandelions and put the petals in a quart jar.
- Pour 4 cups of boiling water over the flowers. Once the jar has cooled down, refrigerate for 24 hours.
- Prepare all the equipment. Wash the jars and sterilize them if necessary. Add water to the canner but wait to boil.
- Strain dandelions and squeeze out any remaining tea before discarding them. This should result in a little less than 4 cups of dandelion tea.
- Boil the tea with lemon juice and pectin in a large pot.
- Add sugar and bring the mixture back to a boil for two minutes before removing the jelly from its heat source.
- Funnel the jelly into a heated jar, leaving ¼ inch of space. Wipe the jar's rim and put on the lid. Using a jar lifter, gently place the jars in the canner, making sure there are 1-2 inches of water above them.
- Bring the canner to a boil and let it process for 10 minutes. Adjust time for altitude differences.

- After the time is up, turn off the heat and remove the canner's lid. Let it stand for five minutes before removal. To remove the jars, use your jar lifter and let them cool for 24 hours before checking the seal.

Plum Out of Puns Jelly

I promise this is the last fruit-related pun. Wild plum trees are highly adaptable, and that is why they can grow all across the United States. From Massachusetts to New Mexico, this plant is best used for jelly or other byproducts since it's flavor isn't always consistent. Growing your own plum tree won't be hard to maintain as long as it has enough sunlight. Late May to August is peak harvest for these versatile fruits.

Amount: Four pint jars

Ingredients: *(See page 172 for Measurement Conversion)*

- 5 pounds of ripe plums
- 1 ½ cups of water
- 1.75 ounces of pectin
- 1 Tablespoons of unsalted butter
- 6 ½ cups of sugar

Directions:

- Plums should be pitted and cut in half. Peeling is unnecessary.
- Prepare all the canning equipment. Wash the jars and sterilize them if necessary. Add water to the canner but wait to boil.
- In a large pot, add the water to the plums and bring it to a boil. Cover the pot and let it simmer for 10 minutes.
- Use a fine mesh strainer to strain the juice. Let this drain for 30 minutes before discarding the fruit. This should result in 5 ½ cups of fruit juice.

- Pour the juice back into the pot and add the butter and pectin. Bring this mixture to a rolling boil.
- Add the sugar and boil for one minute before removing the jelly from the heat source. Skim off any foam.
- Funnel the jelly into a heated jar, leaving ¼ inch of space. Wipe the jar's rim and put on the lid. Using a jar lifter, gently place the jars in the canner, making sure there are 1-2 inches of water above them.
- Bring the canner to a boil and let it process for 10 minutes. Adjust time for altitude differences. After the time is up, turn off the heat and remove the canner's lid. Let it stand for five minutes before removal.
- To remove the jars, use your jar lifter and let them cool for 24 hours before checking the seal.

Key Chapter 3 Takeaways

12. Jam, marmalade, chutney, and jelly are all different ways to prepare and preserve fruit.
13. Different harvest seasons affect when to get the freshest fruit.
14. Fruit grows all across the United States but most can be found in California due to the warm climate.
15. The best ingredient in any jam, marmalade, chutney, or jelly is fresh fruit gardened at home or grown locally.
16. Though many fruits can be grown locally, the United States doesn't have the climate for limes.

Chapter 4
Desserts

"Life is short and unpredictable. Eat the dessert first."

- Jacques Torres

Canning Desserts 101

Many of the main ingredients in common desserts are not eligible to be canned in any capacity whether it is a water bath canner or a pressure canner. Water bath canning is mostly just suitable for fruit-related desserts. This doesn't mean pies in their whole capacities though. Not only would it completely lose its shape in the jar, but grains can't be safely processed. The temperature in a water bath canner can't cook raw dough. Also, grains don't hold heat well enough to kill off bacteria, and canning them could result in botulism. This means any dessert that contains bread, rice, pie dough, biscuits, or crackers should not be canned. Pie filling is regularly canned, though, because it does not have any ingredients that aren't safe.

Any desserts that contain dairy products can not be canned at all either. Milk is so low in acid that even a pressure canner can't get rid of any possible botulism spores. Butter, cheese, and cream all have the same consequences as well. That means chocolate, whipped cream, yogurt parfaits, pudding, and cheesecake filling can't be preserved. This rule doesn't just apply to cow's milk either—no milk of any kind will work, including goat's milk. Soy and tofu have the same problem, and can't be used as alternatives. Dairy is healthier and better tasting if it is served fresh.

Other desserts that won't work are sweets such as caramel and marshmallow. The largest problem with these are the amount of fats they contain. Oftentimes, the fat will impede the sealing process, and the jar will be exposed to airborne bacteria. Even if the jar does seal, the fat will most likely spoil and will ruin the food since it won't properly cook. Any dessert ingredients with nuts, such as Nutella or peanut butter, have too much oil. The oil found in nuts protects botulism spores from the heating process.

When it comes to canning desserts there are a couple of ways you can substitute healthier options for sugar. You can use water instead of sugar and the process will still work; however, the fruit's shape won't hold as well. Honey has numerous health benefits, but it does have more calories. It's also sweeter, so you don't have to use as much. Calorie-wise, this kind of evens out, but unsweetened juice is a good lower-calorie option as well. If you are working with peaches, pears, apricots, plums, and red or white sweet cherries, then a diluted frozen apple juice concentrate will do the job. The artificial sweetener Splenda doesn't have preserving-properties like sugar does, and can't be used to pickle, but it won't affect jam or jelly.

Fruit Recipes

Blasting Blueberries

This recipe is a great place to start for beginner canners. You don't need many ingredients, just blueberries and water. Blueberries are often considered a superfood due to their numerous health benefits. This fruit is full of antioxidant compounds such as anthocyanin, which can help with heart disease. Once frozen, blueberries can lose these properties, so canning is the better option when it comes to preservation. Blueberries grow all over the United States and are easy to produce in home gardens. Peak harvest for this fruit is between June and August.

Amount: Two quarts

Ingredients: *(See page 172 for Measurement Conversion)*

- 2 quarts of fresh blueberries
- 6 cups of water

Directions:

16. Prepare all the canning equipment and wash and remove stems from fruit. Wash the jars and sterilize them if necessary. Add water to the canner but wait to boil.
17. Blanch the blueberries in small portions at 30 second intervals at a time.
18. Remove the blueberries from the pan using a sieve.
19. Once you are finished blanching, fill the quart jars with the blueberries, leaving room for blanching juice and ¼ inch of space at the top.
20. If you run out blanching liquid, boil water to fill the rest of the space.
21. Wipe the jar's rim and put on the lid. Using a jar lifter, gently place the jars in the canner, making sure there are 1-2 inches of water above them.
22. Bring the canner to a boil and let it process for 15 minutes. Adjust time for altitude differences.
23. After the time is up, turn off the heat and remove the canner's lid. Let it stand for five minutes before removal.
24. To remove the jars, use your jar lifter and let them cool for 24 hours before checking the seal.
25. Enjoy your Blasting Blueberries!

Rockin Raspberries

While this recipe isn't as healthy as the previous one, it's still an easy place to start on your canning journey. For your first recipe, you'll want to start with a short ingredients list that is easy to find, like raspberries and sugar. The small fruit require little to no preparation before they are placed in the jars. Raspberries, like most fruit in the U.S., are commercially grown on the west coast but they can make a great addition to any home garden. The best time to pick them is from July to early fall.

Amount: Six pint jars

Ingredients: *(See page 172 for Measurement Conversion)*

- 8 pints of fresh raspberries
- 2 ½ cups of sugar
- 6 cups of water

Directions:

- Raspberries are small enough that they don't need to be chopped, but always wash the fruit before you begin.
- Prepare all the canning equipment. Wash the jars and sterilize them if necessary. Add water to the canner but wait to boil.
- Prepare syrup by bringing a mixture of sugar and water to a boil and then letting it simmer.
- Pour syrup into hot jars and then add the raspberries. Gently shake the jars to make more room and a tighter pack.
- Add more syrup if necessary and leave ¼ inch of space at the top of the jar. Make sure to get rid of any air bubbles.
- Wipe the jar's rim and put on the lid. Using a jar lifter, gently place the jars in the canner, making sure there are 1-2 inches of water above them.
- Bring the canner to a boil and let it process for 15 minutes. Adjust time for altitude differences.
- After the time is up, turn off the heat and remove the canner's lid. Let it stand for five minutes before removal.

- To remove the jars, use your jar lifter and let them cool for 24 hours before checking the seal.
- Enjoy your Rockin Raspberries!

Krazy Kiwi

Despite their prickly texture, kiwis have a sweet taste. They will have a milder flavor after canning, though, and the color may fade as well. The Golden State, California, is the leading producer of this hairy fruit. Kiwis aren't the obvious choice for a home garden, but with a little care they can yield wonderful results. The U.S. kiwi season is from October through May.

Amount: Varies

Ingredients: *(See page 172 for Measurement Conversion)*

- Fresh kiwi
- 2 cups of sugar
- 4 cups of water

Directions:

- Slice the kiwi in half and scoop out the inside. Cut the chunks any way you desire. I like to thinly slice them and turn the slices into fun shapes for a more aesthetic look.
- Prepare all the canning equipment. Wash the jars and sterilize them if necessary. Add water to the canner but wait to boil.
- In a pan, simmer the water and slowly add the sugar until it dissolves.
- Gently boil the syrup for three minutes and make sure to keep the mixture warm before it goes into the jars.
- Fill the jars with kiwi and then add the syrup, leaving ¼ inch of space.

- Wipe the jar's rim and put on the lid. Using a jar lifter, gently place the jars in the canner, making sure there are 1-2 inches of water above them.
- Bring the canner to a boil and let it process for 20 minutes. Adjust time for altitude differences.
- After the time is up, turn off the heat and remove the canner's lid. Let it stand for five minutes before removal.
- To remove the jars, use your jar lifter and let them cool for 24 hours before checking the seal.
- Enjoy your Krazy Kiwi!

Pie Filling Recipes

Granny's Apple Pie Filling

This apple pie filling isn't actually my grandmother's recipe. The "granny" in the title refers to the Granny Smith apples I use to give the pie filling its sweet taste. Any pie apple will do in this recipe, but these apples are my personal recommendation. Granny Smiths are easy to obtain all year round, and work well when they are mixed with other pie apples, such as Honey Crisps or Pink Ladies. The filling is good to eat straight out of the jar into a precooked crust. *(Note: Some of these recipes use Clear Jel. Clear Jel is a chemically modified corn starch. It produces superb consistency even after your filling is baked or canned. It helps prevent your sauce becoming runny. It is popular in the USA but difficult to come by in other countries. Please research some suitable alternatives in your area. Substitutes that I have come across include Tapioca Starch and Gum Arabic Powder.)*

Amount: Seven pint jars

Ingredients: *(See page 172 for Measurement Conversion)*

- 12 cups of apple slices, peeled, cored, and splashed with lemon juice to prevent

browning
- 2 ¾ cups of sugar
- ¾ cup of Clear Jel
- 1 teaspoon of ground cinnamon
- ½ teaspoon of ground nutmeg
- 1 ¼ cups of water
- 2 ½ cups of apple juice
- ½ cups lemon juice

Directions:

- Prepare all the canning equipment. Wash the jars and sterilize them if necessary. Add water to the canner but wait to boil.
- Blanch the apples in boiling water for one minute. Strain the apples and cover them to keep them warm.
- Mix the water, sugar, Clear Jel, ground cinnamon, ground nutmeg, and apple juice in a large saucepan. Bring the mixture to a boil before adding the lemon juice. Return to a boil for one minute
- Stir in the apples.
- Funnel the filling into a heated jar, leaving 1 inch of space. Remove any air bubbles. Wipe the jar's rim and put on the lid.
- Using a jar lifter, gently place the jars in the canner, making sure there are 1-2 inches of water above them.
- Bring the canner to a boil and let it process for 25 minutes. Adjust time for altitude differences.
- After the time is up, turn off the heat and remove the canner's lid. Let it stand for five minutes before removal.
- To remove the jars, use your jar lifter and let them cool for 24 hours before

- checking the seal.
- Enjoy your Granny's Apple Pie!

The Great Rhubarb Pie Filling

While this pie is great tasting, it is actually named after the empress of Russia, Catherine the Great. During her reign she banned the export of rhubarb seeds to give her country a monopoly over the root. Lucky for us, a Russian physician smuggled them into Europe, and now we have delicious rhubarb pie. Rhubarb grows anywhere in the U.S., but mostly comes from the northern west coast. The season for this vegetable starts in the spring and goes into early summer.

Amount: Two pint jars

Ingredients: *(See page 172 for Measurement Conversion)*

17. 3½ cups of chopped rhubarb
18. 1 cup of sugar
19. ¼ cup of Clear Jel
20. 4 tablespoons of lemon juice

Directions:

- Prepare all the canning equipment. Wash the jars and sterilize them if necessary. Add water to the canner but wait to boil.
- Mix the chopped rhubarb with sugar and let it sit for 15-30 minutes. Wait until juice appears.
- Mix the Clear Jel and water before cooking it on medium. As soon as it thickens add the lemon juice and cook for one minute. Heat up the rhubarb separately.
- Add the heated up rhubarb to the mixture and cook for three more minutes.

Stir carefully as you go before finishing and removing it from the heat source.
- Funnel the pie filling into a heated jar, leaving 1 inch of space. Wipe the jar's rim and put on the lid.
- Using a jar lifter, gently place the jars in the canner, making sure there are 1-2 inches of water above them.
- Bring the canner to a boil and let it process for 30 minutes. Adjust time for altitude differences.
- After the time is up, turn off the heat and remove the canner's lid. Let it stand for five minutes before removal.
- To remove the jars, use your jar lifter and let them cool for 24 hours before checking the seal.
- Enjoy your Great Rhubarb Pie!

Cherry Bomb Pie Filling

This pie has an explosion of flavor. Get it? For the most part, sour cherries are more often used in pies than sweet ones. I prefer the juicier consistency, but if you want to use less sugar, you can always use sweet cherries to even out the taste. Cherries are grown throughout the U.S. and you could easily plant your own as long as you have sunlight and deep, well-drained soil. Depending on where in the States the cherries are coming from, the season differs. Peaks can be from anywhere between May and August.

(Note: This recipe use Clear Jel. Clear Jel is a chemically modified corn starch. It produces superb consistency even after your filling is baked or canned. It helps prevent your sauce becoming runny. It is popular in the USA but difficult to come by in other countries. Please research some suitable alternatives in your area. Substitutes that I have come across include Tapioca Starch and Gum Arabic Powder.)

Amount: Eight pint jars

Ingredients: *(See page 172 for Measurement Conversion)*

- 10 lbs of red cherries
- 3 ½ cups of sugar
- 1 cup of Clear Jel
- ½ teaspoon ground cinnamon
- ¼ cup of lemon juice

Directions:

11. Wash and strain the juice and remove any pits from the cherries. Keep at least 4 cups of juice for later.
12. Prepare all the canning equipment. Wash the jars and sterilize them if necessary. Add water to the canner but wait to boil.
13. In a large saucepan, mix cherry juice, sugar, Clear Jel, and cinnamon together and bring it to a boil.
14. Once thickened add lemon juice and return to boil.
15. Finally add the remaining cherries and return to boil again. Stir thoroughly.
16. Remove the sauce from the heat source and funnel the filling into a heated jar, leaving 1 inch of space. Wipe the jar's rim and put on the lid.
17. Using a jar lifter, gently place the jars in the canner, making sure there are 1-2 inches of water above them.
18. Bring the canner to a boil and let it process for 35 minutes. Adjust time for altitude differences. After the time is up, turn off the heat and remove the canner's lid. Let it stand for five minutes before removal.
19. To remove the jars, use your jar lifter and let them cool for 24 hours before checking the seal.

20. Enjoy your Cherry Bomb Pie Filling!

Fruit Sauce Recipes

Lemon Zest Blueberry Sauce

This sauce is one of my favorite additions to plain cheesecake, but if you're looking for a healthier way to use it, I also enjoy it with plain Greek yogurt. It's a great topping for breakfast foods such as waffles or pancakes, as well. For a quicker breakfast option, it pairs well with oatmeal. For a special treat, you can also use it as an ice cream topping. If you want more information on lemons or blueberries, you can find it in the Blasting Blueberries recipe from earlier in this chapter, or the Simply the Zest lemon marmalade recipe from Chapter 3.

Amount: Four pint jars

Ingredients: *(See page 172 for Measurement Conversion)*

- 8 cups of fresh blueberries
- 6 cups granulated sugar
- 2 teaspoon fresh lemon zest
- 2 tablespoon fresh lemon juice
- 6 ounces of pectin

Directions:

- Prepare all the canning equipment. Wash the jars and sterilize them if necessary. Add water to the canner but wait to boil.
- Slightly crush the blueberries without fully mashing them.
- In a large pot, mix the berries, lemon juice, sugar, and lemon zest, and bring

it to a rolling boil.
- Add pectin then continue boiling for one minute. After you remove the sauce from the heat source, skim off any foam.
- Funnel the sauce into a heated jar, leaving ¼ inch of space. Wipe the jar's rim and put on the lid.
- Using a jar lifter, gently place the jars in the canner, making sure there are 1-2 inches of water above them.
- Bring the canner to a boil and let it process for 10 minutes. Adjust time for altitude differences.
- After the time is up, turn off the heat and remove the canner's lid. Let it stand for five minutes before removal.
- To remove the jars, use your jar lifter and let them cool for 24 hours before checking the seal.
- Enjoy your Lemon Zest Blueberry Sauce!

Awesomesauce Applesauce

This is a quick and easy applesauce recipe that I would consider to be a canning staple for any pantry. It saves a lot of time on cooking due to its versatility as a side. It goes with just about anything, but my recommendation is pork chops. It's also a blessing if you have young children or grandchildren. Even the most picky of eaters will enjoy this recipe. If you are curious about apple production in the U.S. more information is available in the Apple-Solutely Delicious Jam recipe in Chapter 3.

Amount: Six pints

Ingredients: *(See page 172 for Measurement Conversion)*

- 8 pounds tart cooking apples
- 2 cups of water
- 1 cup of sugar

Directions:

11. Prepare all the canning equipment. Wash the jars and sterilize them if necessary. Add water to the canner but wait to boil.
12. Prepare the apples by coring them and cutting them in quarters. Boil the apples in water and let simmer for 30 minutes or until tender.
13. Press the apples through a sieve or food mill.
14. Add the apple pulp back to the pot and stir in sugar. Add more water if necessary. Bring mixture to a boil.
15. Funnel the sauce into a heated jar, leaving ½ inch of space. Wipe the jar's rim and put on the lid.
16. Using a jar lifter, gently place the jars in the canner, making sure there are 1-2 inches of water above them.
17. Bring the canner to a boil and let it process for 15 minutes. Adjust time for altitude differences.
18. After the time is up, turn off the heat and remove the canner's lid. Let it stand for five minutes before removal.
19. To remove the jars, use your jar lifter and let them cool for 24 hours before checking the seal.
20. Enjoy your Awesomesauce Applesauce!

Cinnamon Pear Sauce

Pear sauce is great if you need an alternative to applesauce. Adding cinnamon to pear sauce gives the recipe just the slightest kick. The result is delicious. Cinnamon is one of my favorite ingredients to cook with due to its wonderful aroma, and this recipe is no different. If you want your home to smell like a cinnamon sugar dreamland, then I urge you to try it. Want to know more about pear production in the U.S.? Check out the Pear-Fect Chutney recipe in Chapter 3.

Amount: Three pints

Ingredients: *(See page 172 for Measurement Conversion)*

- 7 large pears, quartered and cored
- 1 juicy lemon, zested and juiced
- ¾ cup of water
- ¼ cup of white sugar
- ¼ teaspoon ground cinnamon

Directions:

- Prepare all the canning equipment. Wash the jars and sterilize them if necessary. Add water to the canner but wait to boil.
- In a large pan mix the lemon juice, zest and water. Slowly add in the pears as you cook. Simmer for 10 minutes or until the pears are tender.
- Gently mash the pears and simmer for 10 more minutes.
- Puree the mixture with either an immersion blender or a food mill.
- Simmer puree and add sugar and cinnamon. Cook until desired consistency is attained.
- Funnel the sauce into a heated jar, leaving ½ inch of space. Wipe the jar's rim and put on the lid.
- Using a jar lifter, gently place the jars in the canner, making sure there are 1-2 inches of water above them.
- Bring the canner to a boil and let it process for 10 minutes. Adjust time for altitude differences. After the time is up, turn off the heat and remove the canner's lid. Let it stand for five minutes before removal.
- To remove the jars, use your jar lifter and let them cool for 24 hours before

checking the seal.
- Enjoy your Cinnamon Pear Sauce!

Key Chapter 4 Takeaways

11. Most ingredients in desserts cannot be canned including nuts, dairy, and grains.
12. There are several healthy alternatives to the sugar commonly found in most water bath canning recipes.
13. Blueberries make a wonderful dessert option because not only are they sweet in taste but they can also prevent heart disease.
14. Tart apples such as Granny Smith make the best pie apples.
15. Rhubarb has so many bountiful health benefits that Russia tried to create a monopoly on it in the 18th century.

Chapter 5
Pickles

"Good ideas, like good pickles, are crisp, enduring, and devilishly hard to make."

- **Rushworth Kidder**

Pickling 101

Pickling is one of the oldest forms of preservation. For centuries, people have been fermenting fruits and vegetables in brines. While the process is similar to older practices, it has evolved, so make sure to follow a recipe that aligns with the USDA's canning guidelines. Pickling gives the produce a unique flavor, different from its original taste. The most commonly pickled vegetable is a cucumber. This is what commercially sold pickles are made out of. (Though, technically, anything that has gone through the process of pickling can be called a pickle.) While the process of pickling isn't difficult, it does take a while. Home canners who are just starting out can easily accomplish pickling as long as they have the time.

There are a couple of ways to successfully pickle any fruit or vegetable. The fastest is the quick-pack method. This would be the best place to start for new canners. Instead of using lactic acid in fermentation, this method utilizes the acetic acid in vinegar. Most recipes will call for white distilled or cider vinegar. With either ingredient, make sure it has 5% acidity. While homemade products are usually better, not when pickling. Homemade vinegar often isn't acidic enough. If you choose the quick-pack method don't add alum as a firming agent. Alum only works when the pickles are fermented. Even with a quick-pack, the flavor of the produce takes weeks to develop. Keep this in mind when choosing a time to use your canned pickles.

The method of fermenting or brining the produce will take several weeks to cure. You will know that your product has cured once the texture and color has changed. Sodium is a very important part of fermenting, so make sure not to use reduced salt products. There are different methods to fruit and relish involving sugar. Recipes will usually call for brown or white but keep in mind brown causes a darker brine. Adding in spices can also do this. This is normal and you shouldn't be afraid to experiment with different spices to find what works best for your pickles. If you are curious about the process of sun pickles, it's not USDA approved. The yeast inside a jar sitting out in sunlight will die and ruin the fermentation of the pickles.

Like most water bath canning, there is a science to pickling. It's important to double check your ingredients and pay attention to how much of everything you need. If something is off, it can result in a less-than-ideal final product. Recipes that aren't approved by the USDA can ruin the product and you'll end up with unnecessary waste.

For the best results, only pickle fresh and firm ingredients. The best time to do this is less than 24 hours after obtaining them. Double check for spoilage before you begin working with any fruits or vegetables. The pickling process will not improve any structural or flavor quality. If you have any specific question about pickling, you can always get in contact with your local extension service.

Pickled Vegetables

Dill With It Pickles

Why not start pickling with a classic? Pickling may seem daunting at first, but just like water bath canning, you'll be pickling everything you can like a pro in no time. Every year, Americans eat nine pounds of pickles per person. With over 300 million people, that's a lot of pickles. Traditional pickles come from fermented cucumbers. Cucumbers are harvested in the summer, around 50 to 70 days after being planted. They will need a good amount of room to grow, but they're still an essential plant for any home garden.

Amount: Four pints

Ingredients: *(See page 172 for Measurement Conversion)*

- 3 lbs pickling cucumbers
- 4 teaspoons dill seeds
- 2 teaspoons mustard seeds
- 4 cloves garlic
- 16 whole black peppercorns
- 2 cups water
- 1 ½ cups white vinegar
- 2 tablespoons pickling salt
- 1 tablespoons sugar

Directions :

- Prepare all the canning equipment. Wash the jars and sterilize them if necessary. Add water to the canner but wait to boil.
- Cut the cucumbers into small pieces that will fit in a jar and divide them up between the pints.
- Before adding the brine to the jar, put in a mixture of 1 teaspoon dill seeds, ½ teaspoon mustard seeds, 1 clove garlic and 4 whole peppercorns into each.
- To make the brine, combine water, white vinegar, pickling salt and sugar into a pot. Boil over medium heat to dissolve sugar and salt.
- Pour the brine into the jars, leaving ½ inch of space. Wipe the jar's rim and put on the lid.
- Using a jar lifter, gently place the jars in the canner, making sure there are 1-2 inches of water above them.
- Bring the canner to a boil and let it process for 10 minutes. Adjust time for altitude differences.
- After the time is up, turn off the heat and remove the canner's lid. Let it stand for five minutes before removal.
- To remove the jars, use your jar lifter and let them cool for 24 hours before

checking the seal.
- Enjoy your pickles!

In a Real Pickle Pickled Onions

Did you know that the Shakespeare play *The Tempest* coined the phrase, "in a pickle?" This was used then how we still use the phrase today, to mean being in a difficult situation. What does this have to do with onions? Not a thing, but it will come in handy for any Shakespeare trivia nights. Onions can be harvested at the end of summer or early fall. This is signaled by the leaves on the neck of the plant starting to slump over. Onions have developed a reputation as being difficult to grow at home, but with a little care and a lot of love, you can make it work.

Amount: Four half pints

Ingredients: *(See page 172 for Measurement Conversion)*

12. 8 cups thinly sliced sweet onions
13. 2 tablespoons canning salt
14. 1 cups white vinegar
15. 1 cup sugar
16. 1 teaspoon dried thyme

Directions :

- Prepare all the canning equipment. Wash the jars and sterilize them if necessary. Add water to the canner but wait to boil.
- In a colander, sprinkle salt over your prepared onions and toss to ensure coverage. Let stand for one hour before washing and draining the onions.
- In a Dutch oven, combine vinegar, sugar, and thyme. Bring the mixture to a boil.

- Add onions and return to a boil. Then let simmer, uncovered, for 10 minutes.
- Funnel the brine into the jar, leaving ½ inch of space. Wipe the jar's rim and put on the lid.
- Using a jar lifter, gently place the jars in the canner, making sure there are 1-2 inches of water above them.
- Bring the canner to a boil and let it process for 10 minutes. Adjust time for altitude differences.
- After the time is up, turn off the heat and remove the canner's lid. Let it stand for five minutes before removal.
- To remove the jars, use your jar lifter and let them cool for 24 hours before checking the seal.
- Enjoy your pickled onions!

Rise and Brine Pickled Vegetable Mix

Fun pickle fact #3—In 2000, the Philadelphia Eagles attributed drinking pickle juice to their enormous win against the Cowboys. While pickle juice is healthy for you, I don't think it endows football players with amazing game-winning abilities. I could be wrong, though. Now imagine what powers the brine of all these vegetables combined could do. With an ingredient list as big as this, it's important to invest in as many fresh veggies as possible. Especially if you have a match coming up.

Amount: Six pints

Ingredients: *(See page 172 for Measurement Conversion)*

- 2 ears of corn
- 3 cups cauliflower florets
- 3 medium red sweet peppers, seeded and cut into 1-inch pieces
- 12 ounces green beans, trimmed and cut into 1-inch pieces

- 3 medium carrots, cut into 1/2-inch slices
- 2 medium onions, cut into small wedges
- 3 cups water
- 3 cups white vinegar
- 1 cup sugar
- 1 tablespoon kosher salt
- 18 cloves garlic, smashed
- 1 ½ teaspoons crushed red pepper

Directions:

10. Prepare all the canning equipment and prepare corn by husking it and cutting the cobs into small 1-inch pieces. Wash the jars and sterilize them if necessary. Add water to the canner but wait to boil.
11. In a large pot, combine the corn, cauliflower, sweet peppers, green beans, carrots, onions with enough water to cover it. Bring vegetables to boiling. Cook, uncovered, for three minutes
12. Remove the vegetables from the heat and drain them before packing them into the jars.
13. Add cloves and crushed pepper to each jar.
14. In another pot combine the water, vinegar, sugar, and salt to make the brine. Bring this mixture to boiling and stir to dissolve sugar.
15. Funnel the brine into the jars, leaving ½ inch of space. Wipe the jar's rim and put on the lid.
16. Using a jar lifter, gently place the jars in the canner, making sure there are 1-2 inches of water above them.
17. Bring the canner to a boil and let it process for 10 minutes. Adjust time for

altitude differences. After the time is up, turn off the heat and remove the canner's lid. Let it stand for five minutes before removal.
18. To remove the jars, use your jar lifter and let them cool for 24 hours before checking the seal.
19. Enjoy your pickled vegetable mix!

Pickled Fruit

Perfect Pickled Peaches

Veggies aren't the only thing that can be pickled. Pickled peaches result in a tangy, sweet but sour, and very unique taste. Peaches are probably one of the most popular fruits to be pickled. My favorite way to use pickled peaches is to pair them with roasted pork or a salad for a lighter option. If you're curious about peaches and the harvest times, I have provided the information in Chapter 3 under the recipe Peachy Keen

Chutney.

Amount: Four quarts

Ingredients: *(See page 172 for Measurement Conversion)*

- 4 pounds peaches, blanched and peeled
- 4 cups sugar
- 1 cup white vinegar
- 1 cup water
- 2 tablespoons cloves, whole
- 5 cinnamon sticks

Directions:

- Prepare all the canning equipment. Wash the jars and sterilize them if necessary. Add water to the canner but wait to boil.
- In a large pot, combine the sugar, vinegar, and water. Bring the mixture to a boil for five minutes.
- Press one or two cloves into each peach before adding them to the pot.
- Boil for 20 minutes, or until peaches are tender.
- Spoon in the peaches and then funnel the brine into the jars, leaving ½ inch of space. Wipe the jar's rim and put on the lid.
- Using a jar lifter, gently place the jars in the canner, making sure there are 1-2 inches of water above them.
- Bring the canner to a boil and let it process for 10 minutes. Adjust time for altitude differences.
- After the time is up, turn off the heat and remove the canner's lid. Let it stand for five minutes before removal.

- To remove the jars, use your jar lifter and let them cool for 24 hours before checking the seal.
- Enjoy your pickled peaches!

Picturesque Pickled Apricots

Another great fruit to pickle is apricots. Apricots and peaches are similar fruits, but they do have different tastes. Apricots tend to be more tart than the sweet peach. Harvest season for apricots begins at the end of summer. They are mostly grown in California due the sunny weather conditions. Growing your own apricot tree is possible anywhere in the United States, just make sure you provide the right soil.

Amount: Five half pints

Ingredients: *(See page 172 for Measurement Conversion)*

9. 2 pounds ripe apricots
10. 1 cup white balsamic vinegar
11. ½ cup sweet vermouth
12. ½ cup honey
13. ½ cup water
14. 2, 3-inch sticks cinnamon, broken
15. 6 whole cloves

Directions:

- Prepare all the canning equipment. Wash the jars and sterilize them if necessary. Add water to the canner but wait to boil.
- In a saucepan, combine the vinegar, vermouth, honey, water, cinnamon, and cloves. Bring mixture to boiling before letting it simmer, uncovered, for five

minutes.
- Remove from the heat source and let it stand for 30 minutes. Remove and discard cinnamon and cloves from mixture.
- In a different large saucepan, blanch the apricots before removing skins.
- To prepare the apricots for going into the jars, Cut quarters and remove pits.
- Back to the syrup mixture. Return it to a boil.
- Funnel the syrup into a heated jar, leaving ½ inch of space. Wipe the jar's rim and put on the lid. Using a jar lifter, gently place the jars in the canner, making sure there are 1-2 inches of water above them.
- Bring the canner to a boil and let it process for 10 minutes. Adjust time for altitude differences. After the time is up, turn off the heat and remove the canner's lid. Let it stand for five minutes before removal.
- To remove the jars, use your jar lifter and let them cool for 24 hours before checking the seal.
- Enjoy your pickled apricots!

Popular Pickled Fruit Cocktail

You can pickle really any fruit, as demonstrated in the recipe below. Just make sure to choose a combination that complement each other. This might take some time through trial and error. Some of my favorite ingredients to use are cherries, strawberries, and peaches. Make sure to research the process of pickling whichever fruit you choose to make sure you have the proper way to process them.

Amount: Three pints

Ingredients: *(See page 172 for Measurement Conversion)*

- 2 cups of fresh fruit
- 1 cup vinegar

- 1 cup water
- ½ cup sugar
- 1 tablespoons salt
- Add any spice or herb to flavor

Directions:

10. Prepare all the canning equipment. Wash the jars and sterilize them if necessary. Add water to the canner but wait to boil.
11. Prep the fruit by washing and cutting it.
12. Divide the fruit evenly between jars.
13. In a saucepan, combine the vinegar, sugar, water, and salt. Bring the mixture to boiling before letting it simmer, uncovered, for five minutes.
14. Funnel the brine into a heated jar, leaving 1/2 inch of space. Add spices and herbs to top it off.
15. Wipe the jar's rim and put on the lid. Using a jar lifter, gently place the jars in the canner, making sure there are 1-2 inches of water above them.
16. Bring the canner to a boil and let it process for 20 minutes. Adjust time for altitude differences.
17. After the time is up, turn off the heat and remove the canner's lid. Let it stand for five minutes before removal.
18. To remove the jars, use your jar lifter and let them cool for 24 hours before checking the seal.
19. Enjoy your pickled fruit cocktail!

Relish

Relished Dill Pickled Relish

Despite the fact that people have been pickling for centuries, relish has only been around since the 19th century. Relish, like pickles, doesn't have to be made from just cucumbers. You can make relish from just about any fruit or vegetable. That said, I have ignored this fact and have only compiled cucumber-based recipes. Don't worry, they are all still delicious and unique. It may be basic, but there's a reason why dill is so popular. This recipe makes for the perfect addition to any cookout. The trick to any relish recipe is mastering your herbs and spices.

Amount: Seven pints

Ingredients: *(See page 172 for Measurement Conversion)*

- 9 pounds pickling cucumber
- ½ cup pickling salt
- 2 teaspoons turmeric
- 4 cup water
- 3 cups white vinegar
- 1 cup apple cider vinegar
- 1 ½ cups white onion, diced
- 1 tablespoons sugar
- 2 tablespoons dill seed
- ¼ cup red pepper

Directions:

- Wash, cut, and deseed the cucumbers. Pulse them in a food processor to get

desired size. Dice the onion and pepper as well.
- Prepare all the canning equipment. Wash the jars and sterilize them if necessary. Add water to the canner but wait to boil.
- Put the cucumber in a bowl and sprinkle it with salt and turmeric before adding the water. Let sit for two hours uncovered. Afterwards drain the cucumbers.
- In a saucepan, mix the cucumber with onion, pepper, sugar, and dill seed. Pour both vinegars over the mixture before bringing it to a boil.
- Funnel the relish into the jar, leaving ¼ inch of space. Wipe the jar's rim and put on the lid.
- Using a jar lifter, gently place the jars in the canner, making sure there are 1-2 inches of water above them.
- Bring the canner to a boil and let it process for 15 minutes. Adjust time for altitude differences.
- After the time is up, turn off the heat and remove the canner's lid. Let it stand for five minutes before removal.
- To remove the jars, use your jar lifter and let them cool for 24 hours before checking the seal.
- Enjoy your dill pickled relish!

Relished Sweet Pickled Relish

Sweet pickled relish is another classic version of cucumber-based relish. The big difference between the two is the taste. Dill is more savory while sweet relish is, you guessed it, sweet. If you are having a hard time choosing between the two then you're outta luck. Both are healthy, delicious, and go well with hot dogs. It's all about personal flavor, and personally, I like both flavors. It's a good choice to can both and let your food mood decide what you want to eat that day. It is better to be prepared than disappointed when it comes to relish.

Amount: Four pints

Ingredients: *(See page 172 for Measurement Conversion)*

10. 4 cups finely chopped cucumbers
11. 2 cups finely chopped sweet peppers red or yellow
12. 2 cups finely chopped onion
13. ¼ cup kosher salt
14. 3 ½ cups sugar
15. 2 cups cider vinegar
16. 1 tablespoon mustard seed
17. 1 tablespoon celery seed

Directions:

- In a food processor, chop up onion, pepper, and cucumber. Measure out what you need before placing it all in a bowl.
- Stir in salt before covering it with ice water and setting it aside for two hours.
- Prepare all the canning equipment. Wash the jars and sterilize them if necessary. Add water to the canner but wait to boil.
- In a large stock pot, combine sugar, vinegar, celery seed, and mustard seed. Bring mixture to a boil.
- Stir in drained vegetables and let simmer for 10 minutes.
- Funnel the relish into a heated jar, leaving ¼ inch of space. Wipe the jar's rim and put on the lid. Using a jar lifter, gently place the jars in the canner, making sure there are 1-2 inches of water above them.
- Bring the canner to a boil and let it process for 15 minutes. Adjust time for altitude differences.

- After the time is up, turn off the heat and remove the canner's lid. Let it stand for five minutes before removal.
- To remove the jars, use your jar lifter and let them cool for 24 hours before checking the seal.
- Enjoy your sweet pickled relish!

Relished Jalapeno Relish

For the finale to this cucumber-based relish trilogy I offer a spicy alternative to the previous two recipes. This relish is made with the addition of jalapenos. This pepper brings a perfect amount of heat to one of the world's most favorite condiments. Jalapenos are similar to the chili pepper, but tend to be hotter in flavor. They are commercially grown in relatively the same places though, such as Texas and New Mexico. This spicy pepper makes for a great garden vegetable as well. Jalapenos take 90 days to grow to full size. Harvesting should usually take place around June.

Amount: Seven pints

Ingredients: *(See page 172 for Measurement Conversion)*

- 1 1/2 quarts jalapenos, finely chopped
- 1 quart cucumber, finely chopped
- 2 large onions, finely chopped
- 1/4 cup salt
- 5 1/4 cups sugar
- 3 cups cider vinegar
- 4 teaspoons pickling spices

Directions:

1. In a large bowl, combine jalapenos, cucumbers, onions, and salt. Cover the

mixture with cold water and let it stand for two hours.

2. Prepare all the canning equipment. Wash the jars and sterilize them if necessary. Add water to the canner but wait to boil.
3. In a large pot, combine the sugar and vinegar. Use a cheesecloth to add in the spices.
4. Bring to a boil and simmer for 15 minute.
5. Add in the vegetables and let simmer for another 10 minutes before removing the cheesecloth.
6. Funnel the relish into a heated jar, leaving ¼ inch of space. Wipe the jar's rim and put on the lid.
7. Using a jar lifter, gently place the jars in the canner, making sure there are 1-2 inches of water above them.
8. Bring the canner to a boil and let it process for 10 minutes. Adjust time for altitude differences. After the time is up, turn off the heat and remove the canner's lid. Let it stand for five minutes before removal.
9. To remove the jars, use your jar lifter and let them cool for 24 hours before checking the seal.
10. Enjoy your jalapeno relish!

Key Chapter 5 Takeaways

- The art of pickling had been around for centuries.
- There are a couple ways to pickle your produce, like quick-packing or fermentation.

- Pickling vegetables is an easy way to raise the acidity so they can be processed in a water bath canner.
- Vegetables aren't the only thing that can be pickled; fruit makes for great pickled treats are well.

Chapter 6
Tomatoes

"Canned tomatoes are like summer saved all that deep sun-kissed flavor ready to be enjoyed."

- Better Homes and Gardens

Tomato Recipes

Dice to Meet You Diced Tomatoes

Everyone knows by now that tomatoes are a fruit. Well, at least everyone else but Americans. For custom regulations, the U.S. supreme court ruled tomatoes as a vegetable. I'm not a politician, but I can tell you tomatoes have seeds and are by all definitions a fruit. To be fair, they probably wouldn't taste good in a fruit salad. On the other side of the coin, who are we to make judgements when we are only the second largest producer in the world. China takes the number one spot. Tomatoes are usually ready to be harvested around 60 to 85 days after planting them. This is usually done in the summer for the best results.

Amount: Nine pints

Ingredients: *(See page 172 for Measurement Conversion)*

- 9 pounds tomatoes
- 9 tablespoons bottled lemon juice

Directions:

11. Prepare all the canning equipment. Wash the jars and sterilize them if necessary. Add water to the canner but wait to boil.
12. Blanch tomatoes and remove skin. Then core and dice them as well. Save any excess of juice
13. Add a teaspoon of lemon juice to the bottom of each jar.
14. Funnel the tomatoes into a heated jar, leaving 1/2 inch of space. Press in the tomatoes with a spoon to release juices. If needed add more juice to fill the jar.
15. Wipe the jar's rim and put on the lid.
16. Using a jar lifter, gently place the jars in the canner, making sure there are 1-2 inches of water above them.
17. Bring the canner to a boil and let it process for 85 minutes. Adjust time for altitude differences.
18. After the time is up, turn off the heat and remove the canner's lid. Let it stand for five minutes before removal.
19. To remove the jars, use your jar lifter and let them cool for 24 hours before checking the seal.
20. Enjoy your diced tomatoes!

Cherished Cherry Tomatoes

Cherry tomatoes, in layman terms, are just tiny tomatoes. They are a great source of vitamin A, C, and E, and are often considered a superfood. While cherry tomatoes make for a healthy snack raw, they can also be canned whole. Since they are so small, the process is similar to how you would can a berry. When it comes to choosing between cherry tomatoes and regular-sized tomatoes, it doesn't matter. Their nutritional value is pretty much the same. Despite their name, cherry tomatoes can come in a variety of colors such as orange, purple, or yellow.

Amount: Four pints

Ingredients: *(See page 172 for Measurement Conversion)*

- 10 cups cherry tomatoes
- 1 tablespoon bottled lemon juice
- 1 teaspoon salt

Directions:

- Prepare all the canning equipment. Wash the jars and sterilize them if necessary. Add water to the canner but wait to boil.
- In a pan mix the tomatoes with a little bit of water. For five cups of tomatoes, add one cup of water.

- On medium-high, bring the tomatoes to a boil. Let boil for five minutes.
- Funnel the cherry tomatoes into a heated jar, leaving 1/2 inch of space.
- Add salt and lemon juice to each jar.
- Wipe the jar's rim and put on the lid. Using a jar lifter, gently place the jars in the canner, making sure there are 1-2 inches of water above them.
- Bring the canner to a boil and let it process for 35 minutes. Adjust time for altitude differences.
- After the time is up, turn off the heat and remove the canner's lid. Let it stand for five minutes before removal.
- To remove the jars, use your jar lifter and let them cool for 24 hours before checking the seal.
- Enjoy your cherry tomatoes!

Whole Lotta Whole Tomato

It can not be more simple to can whole tomatoes. While you can't actually can a whole tomato, mostly because it wouldn't fit, you can can them in large halves. Fun fact about tomatoes, more than 600,000 seeds were sent up to outer space. The seeds weren't grown out there, but they did spend time on the international space station before being grown back on earth for an experiment. That is quite an amazing feat for a fruit that's lying about being a vegetable. The good news is that if space tomato seeds can grow, so can normal ones in your own garden.

Amount: Nine pints

Ingredients: *(See page 172 for Measurement Conversion)*

10. 13 pounds Roma tomatoes
11. 9 tablespoons. concentrated lemon juice.

Directions:

- Prepare all the canning equipment. Wash the jars and sterilize them if necessary. Add water to the canner but wait to boil.

- Blanch tomatoes and remove skin. Save any juices.

- Add a teaspoon of lemon juice to the bottom of each jar.

- Funnel the tomatoes into a heated jar, leaving ½ inch of space. You may need to cut the tomatoes into large but smaller pieces.

- Wipe the jar's rim and put on the lid.

- Using a jar lifter, gently place the jars in the canner, making sure there are 1-2 inches of water above them.

- Bring the canner to a boil and let it process for 85 minutes. Adjust time for altitude differences.

- After the time is up, turn off the heat, and remove the canner's lid. Let it stand for five minutes before removal.

- To remove the jars, use your jar lifter and let them cool for 24 hours before checking the seal.

- Enjoy your whole tomatoes!

Salsa Recipes

Mild Salsa

Whether you're using it as a dip for corn chips or to spice up your tortilla, Taco Tuesday is not complete without salsa. This recipe provides a mild version to the Mexican-American food staple we're used to. There are many ways to make salsa and when it comes to your canning pantry, I suggest having a variety of types. Mild salsa is one of the easiest salsas to make, but to prevent canning fatigue, you'll want more flavors, especially if you're canning months ahead. Follow this recipe and the next two below for a fuller canning pantry.

Amount: Nine pints

Ingredients: *(See page 172 for Measurement Conversion)*

- 10 cups tomatoes, peeled and cored
- 6 cups diced peppers, mixture of mild and hot

- 4 cups chopped onions (about 6 medium onions)
- 3 cloves garlic, peeled
- 2 tablespoons cilantro, finely chopped
- 1 tablespoon salt
- ½ teaspoon black pepper
- 1 cup white vinegar

Directions:

9. Prepare all the canning equipment. Wash the jars and sterilize them if necessary. Add water to the canner but wait to boil.
10. Blanch the tomatoes to remove skin. Then squeeze the juice and pulp out.
11. Dice the tomatoes. Remove seeds from the peppers before chopping them up and chop up the onion and garlic in a food processor.
12. In a large pot add the tomatoes, the pepper, the onions, garlic, cilantro, salt, pepper, and vinegar.
13. On medium-high heat bring mixture to a boil then simmer for 15 minutes,
14. Funnel the salsa into a heated jar, leaving ½ inch of space. Wipe the jar's rim and put on the lid. Using a jar lifter, gently place the jars in the canner, making sure there are 1-2 inches of water above them.
15. Bring the canner to a boil and let it process for 15 minutes. Adjust time for altitude differences.
16. After the time is up, turn off the heat and remove the canner's lid. Let it stand for five minutes before removal.
17. To remove the jars, use your jar lifter and let them cool for 24 hours before checking the seal.
18. Enjoy your mild salsa!

Spicy Salsa

Spicy salsa is a great way to use up any leftover peppers from your garden. Even if you don't have a garden, it is still worth the time to make this great salsa for Taco Tuesday. The secret to this salsa's success is the diversity of produce. You'll need two different types of bell peppers, three different types of peppers in total, and two different types of tomatoes. With the addition of onion, that might seem like a lot, but it actually produces a wonderful cacophony of flavor. For more information on the hot pepper, check out Chapter 7's hot sauce recipe.

Amount: Seven pints

Ingredients: *(See page 172 for Measurement Conversion)*

- 5 lbs tomatoes, ½ regular, ½ Romas
- 2 lbs peppers, mix of red and green bell peppers with 6 hot peppers
- 1 lb white onions, diced
- 5 cloves garlic
- 1 cup apple cider vinegar
- 2 teaspoons ground cumin
- 1 ½ teaspoons chili powder
- 2 ½ teaspoons espresso powder
- ½ teaspoon ground black pepper
- 3 teaspoons kosher salt
- 1/2 cup chopped fresh cilantro

Directions:

- Prepare all the canning equipment. Wash the jars and sterilize them if necessary. Add water to the canner but wait to boil.
- In an oven, broil the tomatoes and peppers until the skin is visibly blistering.

- Flip and roast the other side. Remove stems and core but keep the skin.
- In a blender, blend the roasted tomatoes, all the juices from the pan, garlic, and ½ of the diced onions until smooth.
- In a saucepan, add all the ingredients, including the diced peppers and remaining diced onions, and bring to a boil. Simmer for 10 minutes, stirring occasionally.
- Funnel the salsa into a heated jar, leaving ½ inch of space. Wipe the jar's rim and put on the lid.
- Using a jar lifter, gently place the jars in the canner, making sure there are 1-2 inches of water above them.
- Bring the canner to a boil and let it process for 15minutes. Adjust time for altitude differences.
- After the time is up, turn off the heat and remove the canner's lid. Let it stand for five minutes before removal.
- To remove the jars, use your jar lifter and let them cool for 24 hours before checking the seal.
- Enjoy your spicy salsa!

Salsa Verde

Salsa Verde is made with tomatillos. In Spanish this translates to "little tomatoes," but tomatillos aren't little tomatoes. To further complicate their identity crisis, they are also referred to as "husk tomatoes." They are pretty similar and are considered fruits for the same reason tomatoes are but they have different flavors. Tomatillos have to be husked like corn does, but they grow on stems like a tomato instead of a stalk. For the most part, this peculiar plant is grown in Mexico, but places in the United States like Texas and New Mexico have had success planting them. Tomatillos are harvested in the morning hours during midsummer to fall.

Amount: Five half pints

Ingredients: *(See page 172 for Measurement Conversion)*

11. 5 ½ cups tomatillos, chopped husked and cored
12. 1 cup chopped onion
13. 1 cup peppers, chopped, mix of green bell, jalapenos, and Thai chili
14. 6 cloves garlic, minced
15. ⅓ cup cilantro, minced
16. 1 tablespoon cumin
17. 1 teaspoon paprika
18. 1 ½ teaspoons salt
19. ½ cup white vinegar
20. 3 tablespoons lime juice

Directions:

- Prepare all the canning equipment. Wash the jars and sterilize them if necessary. Add water to the canner but wait to boil.
- Preheat the oven to 500 °F. On a baking sheet place ¾ of your tomatillos and roast for 20 minutes.
- Chop up onions and pepper in a food processor.
- Remove hot tomatillo and let them cool before pulsing through the food processor with the remaining ¼ of raw tomatillos.
- In a saucepan, add onions, peppers, tomatillos, garlic, cumin, paprika, salt, vinegar, and lime juice. Bring mixture to a boil and then let simmer for 12 minutes.
- Funnel the salsa into a heated jar, leaving ½ inch of space. Wipe the jar's rim and put on the lid.
- Using a jar lifter, gently place the jars in the canner, making sure there are 1-2

inches of water above them.
- Bring the canner to a boil and let it process for 15 minutes. Adjust time for altitude differences. After the time is up, turn off the heat and remove the canner's lid. Let it stand for five minutes before removal.
- To remove the jars, use your jar lifter and let them cool for 24 hours before checking the seal.
- Enjoy your salsa verde!

Tomato Sauce Recipes

Pasta La Vista, Baby Sauce

Before you start making tomato-based sauces, it's important to know pasta sauce is technically not the same thing as marinara sauce. Pasta sauce has meat or vegetables in it, while marinara typically doesn't. Water bath canners cannot can meat or vegetables. That can only be done in a pressure canner. Below I've provided a recipe to the base of the pasta sauce. Meat or vegetables can be added to the actual food when the jar's contents are ready to be eaten. Okay, maybe it's not that important to know pasta sauce isn't marinara sauce because the technicalities have no bearing on the recipe below.

Amount: Nine quarts

Ingredients: *(See page 172 for Measurement Conversion)*

- 25 pounds tomatoes
- 4 large green peppers
- 4 large onions, cut
- 24 ounces tomato paste

- 1/4 cup canola oil
- 2/3 cup sugar
- 1/4 cup salt
- 8 garlic cloves, minced
- 2 teaspoons dried parsley flakes
- 2 teaspoons dried basil
- 2 teaspoons crushed red pepper flake
- 2 teaspoons Worcestershire sauce
- 2 bay leaves
- 1 cup 2 tablespoons bottled lemon juice

Directions:

9. Prepare all the canning equipment. Wash the jars and sterilize them if necessary. Add water to the canner but wait to boil.
10. Blanch the tomatoes before peeling and quartering them.
11. In a food processor, pulse green peppers and onions until finely chopped.
12. In a stockpot, mix in all ingredients except lemon juice. Cover with water and bring to a boil. Then let simmer, for 4-5 hours uncovered, stirring occasionally.
13. Add 2 tablespoons lemon juice to each jar.
14. Funnel the sauce into a heated jar, leaving ½ inch of space. Wipe the jar's rim and put on the lid. Using a jar lifter, gently place the jars in the canner, making sure there are 1-2 inches of water above them.
15. Bring the canner to a boil and let it process for 40 minutes. Adjust time for altitude differences.
16. After the time is up, turn off the heat and remove the canner's lid. Let it stand for five minutes before removal.

17. To remove the jars, use your jar lifter and let them cool for 24 hours before checking the seal.
18. Enjoy your pasta sauce!

Marinara Sauce

If you liked the last recipe name and were disappointed to find this is just called marinara sauce, I'm sorry, but I've peaked when it comes to tomato-sauce-related puns. So what's the difference between canning pasta sauce and marinara sauce? Time mostly. It's just a simpler version of tomato sauce than pasta is. Marinara is commonly used as a dipping sauce and doesn't need to shine as much as pasta sauce does. Don't worry, if you use marinara sauce as pasta sauce it's not going to rip a hole in the time-space continuum. Marinara sauce is often used as pasta sauce even though technically they are not the same thing. In conclusion, when it comes to your pasta, do whatever you want.

Amount: Nine quarts

Ingredients: *(See page 172 for Measurement Conversion)*

- 12 pounds tomatoes
- ½ cup minced onion
- 6 cloves garlic, minced
- ¼ cup extra virgin olive oil
- 3 tablespoons brown sugar
- 2 tablespoons sea salt
- 1 tablespoon dark balsamic vinegar
- 1 ½ teaspoons dried rosemary
- 1 ½ teaspoons dried oregano
- 1 ½ teaspoons dried basil

- 1 ½ teaspoons dried thyme
- 1 teaspoon crushed fennel seeds
- ½ teaspoon dried ground sage
- ½ teaspoon freshly ground black pepper
- 2 bay leaves
- 1 tablespoon lemon juice

Directions:

- Prepare all the canning equipment. Wash the jars and sterilize them if necessary. Add water to the canner but wait to boil.
- Blanch the tomatoes before peeling and squeezing out the seeds. Chop up the tomatoes.
- In a large pot, mix in all the ingredients except lemon juice. Bring to a boil. Then let simmer, for two hours uncovered, stirring occasionally.
- In an immersion blender, puree the mariner to a desired consistency
- Add 2 tablespoons lemon juice to each jar.
- Funnel the sauce into a heated jar, leaving ½ inch of space. Wipe the jar's rim and put on the lid.
- Using a jar lifter, gently place the jars in the canner, making sure there are 1-2 inches of water above them.
- Bring the canner to a boil and let it process for 40 minutes. Adjust time for altitude differences. After the time is up, turn off the heat and remove the canner's lid. Let it stand for five minutes before removal.
- To remove the jars, use your jar lifter and let them cool for 24 hours before checking the seal.
- Enjoy your marinara sauce!

Pizza Sauce

Wait a minute, isn't pizza sauce just marinara sauce which is pasta sauce without the meat? No, it's slightly different. Pizza sauce needs to spread gracefully across the crust. Marinara is too chunky to achieve this. While the ingredients are similar and the taste has a minute difference, they are made with different methods. Could you put marinara on a pizza? Probably, but it won't spread as nicely. Does this small difference in texture really deserve a different name though? It's not up to us, it's up to the tomato gods and they have spoken. Pasta sauce goes on pasta, marinara is a dip, and pizza sauce goes on pizza.

Amount: Seven pints

Ingredients: *(See page 172 for Measurement Conversion)*

13. 22 pounds tomatoes
14. 3 cups onions, chopped
15. 6 cloves garlic, minced
16. ¼ cups olive oil
17. 2 tablespoons dried basil
18. 1 tablespoon dried oregano
19. 1 tablespoon dried thyme
20. ½ tablespoon black pepper
21. 1 tablespoon sugar or honey
22. 2 tablespoons salt
23. 1 teaspoon crushed red pepper flakes
24. 1 tablespoon lemon juice

Directions:

- Wash, core, and halve tomatoes. Then, in a stockpot, bring the tomatoes to a boil. Strain to remove seeds and peels.
- Prepare all the canning equipment. Wash the jars and sterilize them if necessary. Add water to the canner but wait to boil.
- In a larger stockpot, cook onions and garlic in olive oil over medium heat for 5-10 minutes.
- Add tomato puree and all the seasonings before bringing mixture to a boil. Reduce heat and cook for about 30 minutes, uncovered.
- Process with an immersion blender to make a smoother sauce
- Bring back to a boil; reduce heat and simmer, uncovered, for one hour. Stir occasionally.
- Funnel the sauce into a heated jar, leaving ½ inch of space. Wipe the jar's rim and put on the lid. Using a jar lifter, gently place the jars in the canner, making sure there are 1-2 inches of water above them.
- Bring the canner to a boil and let it process for 35 minutes. Adjust time for altitude differences. After the time is up, turn off the heat and remove the canner's lid. Let it stand for five minutes before removal.
- To remove the jars, use your jar lifter and let them cool for 24 hours before checking the seal.
- Enjoy your pizza sauce!

Tomato Juice Recipes

Tomato Juice

There are a million uses for tomato juice. You can drink it, you can add it to a cocktail, and you can even use it to get the smell of skunk off of you. Tomato juice is very rich in nutrients and provides several important vitamins. Like blueberries, it can also be a source of antioxidants. Store-bought tomato sauce can be full of unnecessary sugar and salt, so the best way to take advantage of the nutritional value of tomato sauce is to make your own at home. The recipe below is a quick way to turn any garden yields into a tasty and healthy drink.

Amount: Six pint jars

Ingredients: *(See page 172 for Measurement Conversion)*

- 1 bushel of tomatoes. half Roma and half regular
- 15 teaspoons salt

Directions :

11. Prepare all the canning equipment. Wash the jars and sterilize them if necessary. Add water to the canner but wait to boil.
12. Core and peel tomatoes.
13. Place a few of the tomatoes in a large stock pot and squish them with a potato masher. Add the rest of the tomatoes while bringing the pot to a boil.
14. Put the mixture through a food mill and discard the pulp. Put the juice back in the stock pot.

15. Bring to a full rolling boil.
16. Add salt.
17. Funnel the juice into a heated jar, leaving ½ inch of space. Wipe the jar's rim and put on the lid. Using a jar lifter, gently place the jars in the canner, making sure there are 1-2 inches of water above them.
18. Bring the canner to a boil and let it process for 25 minutes. Adjust time for altitude differences. After the time is up, turn off the heat and remove the canner's lid. Let it stand for five minutes before removal.
19. To remove the jars, use your jar lifter and let them cool for 24 hours before checking the seal.
20. Enjoy your tomato juice!

Fresh From the Garden Vegetable Juice

The magic of the tomato and lemon juice is that they make low-acid vegetables water bath canner friendly. Usually with some of the vegetables listed below you would use a pressure canner, which is a lot more maintenance than a water bath canner. Garden vegetable juice is a great way to use up your extra veggies without all the effort. My favorite part, as the name implies, is that you can get all the ingredients from a home garden. As someone who likes to limit their waste as much as possible, this is one of the easiest yet tastiest ways to can up extra produce.

Amount: Seven quart jars

Ingredients: *(See page 172 for Measurement Conversion)*

- 22 lbs tomatoes
- ¾ cup celery, diced
- ¾ cup bell pepper, seeded, diced
- ¾ cup carrot, peeled, diced
- ½ cup onion, peeled, diced

- ¼ cup parsley, chopped
- 1 tablespoon salt
- lemon juice

Directions:

- Prepare all the canning equipment. Wash the jars and sterilize them if necessary. Add water to the canner but wait to boil.
- In a large pot, mix everything but the salt and lemon juice. let it simmer for 20 minutes.
- Put the mixture through a food mill before putting it back in the pot.
- Add salt and reheat but don't boil the mixture.
- Funnel the juice into a heated jar, leaving ½ inch of space. Wipe the jar's rim and put on the lid.
- Using a jar lifter, gently place the jars in the canner, making sure there are 1-2 inches of water above them.
- Bring the canner to a boil and let it process for 40 minutes. Adjust time for altitude differences.
- After the time is up, turn off the heat and remove the canner's lid. Let it stand for five minutes before removal.
- To remove the jars, use your jar lifter and let them cool for 24 hours before checking the seal.
- Enjoy your garden vegetable juice!

Bloody Mary

This recipe is not the actual alcoholic drink. It is the mix to make the alcoholic drink. After you're done canning you can decide for yourself if you'd like to upgrade to a more adult option by adding vodka or to keep it virgin. This iconic cocktail is only 100 years old. It's believed to have been created by a Parisian bartender in the early 1920s. It was a great way to start off the roaring '20s. Before the invention of the Bloody Mary, a similar mixture to the one below was actually used to cure hangovers. Whichever way you choose to use it, it will make a delightful addition to any brunch.

Amount: Six pint jars

Ingredients: *(See page 172 for Measurement Conversion)*

- 30 pc. medium tomatoes, quartered
- 1 ½ cups green peppers, chopped
- 1 cup carrots, diced
- ½ cup celery, diced
- 1 pc. small onions, diced
- 2-3 pc. garlic cloves, minced
- ¼ cup parsley, minced
- ¼ cup sugar
- ¼ cup lemon juice
- 1 1/2 tablespoon salt
- 1 tablespoon Worcestershire sauce
- ¼ cup medium jalapeno, diced including seeds

Directions:

- Prepare all the canning equipment. Wash the jars and sterilize them if necessary. Add water to the canner but wait to boil.
- In a large Dutch oven, cook the tomatoes, green peppers, carrots, celery, onion, garlic, parsley, and hot peppers for 30-45 minutes.
- After this, blend the mixture in an immersion blender until smooth.
- Place the mixture back in the pot and add the sugar, lemon juice, Worcestershire sauce, and salt. Bring to a boil over medium, stirring frequently.
- Funnel the mix into a heated jar, leaving ½ inch of space. Wipe the jar's rim

and put on the lid.
- Using a jar lifter, gently place the jars in the canner, making sure there are 1-2 inches of water above them.
- Bring the canner to a boil and let it process for 40 minutes. Adjust time for altitude differences.
- After the time is up, turn off the heat and remove the canner's lid. Let it stand for five minutes before removal.
- To remove the jars, use your jar lifter and let them cool for 24 hours before checking the seal.
- Enjoy your Bloody Mary!

Key Chapter 6 Takeaways

- From sauces to alcoholic beverages, there's a lot you can do with tomatoes.
- Different-sized cuts of tomatoes need different cooking times to properly be processed.
- Tomatoes are a fruit and not a vegetable due to their high acidity and ability to be canned in a water bath canner.
- Marinara sauce and pasta sauce are very similar but can still be considered two different products.
- Roma tomatoes are usually the best tomatoes to work with.

Chapter 7
Condiments

"Failure is the condiment that gives success its flavor."

-Truman Capote

Basic Condiments

Knock 'Em Out Ketchup

Ketchup is one of America's most beloved condiments. It pairs with just about any meat and is a must-have for any cookout. Just 4 tablespoons of ketchup has the same nutritional value as an entire medium-sized tomato. It was first sold in 1876 by the F. & J. Heinz company, which is still a main producer of the condiment today. Back then it was called "catsup," before the producers decided to change the name to ketchup. Since it comes from tomatoes, ketchup's taste is completely dependent on the quality of the crop. Check out Chapter 6 for more information on the harvest season.

Amount: Three pint jars

Ingredients: *(See page 172 for Measurement Conversion)*

10. 4 quarts tomato puree
11. 1 cup onion, chopped
12. ½ cup sweet pepper, chopped
13. 1 ½ cups vinegar
14. 1 tablespoon canning salt
15. ¼ teaspoon ground allspice
16. 1 stick cinnamon

17. ¾ cup sugar

Directions:

- Prepare all the canning equipment. Wash the jars and sterilize them if necessary. Add water to the canner but wait to boil.
- In a large pot, combine 1 quart of the tomatoes, all of the onions and sweet pepper in. Simmer until vegetables are soft.
- Press remaining tomatoes, and the tomato mixture through a food mill to remove the seeds and skins
- in a stockpot, bring mixture to a boil. Boil rapidly for one hour or until thickened.
- Add vinegar, salt, sugar, cinnamon, and other seasonings.
- Place sauce in a slow cooker on high with the cover removed until desired consistency.
- Funnel the ketchup into a heated jar, leaving ¼ inch of space. Wipe the jar's rim and put on the lid. Using a jar lifter, gently place the jars in the canner, making sure there are 1-2 inches of water above them.
- Bring the canner to a boil and let it process for 10 minutes. Adjust time for altitude differences. After the time is up, turn off the heat and remove the canner's lid. Let it stand for five minutes before removal.
- To remove the jars, use your jar lifter and let them cool for 24 hours before checking the seal.
- Enjoy your ketchup!

Better Barbecue Sauce

This American classic has been around for centuries and works as more than just a condiment. It can be used for marinating or basting pork, beef, or chicken. It's sweet but tangy flavor also makes it ideal for a topping to meat products. Many celebrity chefs have their own specific recipes, making barbecue sauce a must-have for any canning pantry. Stemming from its popularity in the south, barbecue sauce is undoubtedly one of the biggest condiments of soul food. If you're curious about any information about tomatoes or onions, check out Chapter 6, and Chapter 5's pickled onions recipe.

Amount: Six pint jars

Ingredients: *(See page 172 for Measurement Conversion)*

- 12 lbs tomato, peeled
- 3 cups onion, finely chopped
- 4 cloves garlic, chopped
- 1 ½ cups apple cider vinegar
- ½ cup bourbon
- 2 cups dark brown sugar, packed
- 1 tablespoon garlic powder
- 1 tablespoon mustard powder
- 2 tablespoons smoked paprika
- 1 teaspoon cayenne pepper
- 2 teaspoons chili flakes
- 2 tablespoons salt

Directions:

12. Prepare all the canning equipment. Wash the jars and sterilize them if necessary. Add water to the canner but wait to boil.
13. In a large stock pot, combine tomatoes, onion, and garlic and bring to a boil. Let simmer for 30 minutes.
14. Puree vegetables until smooth in the food processor.
15. Return tomato mixture to the pot and add remaining ingredients. Bring to a boil over high heat, stirring frequently. Let simmer for two hours or until mixture has thickened and darkened in color, stirring occasionally.
16. Funnel the barbecue into a heated jar, leaving ½ inch of space. Wipe the jar's rim and put on the lid.
17. Using a jar lifter, gently place the jars in the canner, making sure there are 1-2 inches of water above them.
18. Bring the canner to a boil and let it process for 20 minutes. Adjust time for altitude differences.
19. After the time is up, turn off the heat and remove the canner's lid. Let it stand for five minutes before removal.
20. To remove the jars, use your jar lifter and let them cool for 24 hours before checking the seal.
21. Enjoy your barbeque!

Marry Me Mustard

Will this recipe get you a wedding ring? Crazier things have happened, but even if you end up alone with 50 cats at least you'll have a delicious addition to your pantry. Mustard is centuries older than ketchup, first appearing in the 13th century in Dijon, France. The mustard seed comes from the mustard plant. If you're a gardener and want to try to harvest your own, the best season to grow this plant would be the spring or fall. This recipe makes a good companion to hamburgers or chicken tenders, but my personal favorite use for Marry Me Mustard is as a dip for hot pretzels.

Amount: Eight four oz jars

Ingredients: *(See page 172 for Measurement Conversion)*

- 2 cups onion, chopped
- 2 cups Pinot Grigio
- 1 cup white wine vinegar
- 1 teaspoon table salt
- 6 medium garlic cloves, coarsely chopped
- 4 whole black peppercorns
- 1 sprig fresh rosemary
- 1 cup yellow mustard seeds
- ⅓ cup dry mustard
- 2 ⅔ cups water

Directions:

1. Prepare all the canning equipment. Wash the jars and sterilize them if necessary. Add water to the canner but wait to boil.

2. In a saucepan, combine the onions, Pinot Grigio, vinegar, salt, garlic cloves, peppercorns, and rosemary and bring to a boil. Then reduce heat and let simmer for 20 minute to soften the onion.

3. Strain the mixture through a mesh strainer.

4. Add the mustard seed and dry mustard to the liquid. Cover and let sit for 24 hours at room temperature.

5. Process the mix in a blender before boiling it in a saucepan. Let simmer for 5 minutes.

6. Funnel the mustard into a heated jar, leaving ¼ inch of space. Wipe the jar's rim and put on the lid. Using a jar lifter, gently place the jars in the canner, making sure there are 1-2 inches of water above them.

7. Bring the canner to a boil and let it process for 10 minutes. Adjust time for altitude differences.

8. After the time is up, turn off the heat and remove the canner's lid. Let it stand for five minutes before removal.

9. To remove the jars, use your jar lifter and let them cool for 24 hours before checking the seal.

10. Enjoy your mustard!

Advanced Condiments

Serenading Sweet Chili Sauce

Bored of plain old ketchup or mustard? Want to try something with a little more spice? Well I got the recipe for you. This serenading sweet chili sauce is sure to kick up any meal a notch. The sweetness comes from the sugar and tomatoes but then the vinegar and peppers provide a nice contradictory sourness to the sauce. Adding a recipe like this to the pantry is a great way to avoid canning fatigue. In the traditional recipes of Thailand, sweet chili sauce is often made with hot red peppers but I've chosen a bell pepper recipe down below for a more mild taste.

Amount: Four pints

Ingredients: *(See page 172 for Measurement Conversion)*

12. 16 cups small tomatoes, peeled and chopped
13. 1 ¾ cups white vinegar
14. 2 cups sugar
15. 1 cup finely chopped onions
16. 1 ½ cups finely chopped celery
17. ¾ cup finely chopped bell pepper of any color
18. 2 ¼ teaspoons pickling or kosher salt
19. 1 ½ teaspoons ground cinnamon
20. 1 ½ teaspoons ground ginger
21. 1 teaspoons mustard seed

Directions:

- Wash and chop up tomatoes and all vegetables.
- Prepare all the canning equipment. Wash the jars and sterilize them if

necessary. Add water to the canner but wait to boil.
- In a large saucepan, combine the tomatoes, vinegar, sugar, onions, celery, bell peppers, salt, cinnamon, ginger, and mustard seeds.
- Bring to a boil, stirring to dissolve the sugar. Let simmer for two hours, stir frequently.
- Funnel the sauce into a heated jar, leaving ½ inch of space. Wipe the jar's rim and put on the lid.
- Using a jar lifter, gently place the jars in the canner, making sure there are 1-2 inches of water above them.
- Bring the canner to a boil and let it process for 15 minutes. Adjust time for altitude differences.
- After the time is up, turn off the heat and remove the canner's lid. Let it stand for five minutes before removal.
- To remove the jars, use your jar lifter and let them cool for 24 hours before checking the seal.
- Enjoy your sweet chili sauce!

Horseradish Harmony

Despite its name, horseradish is not made of horses and radishes. That would not make a very good sauce. Horseradish comes from the horseradish plant. This is a root vegetable that has been grown for centuries to cultivate its medicinal properties. What makes horseradish so odd is that peak harvest season for the plant is late fall, around October or November. This would be normal if the majority of horseradish's were grown in a state with warmer weather but the horseradish capital of the world is Illinois, U.S.A.. It grows on the floodplains of the Mississippi which makes for great soil but a cold midwestern fall.

Amount: Four half pint jars

Ingredients: *(See page 172 for Measurement Conversion)*

- 1 cup sugar
- 1 tablespoon kosher salt
- 2 cups white vinegar
- 7 cups lightly packed shredded horseradish root.

Directions:

9. Prepare all the canning equipment. Wash the jars and sterilize them if necessary. Add water to the canner but wait to boil.
10. In a saucepan, combine sugar, salt and vinegar. Bring to a boil over medium high heat, stirring to dissolve sugar and salt.
11. Add horseradish and return to a boil.
12. Press down on horseradish for better immersion
13. Funnel the sauce into a heated jar, leaving ½ inch of space. Wipe the jar's rim and put on the lid.
14. Using a jar lifter, gently place the jars in the canner, making sure there are 1-2 inches of water above them.
15. Bring the canner to a boil and let it process for 10 minutes. Adjust time for altitude differences.
16. After the time is up, turn off the heat and remove the canner's lid. Let it stand for five minutes before removal.
17. To remove the jars, use your jar lifter and let them cool for 24 hours before checking the seal.
18. Enjoy your horseradish!

From the Heart Honey Mustard

I'm not sure why all the mustard names are so romantic. I suppose it's because the mustard seed has a history being an aphrodisiac. The ancient Greeks were the first to figure out the benefits it can provide to blood pressure. This is because the seeds are rich with copper, iron, magnesium and selenium. These minerals have been documented to help with blood flow. Along with this benefit, these properties have provided relief to asthma patients. So whether you are having an asthma attack or looking for a romantic meal for an anniversary this recipe will come in handy.

Amount: Two half pint jars

Ingredients: *(See page 172 for Measurement Conversion)*

- ¾ cup mustard powder
- ⅓ cup honey
- 1 cup cider vinegar
- 3 whole eggs, slightly beaten

Directions:

- Prepare all the canning equipment. Wash the jars and sterilize them if necessary. Add water to the canner but wait to boil.
- Place a double boiler over simmering water
- In a double boiler, combine all the ingredients, stirring until smooth and fully mixed.
- Cook for 10 minutes or until thick and smooth.
- Funnel the sauce into a heated jar, leaving ½ inch of space. Wipe the jar's rim and put on the lid.
- Using a jar lifter, gently place the jars in the canner, making sure there are 1-2 inches of water above them.
- Bring the canner to a boil and let it process for 10 minutes. Adjust time for

altitude differences.
- After the time is up, turn off the heat and remove the canner's lid. Let it stand for five minutes before removal.
- To remove the jars, use your jar lifter and let them cool for 24 hours before checking the seal.
- Enjoy your honey mustard!

Dressing and Syrup Recipes

You Won't Regret this Strawberry Vinaigrette

Dressing isn't typically canned. In fact you will have difficulty finding a USDA approved recipe for any dressing. This strawberry vinaigrette is fine because it's ingredients are safe to can. Ranch dressing requires buttermilk and other dressings like French need oil. Both of these ingredients are not ideal for any canner. Another reason is that there isn't really a need for canning dressing. Most dressings can be made any time, there's no peak. There is a peak season for strawberry vinaigrette though. If you're curious about the peak seasons of strawberry check out the very first recipe in chapter 3, strawberry good jam.

Amount: Six half pint jars

Ingredients: *(See page 172 for Measurement Conversion)*

- 7 lbs strawberries
- 4 cups white vinegar
- sugar (should be equal to strawberry liquid)

Directions:

11. Put strawberries in a container and pour the vinegar over them. Cover tightly with plastic wrap and place in a 70 °F location to let stand overnight.
12. Prepare all the canning equipment. Wash the jars and sterilize them if necessary. Add water to the canner but wait to boil.
13. Strain the liquid and berries through a cheesecloth. Discard any pulp and keep clean liquid.
14. In a pot, stir in white sugar equal to the volume of liquid. Bring to a boil and immediately remove from heat.
15. Skim off any foam and discard.
16. Funnel the dressing into a heated jar, leaving ¼ inch of space. Wipe the jar's rim and put on the lid.
17. Using a jar lifter, gently place the jars in the canner, making sure there are 1-2 inches of water above them.
18. Bring the canner to a boil and let it process for 10 minutes. Adjust time for altitude differences. After the time is up, turn off the heat and remove the canner's lid. Let it stand for five minutes before removal.
19. To remove the jars, use your jar lifter and let them cool for 24 hours before checking the seal.
20. Enjoy your strawberry vinaigrette!

Seriously Good Strawberry Syrup

When it comes to regular maple syrup, the extra step of canning is actually unnecessary. Canning usually requires sugar but syrup already has a high amount in it so there's no need to add any more. When preparing syrup, it gets boiled but it's boiling point is well above that of water. When it's added to the jar, the lid just pops and it's sealed. Water bath canning will just ruin the product. What does any of this have to do with strawberry syrup? Nothing because it's a fruit byproduct and you definitely need to water bath can it. Check out the strawberry good jam recipe in chapter 3 for information on picking and growing strawberries.

Amount: Eight half pints

Ingredients: *(See page 172 for Measurement Conversion)*

- 10 cups strawberries, stemmed and crushed
- 3 cups water
- 1 strip (2-inch) lemon peel
- 2 ½ cups granulated sugar
- 3 ½ cups corn syrup
- 2 tablespoons lemon juice

Directions:

- Prepare all the canning equipment. Wash the jars and sterilize them if necessary. Add water to the canner but wait to boil.
- In a large pot, combine strawberries, 1½ cups of the water and the lemon peel. Boil for 5 minutes.
- Place the mixture in a jelly bag and let it drip for at least two hours.
- In a large pot, combine sugar and remaining 1½ cups of water.
- Bring to a boil over medium-high heat, stirring to dissolve sugar, and cook until temperature reaches 230 °F.
- Add strawberry juice and corn syrup. Boil for another 5 minutes, stirring occasionally. Remove from heat and add the lemon juice.
- Funnel the syrup into a heated jar, leaving ¼ inch of space. Wipe the jar's rim and put on the lid. Using a jar lifter, gently place the jars in the canner, making sure there are 1-2 inches of water above them.
- Bring the canner to a boil and let it process for 20 minutes. Adjust time for altitude differences. After the time is up, turn off the heat and remove the

canner's lid. Let it stand for five minutes before removal.
- To remove the jars, use your jar lifter and let them cool for 24 hours before checking the seal.
- Enjoy your strawberry syrup!

Best Blueberry Syrup Around

Since blueberries are one of the healthiest fruits to eat, it is smart to incorporate them into your morning pancakes. This recipe is a healthy alternative to regular maple syrup that has a higher level of sugar. Blueberries are one of the only naturally occurring blue foods. The anthocyanin in the fruit causes its unique color. To reiterate the properties I mentioned in the Blasting Blueberries recipe of Chapter 4, anthocyanin lowers the risk of cancer and helps with insulin production. You can also check out the recipe mentioned above for more information on the harvesting of this amazing fruit.

Amount: One pint jar

Ingredients: *(See page 172 for Measurement Conversion)*

13. 5 cups blueberries
14. 1 cup sugar
15. 2 teaspoons bottled lemon juice
16. 2 ½ tablespoons Clear Jel
17. ⅓ cup water

Directions:

- Prepare all the canning equipment. Wash the jars and sterilize them if necessary. Add water to the canner but wait to boil.

- In a large pot, add blueberries and 1/2 cup of water. Boil for 10 minutes and then let simmer for 20 minutes. Lightly stir to extract juice.
- Put the berries in a jelly bag to let drip for 1 hour.
- In a large pot, measure out 2 cups of blueberry juice and add sugar and lemon juice. Bring blueberry mixture to a boil, stirring to dissolve sugar.
- In a separate small bowl combine water with the Clear Jel and stir until it's smooth. Add to boiling mixture. Stir for one minute.
- Funnel the syrup into a heated jar, leaving ¼ inch of space. Wipe the jar's rim and put on the lid.
- Using a jar lifter, gently place the jars in the canner, making sure there are 1-2 inches of water above them.
- Bring the canner to a boil and let it process for 15 minutes. Adjust time for altitude differences. After the time is up, turn off the heat and remove the canner's lid. Let it stand for five minutes before removal.
- To remove the jars, use your jar lifter and let them cool for 24 hours before checking the seal.
- Enjoy your blueberry syrup!

More Sauces

Can't Be Beat Cranberry Sauce

When it comes to holiday dinners, cranberry sauce has a chokehold on the market. What is Thanksgiving or Christmas without this iconic sauce? Not only will it invoke festive cheer but it's also full of nutritional value. The holidays are the worst time for a diet so implementing a healthy side will limit any post dinner regrets. Since it's low in fat, cranberry sauce is good for your heart. Most of the cranberries in the U.S. come from Massachusetts or Wisconsin. There are two ways to harvest the fruit, dry and wet. Dry harvest is the fresh marketplace cranberries that are used in the recipe below. The wet method, which involves a bog, is used mainly for cranberry juice production.

Amount: Five pint jars

Ingredients: *(See page 172 for Measurement Conversion)*

- 3 lbs fresh cranberries
- 2 cups water
- 2 oranges, juiced and zested
- 1 lemon, juiced and zested
- 4 cups white granulated sugar
- 1 cinnamon sticks
- 2 tablespoons whole cloves
- Pinch of salt

Directions:

14. Prepare all the canning equipment. Wash the jars and sterilize them if necessary. Add water to the canner but wait to boil.
15. In a large pot, combine cranberries, sugar, water, orange zest and juice, lemon zest and juice, and a pinch of salt. Bring to a boil over high heat. Stir frequently.
16. Once a boil has been reached, add the cheese cloth filled with cinnamon and cloves. Continue to boil over high heat for 10-15 minutes. The cranberries should all pop.
17. Once all the cranberries have popped and your desired consistency has been reached remove the pot from the heat. Skim off any foam on the top.
18. Funnel the sauce into a heated jar, leaving ¼ inch of space. Wipe the jar's rim and put on the lid.

19. Using a jar lifter, gently place the jars in the canner, making sure there are 1-2 inches of water above them.
20. Bring the canner to a boil and let it process for 10 minutes. Adjust time for altitude differences.
21. After the time is up, turn off the heat and remove the canner's lid. Let it stand for five minutes before removal.
22. To remove the jars, use your jar lifter and let them cool for 24 hours before checking the seal.
23. Enjoy your cranberry sauce!

Hot Hot Sauce

The hot sauce that we use today has been around for nearly two centuries. Hot peppers are the key ingredient to making this spicy condiment. Hot peppers don't just provide heat to a dish, they also have some health benefits. The active chemical component of hot pepper is called "capsaicin." Capsaicin can help with sinus issues and can work as an antioxidant. Hot peppers grow best in warmer climates such as California but many gardeners have no problem growing their own. You can harvest your hot peppers 60 to 95 days after planting them. You'll know they are ready by their size and ripe color.

Amount: Four pint jars

Ingredients: *(See page 172 for Measurement Conversion)*

- 1 ½ cups hot peppers, chopped, stemmed and seeded
- 2 tablespoons pickling spice
- 8 cups tomatoes, diced
- 4 cups white vinegar
- 2 teaspoons pickling salt

Directions:

- Prepare all the canning equipment. Wash the jars and sterilize them if necessary. Add water to the canner but wait to boil.
- In a large pot, add in all ingredients. The spices should be in a spice bag or cheesecloth. Bring mixture to a boil, uncovered. Then let simmer, uncovered for 20 minutes.
- Press mixture through a food mill.
- Return the liquid to the pot. Bring to a full rolling boil, uncovered for 15 minutes.
- Funnel the sauce into a heated jar, leaving ¼ inch of space. Wipe the jar's rim and put on the lid.
- Using a jar lifter, gently place the jars in the canner, making sure there are 1-2 inches of water above them.
- Bring the canner to a boil and let it process for 10 minutes. Adjust time for altitude differences.
- After the time is up, turn off the heat and remove the canner's lid. Let it stand for five minutes before removal.
- To remove the jars, use your jar lifter and let them cool for 24 hours before checking the seal.
- Enjoy your hot sauce!

The Chicken Wing Sauce

There are so many different kinds of condiments to eat chicken wings with but none as bold as this one. The name alone declares itself as *the* chicken wing sauce. Its ingredients are very similar to barbecue sauce but the execution gives it a unique and perfect pairing for chicken. If you would prefer a healthier option, you can pair it with grilled chicken breast strips instead of the fried wings. You could also use vegan chicken or tofu as plant-based replacements if needed. If you're wondering more about the tomato, check out Chapter 6.

Amount: Four pint jars

Ingredients: *(See page 172 for Measurement Conversion)*

10. 10 cups tomatoes, washed, peeled, cored, and chopped
11. 2 cups onion, chopped
12. ⅓ cup brown sugar
13. ½ teaspoon cayenne pepper
14. 1 ½ cups white vinegar
15. 4 teaspoons salt
16. 2 cloves garlic, minced
17. 1 teaspoon allspice ground
18. 1 teaspoon cinnamon ground
19. 1 teaspoon cloves ground
20. 1 teaspoon ginger ground

Directions:

- Prepare all the canning equipment. Wash the jars and sterilize them if necessary. Add water to the canner but wait to boil.
- In a large pot, add the tomatoes, onions, sugar, and cayenne. Bring to a boil uncovered. Let simmer uncovered for 30 minutes.
- Remove from heat and let it cool before using a blender or food processor to puree the mixture.
- Return mixture to the pot and add all the remaining ingredients. Bring to a boil then let simmer, uncovered, for an hour.
- Funnel the sauce into a heated jar, leaving ½ inch of space. Wipe the jar's rim and put on the lid.
- Using a jar lifter, gently place the jars in the canner, making sure there are 1-2

inches of water above them.
- Bring the canner to a boil and let it process for 15 minutes. Adjust time for altitude differences.
- After the time is up, turn off the heat and remove the canner's lid. Let it stand for five minutes before removal.
- To remove the jars, use your jar lifter and let them cool for 24 hours before checking the seal.
- Enjoy your chicken wing sauce!

Key Chapter 7 Takeaways

- Most condiments have been around for centuries.
- Ketchup was originally called catsup.
- Most dressings shouldn't be home canned.
- Syrup from fruit should be water bathed but maple syrup can seal on its own.
- Cranberry sauce is one of the healthiest options around the holidays.

Chapter 8: Bonus Chapter -
Meals in a Jar

"To eat is a necessity, but to eat intelligently is an art."

- François de Rochefoucald

Meal Preparation

Meal preparation (prepping) is the practice of planning and preparing your meals ahead of time. Not only does it save time but many people utilize the practice for portion control. Nutrition can often take a back seat to the busy goings on of everyday life. This is an option for those who want to reach their health goals but just don't have the time. Nowadays it's easy to go out to your local fast-food joint instead of staying home and cooking a meal with nutritional value. In this fast world, we rarely have time to eat let alone the time to cook. Meal preparation can revolutionize your diet, keeping you healthy and happy.

In most meal prepping communities, Sunday is the day to plan and make your meals for the following week. This is fine if you want to waste your Sunday afternoon slaving away in a kitchen. With water bath canning, you can plan your food months ahead. This is called batch cooking where you only have to prepare food every couple of months. It's a great way to free up your days for more important activities. There are other methods to meal prepping such as individually portioned meals. This is where you portion the meal out and grab and go as you're hungry instead of eating the full prepared food. Another method is to prep the ingredient to cut down on cooking time but not fully eliminate it. Whichever method works best is ultimately up to you but

I'm partial to my beloved water bath canner.

Before you start meal prepping make a list of what you want to achieve with it. This could be weight loss, dietary restrictions, getting nutrition value or anything else you want to do. This list will be the starting point to figure out what kind of meals you'll make to plan. If you're working towards portion control, you won't want to prepare too much food. You'll also want a variety of options for the week so you don't get stuck eating the same thing every day. It's also a good idea to pinpoint the times in your life you're most tempted to eat out or snack on unhealthy foods. Being prepared for these times can help you quit your unhealthy eating habits.

Meal preparation sounds great and all but where do you even start? Cooking the recipes from this book doesn't automatically help you eat healthier. Many of the recipes are condiments to meals, not actual entrees. How are you supposed to make a healthy and nutritious lunch out of pickled peaches? Don't worry I got you. In the next three sections I have prepared breakfast, lunch and dinner options. These are ways to turn water bath canned goods into an actual meal. It's important to know, this is just a jumping off point to help you start your healthy canning meal preparation. It's going to take your own research to come up with a variety of canning that works for your kitchen. Don't worry though, once you get a hold of what to do after the jar, meal prep will be life changing.

What's for Breakfast

Apple Butter on Toast

Apple butter on toast is an easy way to start your day. It only requires the two ingredients of apple butter and whole wheat toast. You can use white bread but whole wheat has less calories and more fiber. Simply spread the butter over your toast and voilà: breakfast is taken care of. So what is coming from your canning pantry? The apple butter. Grains can't be safely preserved so you should never can bread. Simply follow this recipe below to make sure you have a jar of apple in your reserves.

Amount: Three pint jars

Ingredients: *(See page 172 for Measurement Conversion)*

9. 4 pounds of apples
10. 1 cup of apple cider vinegar
11. 2 cups water
12. 4 cups of sugar
13. 2 teaspoons cinnamon
14. ½ teaspoon ground cloves
15. ½ teaspoon allspice
16. 1 tablespoon lemon zest
17. 3 tablespoons lemon juice
18. Pinch of salt

Directions:

- Prepare all the canning equipment. Wash the jars and sterilize them if necessary. Add water to the canner but wait to boil.
- When cutting up the apples don't peel or core them. Put them into a large pot and add apple cider vinegar and water. Cover and boil then simmer for 20 minutes to soften apples.
- Put the mixture through a sieve or food mill.
- Add the rest of the ingredients before putting in a pot and cooking it for 1 to 2 hours. It should be thick, smooth and dark brown in color.
- Funnel the apple butter into a heated jar, leaving ¼ inch of space. Wipe the jar's rim and put on the lid.

- Using a jar lifter, gently place the jars in the canner, making sure there are 1-2 inches of water above them.
- Bring the canner to a boil and let it process for 10 minutes. Adjust time for altitude differences.
- After the time is up, turn off the heat and remove the canner's lid. Let it stand for five minutes before removal.
- To remove the jars, use your jar lifter and let them cool for 24 hours before checking the seal.
- Enjoy your apple butter!

Greek Yogurt with Mango

Another healthy option for breakfast is Greek yogurt with Mango. If you're wondering why use Greek yogurt instead of regular yogurt, it's all about protein. Greek yogurt has half the carbs and sugar but twice the protein. After you've added your mango to the yogurt, feel free to top it off with granola for extra nutrients. So what's from the pantry? The mangos of course. As you know by now yogurt can't be processed and should come directly from the refrigerator. Follow the recipe below to can your mango topping.

Amount: Three pint jars

Ingredients: *(See page 172 for Measurement Conversion)*

- 8 or 9 mangoes, peeled and seeded
- 1/4 cup of sugar
- 2 cups of water
- 2 teaspoons lemon juice

Directions:

10. Prepare all the canning equipment. Wash the jars and sterilize them if necessary. Add water to the canner but wait to boil.
11. When cutting the mangos, you can leave them in larger halves or chop them up.
12. Pack the mangos into a heated jar, leaving ½ inch of space. Add in the lemon juice
13. In a pan, bring sugar and water to a boil. Stirring to dissolve.
14. Pour the syrup into the jars with the mangos in them. Wipe the jar's rim and put on the lid.
15. Using a jar lifter, gently place the jars in the canner, making sure there are 1-2 inches of water above them.
16. Bring the canner to a boil and let it process for 15 minutes. Adjust time for altitude differences.
17. After the time is up, turn off the heat and remove the canner's lid. Let it stand for five minutes before removal.
18. To remove the jars, use your jar lifter and let them cool for 24 hours before checking the seal.
19. Enjoy your mango!

What's for Lunch

Peach Salsa Tacos

Now that it's lunchtime, you're going to want something a little more filling. So why are we doing peach salsa and not regular salsa? Just because we can. If peach isn't the move for you, Chapter 6 has several other salsa options. To make these tacos just grill up your preferred meat (I like chicken), put it in a spinach or tortilla wrap and add your salsa. So what's from the pantry? The peach salsa of course. We all know a wrap from a can would be ridiculous but what about the meat? All fresh meat can be canned but only in a pressure canner. Water bath canning would be too dangerous due to meat's pH levels. Keep reading to find out how to make your own peach salsa.

Amount: Four pint jars

Ingredients: *(See page 172 for Measurement Conversion)*

- 6 cups of peaches, peeled and diced
- 1 cup of granulated sugar
- 1 cup of chopped red bell pepper
- 1 cup of apple cider vinegar
- ½ cup of chopped red onion
- ½ cup of cold water
- ¼ cup of lime juice
- ½ teaspoon kosher salt
- 2 jalapeño peppers, seeded and finely chopped
- 2 garlic cloves, minced
- 1 habanero pepper, seeded and minced
- ¼ cup chopped fresh cilantro

Directions:

- Prepare all the canning equipment. Wash the jars and sterilize them if necessary. Add water to the canner but wait to boil.
- In a Dutch oven, add in all the ingredients except cilantro.
- Bring to a boil and stir until sugar has dissolved. Let it simmer, uncovered, for five minutes.
- Remove the mixture from the heat source and stir in the cilantro.
- Funnel the salsa into a heated jar, leaving ½ inch of space.

- Wipe the jar's rim and put on the lid. Using a jar lifter, gently place the jars in the canner, making sure there are 1-2 inches of water above them.
- Bring the canner to a boil and let it process for 15 minutes. Adjust time for altitude differences.
- After the time is up, turn off the heat and remove the canner's lid. Let it stand for five minutes before removal.
- To remove the jars, use your jar lifter and let them cool for 24 hours before checking the seal.
- Enjoy your peach salsa!

Cowboy Candy Over Salmon

Candy for lunch? Sorry to disappoint but no. These are healthy options, remember? "Cowboy Candy" is just a nickname for candied jalapenos. They have no more sugar in them than most of the other recipes in this book. This meal is just as it sounds, candied jalapenos over grilled Alaskan salmon. If you want to use another type of fish, feel free. Salmon is just my preference since it's one of, if not the, healthiest fish to eat. As long as you're getting protein, it doesn't really matter what meat or meat substitute you use. So what's from the pantry? As you can tell from the recipe below, Cowboy Candy is water bath canner approved.

Amount: Three pints

Ingredients: *(See page 172 for Measurement Conversion)*

9. 1 pound fresh jalapeños/21 peppers
10. 2 cups white sugar
11. ⅔ cup apple cider vinegar
12. 1 teaspoon garlic powder
13. ½ teaspoon celery seed

14. ½ teaspoon ground turmeric
15. ¼ teaspoon red pepper flakes

Directions:

- Prepare all the canning equipment. Wash the jars and sterilize them if necessary. Add water to the canner but wait to boil.
- Wear gloves when cutting the jalapenos into small rounds.
- In a medium pot, add the sugar, apple cider vinegar, garlic powder, celery seed, turmeric, and red pepper flakes. Bring to a rolling boil before letting it simmer for 5 minutes.
- Stir in the jalapenos and bring the mixture back to a boil. Let simmer for 10 minutes.
- Remove jalapenos from the syrup and put them into a heated jar. Pour in the syrup, leaving ¼ inch of space. Wipe the jar's rim and put on the lid.
- Using a jar lifter, gently place the jars in the canner, making sure there are 1-2 inches of water above them.
- Bring the canner to a boil and let it process for 15 minutes. Adjust time for altitude differences.
- After the time is up, turn off the heat and remove the canner's lid. Let it stand for five minutes before removal.
- To remove the jars, use your jar lifter and let them cool for 24 hours before checking the seal.
- Enjoy your candied jalapenos!

What's for Dinner

Spaghetti with Zoodles

I hope you're hungry because we are having spaghetti zoodles for dinner tonight. You may be thinking, why zoodles? I've been eating healthy all day, can't I just for once have my carbs? Sure. I mean, I'm just the person who wrote this book, I can't stop you from enjoying your pasta. I can make you feel bad about it though. Zoodles are an amazing alternative to grained pasta. Not only are they low in calories but they are packed full of vitamins and antioxidants. Whether or not they can be canned is still up in the air. The USDA doesn't recommend it but there are still recipes available. So that means the spaghetti sauce is what we're canning today. The recipe below is a little different from the pasta la vista sauce in chapter 6 but either one will work.

Amount: Four quart jars

Ingredients: *(See page 172 for Measurement Conversion)*

- 12 cups of tomatoes, peeled, drained, and chopped
- 1 cup green bell pepper, finely chopped
- 1 cup red bell pepper, finely chopped
- 2 cups of onions, finely chopped
- 18 ounces of tomato paste
- ½ cup vegetable
- ½ cup granulated sugar
- 3 tablespoons salt
- 2 tablespoons garlic, finely minced
- 1 ½ tablespoons dried oregano
- 1 ½ tablespoons dried basil
- 1 ½ teaspoons dried parsley

- 2 teaspoons Worcestershire sauce
- ½ cup lemon juice

Directions:

11. Prepare all the canning equipment. Wash the jars and sterilize them if necessary. Add water to the canner but wait to boil.
12. In a large pot, combine all ingredients except lemon juice.
13. Stir and bring to a boil. Let simmer for one hour.
14. When that's finished let it cool before blending the mixture until smooth.
15. Add the lemon juice to the bottom of a heated jar then add the sauce, leaving ½ inch of space. Wipe the jar's rim and put on the lid.
16. Using a jar lifter, gently place the jars in the canner, making sure there are 1-2 inches of water above them.
17. Bring the canner to a boil and let it process for 40 minutes. Adjust time for altitude differences.
18. After the time is up, turn off the heat and remove the canner's lid. Let it stand for five minutes before removal.
19. To remove the jars, use your jar lifter and let them cool for 24 hours before checking the seal.
20. Enjoy your spaghetti sauce!

Pickled Beets Salad

For a lighter option, we have pickled beet salad on the menu tonight. This consists of pickled beets, home canned to perfection, poured over a leafy green base and sprinkled with walnuts and feta cheese. Besides the pickled beets, none of the other ingredients are canned and are far superior when they are as fresh as possible. Follow the recipe below so that you can create this fancy entree that's perfect for dinner parties.

Amount: Six pint jars

Ingredients: *(See page 172 for Measurement Conversion)*

- 35-40 small beets, unpeeled
- 2 cups sugar
- 2 cups water
- 2 cups white vinegar
- 1 teaspoon ground cloves
- 1 teaspoon allspice
- 1 tablespoon cinnamon
- 1 teaspoon whole cloves

Directions:

- Prepare all the canning equipment. Wash the jars and sterilize them if necessary. Add water to the canner but wait to boil.
- In a large pot cook the beets until they are tender.
- Let them cool before removing the skins and cutting them into cubes.
- In a saucepan, combine the rest of the ingredients and bring them to a boil. Let simmer for 10 minutes.
- Put the beets into a heated jar and pour in the syrup, leaving ¾ inch of space. Wipe the jar's rim and put on the lid.
- Using a jar lifter, gently place the jars in the canner, making sure there are 1-2 inches of water above them.
- Bring the canner to a boil and let it process for 12 minutes. Adjust time for altitude differences.
- After the time is up, turn off the heat and remove the canner's lid. Let it stand for five minutes before removal.

- To remove the jars, use your jar lifter and let them cool for 24 hours before checking the seal.
- Enjoy your pickled beets!

Key Chapter 8 Takeaways

1. Meal preparation is a great option for monitoring what you eat.
2. There are several methods to this practice including canning foods in bulk so you only have to prepare and plan every couple of months.
3. Can a variety of options to avoid canning fatigue.
4. For a more diverse diet, it's important to pair canned goods with goods that can't be canned in a water bath when eating them.
5. While many water bath canning recipes include sugar there are still healthy ways to prepare the food.

Chapter 9
Everything Else you Need to Know

"Knowledge has no value unless you put it into practice."

-Anton Chekhov

Altitude

Water Bath Canning Chart

Altitude	Increase in Processing time
sea level	no adjustment
1,001-3,000	5 min
3,001 -6,000	10 min
6,001 - 8,000	15 min
8,001 - 10,000	20 min

Chart of the 20 largest cities in the U.S. and their Altitudes

City	State	Altitude	Rank by population
Phoenix	Arizona	1086 ft	5

Denver	Colorado	948 ft	19
Columbus	Ohio	902 ft	15
Charlotte	North Carolina	761 ft	16
Indianapolis	Indiana	719 ft	17
Fort Worth	Texas	653 ft	13
San Antonio	Texas	650 ft	7
Chicago	Illinois	597 ft	3
Dallas	Texas	430 ft	9
Austin	Texas	425 ft	11
Washington	D.C.	409 ft	20
Los Angeles	California	305 ft	2
Seattle	Washington	174 ft	18
Houston	Texas	105 ft	4
San Jose	California	82 ft	10
San Diego	California	62 ft	8
San Francisco	California	52 ft	14
Philadelphia	Pennsylvania	39 ft	6

New York City	New York	33 ft	1
Jacksonville	Florida	16 ft	12

5 cities with the highest altitudes in the U.S.

City	State	Altitude
Alma	Colorado	10,361 ft
Leadville	Colorado	10,150 ft
Blue River	Colorado	10,020 ft
Breckenridge	Colorado	9,600 ft
Flagstaff	Arizona	6,910 ft

Altitude of the 10 largest cities in Canada

City	Province	Altitude	Rank by population
Vancouver,	British Columbia	6,562 ft	8
Calgary	Alberta	3,428 ft	3
Edmonton	Alberta	2,116 ft	5
Hamilton	Ontario	1083 ft	10
Winnipeg	Manitoba	784 ft	7

Montreal	Quebec	764 ft	2
Brampton	Ontario	715 ft	9
Mississauga	Ontario	512 ft	6
Toronto	Ontario	251 ft	1
Ottawa	Ontario	230 ft	4

Measurement Conversion

Cups	Tablespoons	Teaspoons	Milliliters
		1 tsp	5 ml
1/16 cups	1 tbsp	3 tsp	15 ml
⅛ cups	2 tbsp	6 tsp	30 ml
¼ cups	4 tbsp	12 tsp	60 ml
⅓ cups	5 ⅓ tbsp	16 tsp	80 ml
½ cups	8 tbsp	24 tsp	120 ml
⅔ cups	10 ⅔ tbsp	32 tsp	160 ml
¾ cups	12 tbsp	36 tsp	180 ml

| 1 cup | 16 tbsp | 48 tsp | 240 ml |

1 Gallon = 4 quarts = 8 pints =16 cups= 120 oz = 3.8 liters

1 Quart = 2 pints= 4 cups = 32 oz = 950 ml

1 Pint = 2 cups= 16 oz = 480 ml

1 cup = 8oz= 240ml

Cooking Temperatures

Fahrenheit = (Celsius x 1.8) +32

Celsius = (Fahrenheit - 32) x 0.5556

Pounds to Kilograms

1 lb = 0.45 kg   1 kg= 2.22 lbs

2 lbs = 0.90 kg   2 kg= 4.44 lbs

3 lbs = 1.35 kg   3 kg= 6.67 lbs

4lbs = 1.80 kg   4 kg= 8.89 lbs

5 lbs = 2.25 kg   5 kg= 11.11 lbs

6 lbs = 2.70 kg   6 kg= 13.33lbs

7 lbs = 3.15 kg   7 kg= 15.56 lbs

8 lbs = 3.60 kg   8 kg= 17.78 lbs

9 lbs = 4.05 kg   9 kg= 20.00 lbs

10 lbs = 4.50 kg   10 kg= 22.22 lbs

EWG's 2021 "Dirty Dozen"

- Strawberries
- Spinach
- Kale, collard and mustard greens
- Nectarines
- Apples
- Grapes
- Cherries
- Peaches
- Pears
- Bell and hot peppers
- Tomatoes
- Celery

EWG's 2021 "Clean Fifteen"

- Avocados
- Sweet corn
- Pineapples
- Onions
- Papayas
- Sweet peas (frozen)
- Eggplants
- Asparagus
- Broccoli
- Cabbages
- Kiwis
- Cauliflower

- Mushrooms
- Honeydew melons
- Cantaloupes

Fruit and Tomato Canning Charts

Water Bath Canning Fruit Chart

Fruit type	Pack style	Pints	Quarts
apples	hot	20 min	20 min
apricots	raw	25 min	30 min
berries	raw	15 min	20 min
cherry	raw	20 min	25 min
fruit juice	hot	15 min	15 min
fruit jam	hot	10 min	10 min
peaches	hot	20 min	25 min
pears	hot	20 min	25 min
plums	hot	20 min	25 min
rhubarb	hot	10 min	10 min

Water Bath Canning Tomato Chart

Tomato type	Pack style	Pints	Quarts
crushed	hot	45 min	55 min
whole	hot/raw	50 min	55 min
juice	hot	45 min	50 min
sauce	hot	45 min	50 min

Water Bath Canning Pickled Chart

Pickled type	Pack style	Pints	Quarts
dill pickle	raw	15 min	20 min
sweet pickle	raw	10 min	15 min
pickle relish	hot	10 min	Not recommended
bread and butter pickles	hot	15 min	15 min
pickled beets	hot	40 min	40 min

Pesticides

Around 70% of non-organically grown produce in the United States contains residue from pesticides. This residue can be potentially harmful to humans and doesn't go away even after washing and peeling. Of this 90%, 70% was shown to have traces of more than one type of pesticide. Don't let this scare you off from consuming your fruit and vegetables, though. Shopping organically is an easy way to assure your produce is pesticide-free. Consider attending any local farmer markets instead of hitting up big chain marts. The Environmental Working Group (EWG) has compiled a list of the produce that contains the most pesticides. This list is aptly named the dirty dozen. If you're curious as to the produce with the least amount of pesticides, they have also provided a "Clean Fifteen." Both lists from 2021 are provided below.

What Can Go Wrong?

Don't worry, as long as you're a competent cook, you'll probably never have to deal with a kitchen fire. It would be very difficult to set boiling water on fire. You're more likely to have an issue while preparing the food in a saucepan or pot than when using your water bath canner. If you do end up with a tiny fire in your pan, do not try to put it out with water. Grease fires can be taken down by turning off the heat and smoothing the flames with a lid. Don't attempt to move the pan or hot grease could splash you. If you tend to be accident prone, invest in a fire extinguisher.

Water bath canners are very safe as long as they are used correctly. The worst thing that could happen is the lid somehow comes off. Water bath canners process food through the temperature of boiling water. If the lid comes undone you could be splashed by this boiling water and receive severe burns. You could also get burned by any steam that comes out. If the lid falls off, back away from any splash zone and try to kill the heat source. This might seem like it goes without saying but don't ever stick your hand in the water when the heat source is on. The temperature of boiling water is 212 °F. That will be very painful. If you do end up with a minor burn, apply cold water to the area. Any serious burn , seek a medical professional.

The last thing you should look out for is botulism. This is a serious illness that could result in death. Symptoms of botulism include difficulty breathing, blurry vision, nausea, slurred speech, droopy eyelids and even paralysis. Symptoms will usually appear within 18 to 36 hours after exposure. It is very important to seek medical attention immediately if you have any of these symptoms. Even after receiving medical treatment, paralysis can last months following the infection. If not treated right away this can be permanent. Some patients have reported breathing problems and fatigue years afterwards as well. The toxin that causes botulism attacks the nervous system and kills 5 out of every 100 people. Luckily the condition is rare and as long as you know how to avoid it, you'll probably never have to worry about it.

So how do you avoid this? Only use the water bath canner for its intended product. Vegetables with low acid will not be successfully canned in a water bath canner. If you are curious about a certain product and can't find a definitive answer on if it can be safely canned, don't do it. It's better to be safe than sorry. If something doesn't seal properly, you can try to can it again but older goods with a faulty seal should be thrown away. You should also look out for discoloration, foul smells or rotten fat deposits. These are all signs of a weak seal and contamination. Don't play roulette with your health. Follow the USDA and FDA guidelines even if it may seem inconvenient at times. They are there to maintain us as safe canners.

Conclusion

"You don't have to be great to start but you have to start to be great."

- Zig Ziglar

Congratulations, you have made it to the end of the book. An impressive feat considering all the puns you have had to endure. I truly hope you have enjoyed these recipes as much as I have. I believe the quote above is just the right sentiment to end this book on. You don't have to be a dietitian or a good cook to start your canning journey. You can be a certified kitchen disaster and still learn how to make a fantastic mango chutney. It just takes practice and a whole lot of patience. Remember, this is your path to make not follow. Nobody starts off their canning journey as a professional. There's a reason why the USDA doesn't approve of old pickling recipes. Perfection takes time and perhaps more importantly research. You'll get there and when you do, you'll be eating like a champion.

Even if you're only canning for your family, you're still making a huge difference. When you start canning, you start taking accountability for your waste habits. The only thing that can't be reused is the metal lids of the jars since they can't seal right the second time. While we can hope that this tiny issue can be fixed in a few years as canning practices evolve, there are still options for today. The metal lids don't have to contribute to your waste as they are recyclable. You can also reuse them as lids for refrigerated homemade food. If you do this make sure you store the lids in a way that doesn't confuse which ones can be canned. You don't want to waste any by ruining a seal.

There are alternatives to the metal lids as well. You may want to invest in some BPA free plastic lids. BPA just refers to the industrial chemical bisphenol A that seeps into food from the plastic. It could cause potential harm to infants and children so it's important not to only get BPA free plastic. Though they aren't as widely used as the metal ones, plastic lids have unlimited uses. If you choose this option remember that it is contributing to the creation of unnecessary plastic so buy responsibly. You could also use glass as an alternative but it runs the risk of chipping and putting broken glass in your food. They are indefinitely reusable like the plastic ones though. Whichever method you go with, make sure you recycle any waste so your canning can help the world as much as it helps you.

There are going to be some unavoidable expenses when you first start canning. Water bath canning is a cheaper alternative to other methods but you'll still need a large pot, jars, lids, and other equipment. You'll also have to worry about the price of the ingredients you'll be using. This will be your first investment. Stocking up on home canned goods may seem expensive at the moment but it'll save you money in the long run. As long as you utilize canning to the best of your ability you'll make your money back through limiting your annual food spoilage. If you sell your home canned goods, like many canners do, you'll make it back even faster as long as you find your market.

The next investment is time. I've said it once, I've said it a million times but it is sincerely the most important thing. Research everything. Call up your local extension service, haunt the USDA or FDA's websites and can your heart out. If the point of canning is to save time, why should you be spending all this time on it? Like I said, it's an investment. Spend time now, save time in the future. While you still should keep tabs on any changes for the home canning guidelines, canning will become so easy that you won't even think twice about it once you get all your research out of the way.

Despite the limitation on what can be processed, there are still many amazing recipes you can make with your water bath canner. The best place to start would be with a simple fruit canning recipe. They only have a few directions and one or two ingredients. Once you've tested the waters move on to something harder like a jam or jelly. Condiments are going to take more ingredients to really explore their favors.

Canning these will be a fun place to start your transition into harder to make goods such as pickles and relish. Just like with any activity, it's better to start slow and work your way up.

With the 60 compiled recipes in this book, you are well on your way to a diverse and delicious panty. Diverse is the key aspect to being successful with home canning. Having options will help you eat healthier. It may seem easy to just can one recipe in bulk but it could result in canning fatigue. You don't want to get sick of eating a specific food and end up wasting all your work. As most dietitians will tell you, you should be receiving a variety of vitamins each day. This should be reflected in your canning habits. A water bath canner is a great start but you can also invest in a pressure canner for more diversity. With a pressure canner, you can process meat and regular vegetables ending with a more rounded out pantry.

It looks as if we have reached the end of the book, dear reader. I hope you can take the information you have learned and make wonderful things. Remember to have fun and try new recipes whenever you can. If you fail, the next batch will be better. As cliche as it may sound it's very crucial that you don't give up. If people gave up preservation hundreds of years ago we might never have had pickles. We would be in a real pickle then. Sorry, one last pun for the road. I wish you the best of luck and the most delicious food.

Thank You

Dear reader, I would like to take this time to appreciate you. Without your purchase and interest, I wouldn't be able to keep writing helpful books like this one. Once again, THANK YOU for reading this book. I hope you enjoyed it as much as I enjoyed writing it.

Before you go, I have a small favor to ask of you. **Would you please consider posting a review of this book on the platform? Posting a review will help support my writing.**

Your feedback is very important and will help me continue to provide more informative literature in the future. I look forward to hearing from you. Just follow this relevant link below.

US- https://www.amazon.com/review/create-review?&asin=B0B7KCH351

UK- https://www.amazon.co.uk/review/create-review?&asin=B0B7KCH351

CANADA- https://www.amazon.ca/review/create-review?&asin=B0B7KCH351

MEXICO- https://www.amazon.com.mx/review/create-review?&asin=B0B7KCH351

BRAZIL - https://www.amazon.com.br/review/create-review?&asin=B0B7KCH351

SPAIN- https://www.amazon.es/review/create-review?&asin=B0B7KCH351

ITALY- https://www.amazon.it/review/create-review?&asin=B0B7KCH351

FRANCE- https://www.amazon.fr/review/create-review?&asin=B0B7KCH351

INDIA- https://www.amazon.in/review/create-review?&asin=B0B7KCH351

GERMANY - https://www.amazon.de/review/create-review?&asin=B0B7KCH351

Glossary

Acid — Any sour compounds.

Antioxidant — The citric acid of lemon or lime juice, ascorbic acid or a blend of citric and ascorbic acids, that stops oxidation and browning. It also has health properties.

Artificial sweeteners — Synthetic alternatives to sugar. Sweetness can vary.

Brine — salt water solution that is used to pickle fruits and vegetables.

Bacteria — Microorganisms that can be potentially harmful. In canning, bacteria thrives in low acid foods and if not properly processed.

Blanching — Preparation method that boils vegetables or fruit before emerging them in ice water to elongate the food's quality.

Botulism — A potentially fatal illness that attacks the nerves and can cause paralysis.

Canning — Preserving produce in jars by heating it up and killing any bacteria.

Canning rack — Rack used at the bottom of a cooker to elevate the jars from the pot.

Cheesecloth — A woven cloth that can be used to strain juice or infuse herbs and spices during the cooking process.

Chutney — slow cooked fruits or vegetables with the addition of spices such as garlic, ginger or chilies. This dish originates from India.

Clean Fifteen — EGW's list for the top fifteen types of produce that are unlikely to have pesticides.

Condiment — A sweet or savory sauce used to enhance flavors of other food.

Dirty dozen — EGW's list for the top twelve produces that are most likely to have pesticide residue

EPA — An acronym for Environmental protection agency. The mission of this independent executive agency of the United States is to protect the environment and human health.

EGW — An acronym for Environmental Working Group. This activist organization works in researching agricultural populations. Every year they provide a produce pesticide lists called the "dirty dozen" "clean fifteen"

FDA — An acronym for The Food and Drug Administration. This federal agency of the department of health and human services is in charge of food and drug regulations with the goal of protecting and maintaining public health and safety.

Food mill — three part food preparation utensil for sieving and mashing foods. The parts are a bowl, a bottom plate with holes, and a crank with a metal blade that crushes the food and forces it through the holes in the plate.

Hot packing — Packing partially cooked food into jars and then covering them in boiling water, juice or syrup.

Jam — Crushed or chopped fruit that is cooked with sugar or pectin to a thickened but spreadable consistency.

Jar — Glass container used for processing in a canner. Comes in several sizes such as quart, pint and half pint. They have a two piece closure consisting of a metal lid and a band.

Jar lifter — A canning utensil used to place and remove jars from the canner safely.

Jelly — Fruit juice that has been strained from fruit and cooked with sugar or pectin to create a firmer consistency than Jam.

Marmalade — Preserve made from the peel and juice of citrus fruits boiled with sugar and water.

Meal Preparation — This is the process of creating meal plans by scheduling out dishes and preparing them ahead of time.

Pectin — A carbohydrate found in fruits and vegetables that deteriorates as they ripen. This is why produce becomes soft and loses its structure. You can also buy pectin in powdered and liquid forms to make jams, jellies and other soft spreads.

Pesticides — Substance applied to plants that kills and repels insects and other potentially harmful ailments.

pH levels — A way to measure the acidic level of water on a range of 0-14. Seven is neutral, less than seven is acidic and more than seven is considered base.

Pickling — Preservation for produce through immersion in vinegar or anaerobic fermentation.

Pressure Canner — A special appliance that reaches higher temperatures than water bath canning. This is the only approved way to preserve low acid foods such as vegetables and meats.

Raw Packing — Packing uncooked food into jars and then covering them in boiling water, juice or syrup.

Rolling boil — A continuous and strong boil that churns the ingredients from high heat.

Simmer — gently bubbling liquid from a low heat source.

Sieve — A strainer made from a wired mesh used for making pulps, purees and juices.

Syrup — Refers to canning syrup made from sugar and water or juice. This liquid is added to canned produce to help them become processed.

USDA — An acronym for The United States Department of Agriculture. This federal department is responsible for creating and maintaining federal laws about agriculture and food in relation to safety and nutritional quality.

Water Bath Canner — A large pot with a rack that reaches high temperatures for boiling jars and preserving food. This process is only used for food products with high acidic levels.

Index

A

acidic, 255, 257, 311, 400, 401
air bubbles, 267, 298, 301
alkaline, 257
allspice, 286, 287, 352, 370, 375, 383
Apple Butter on Toast, 374
apple cider vinegar, 286, 287, 323, 336, 354, 375, 378, 379, 380
Apple-Solutely Delicious Jam, 274, 306
Apricots, 320, 408
Asparagus, 390
Awesomesauce Applesauce, 306, 307

B

Baby Sauce, 339
Barbecue Sauce, 354, 408
basil, 340, 341, 343, 381
bay leaves, 340, 342
Be Grape-Ful Jelly, 288
beets, unpeeled, 383
berries, 273, 305, 363, 366, 391
berry, 252, 273, 330, 414
black peppercorns, 314, 356
Blasting Blueberries, 296, 297, 305, 365
Bloody Mary, 348, 350, 410
blueberries, 365
Blueberry Syrup Around, 365
boiling water, 255, 257, 268, 272, 291,

301, 393, 400, 401

bourbon, 354

Broccoli, 390

C

Cabbages, 390

Cantaloupes, 391

Cauliflower, 390

cauliflower florets, 316

cayenne pepper, 354, 370

celery seed, 325, 379, 380

celery,, 346, 349, 359

Cherry Bomb Pie Filling, 303, 305

cherry tomatoes, 331

Chicken Wing Sauce, 369

chili powder, 336

Chili Sauce, 358, 413

chopped onion, 284, 325, 338

chutney, 261, 284, 285, 286, 287, 288, 293, 395, 409, 412

Chutney Recipes, 284

cider vinegar, 311, 325, 326, 361

cinnamon, 301, 304, 307, 308, 319, 320, 321, 352, 353, 358, 359, 367, 370, 375, 383, 413

Cinnamon Pear Sauce, 307, 309, 413

clove, 284, 287, 314

Cocktail, 321

Condiments, 352, 358, 396

Cowboy Candy Over Salmon, 379

cranberries, 366, 367, 410

Cranberry Sauce, 366, 410

crystallized ginger, 284

cucumber, 323

cumin, 336, 338

cups of sugar, 275, 280, 281, 284, 291,

292, 298, 299, 301, 304, 375

cups of white sugar, 289

cups sugar, 276

D

dandelion petals, 291

Dandy Dandelion Jelly, 290

Diced Tomatoes, 329, 411

dried rosemary, 341

E

ears of corn, 316

F

fennel seeds, 342

flakes, 284, 340, 343, 354, 380

fresh blueberries, 297, 305

G

garlic, 284, 287, 314, 317, 335, 336, 337, 338, 340, 341, 343, 344, 349, 354, 355, 356, 357, 370, 378, 379, 380, 381, 399

Glad Marmalade, 278

golden raisins, 284, 286

Granny's Apple Pie Filling, 300

granulated sugar, 273, 278, 305, 364, 367, 378, 381

Greek Yogurt with Mango, 376

green bell pepper, 381

Grigio, 356, 357

ground black pepper, 286, 287, 336, 342

ground cloves, 375

ground coriander, 286, 287

H

habanero pepper, 378

Harmony, 359

honey, 273, 274, 284, 320, 343, 361, 362, 408

Honeycrisp apples, 274

Honeydew melons, 391

Horseradish, 359, 409, 411

hot chili pepper, 286

Hot Sauce, 368, 410

J

jalapeño peppers, 378

jalapeños, 379

jam, 261, 273, 274, 275, 276, 277, 293, 296, 362, 364, 391, 396, 408, 411, 413,

414

Jam Recipes, 273

jams, 257, 274, 400

Jellies, 250, 273

jelly, 261, 273, 289, 290, 291, 292, 293, 296, 364, 366, 396, 411, 413

K

Krazy Kiwi, 299, 300

L

large pears, 308

lemon juice, 257, 275, 276, 277, 278, 279, 280, 291, 300, 301, 302, 304, 305, 308, 329, 330, 331, 332, 333, 340, 342, 343, 346, 347, 349, 364, 365, 366, 375, 376, 377, 382

Lemon Zest Blueberry Sauce, 305, 306

light brown sugar, 286, 287

lime juice, 378

low-acid foods, 258

M

mangoes, 284, 376

Marinara Sauce, 341, 411

marmalade, 261, 278, 279, 280, 281, 282, 293, 305, 408, 410, 413, 414

Marmalade Recipes, 278

Marmalades, 273

Marry Me Mustard, 356

Meat, 257, 339

Mild Salsa, 334

minced, 284, 338, 340, 341, 343, 349, 370, 378, 381

Mushrooms, 391

mustard seed, 325, 356, 357, 358, 361

mustard seeds, whole, 284

O

oranges, 278, 279, 367, 413

oregano, 341, 343, 381

P

paprika, 338, 354

parsley, 340, 347, 349, 381

Pasta La Vista, 339

Peach Salsa Tacos, 377

peaches, 285, 286, 296, 318, 319, 320,

321, 374, 378, 391, 409, 412

Peachy Keen Chutney, 285, 319

Pear-Fect Chutney, 287, 308

Pectin, 273, 274, 400

peel, 278, 279, 286, 345, 364, 375, 400

peeled, 281, 284, 286, 287, 288, 300, 319, 334, 335, 346, 354, 358, 370, 376, 378, 381

Persian limes, 281

Pesticides, 393, 400

Pickled Beets Salad, 382

Pickled Onions, 315

Pickled Peaches, 318, 409

pickles, 257, 311, 312, 313, 315, 323, 392, 397, 413, 414

Pickling, 311, 313, 328, 401

pickling cucumbers, 314

pickling spice, 368

Piña Coladas Jam, 276

Pinot, 356, 357

Pizza Sauce, 343, 411

Puns Jelly, 292

pureed pineapple, 276

R

raspberries, 298, 411

red chili pepper, 284

red pepper flake, 340

Relish, 323, 324, 326, 408, 410, 412

Rhubarb Pie Filling, 302, 409

ripe plums, 292

Rockin Raspberries, 297, 299

Roma tomatoes, 332, 350

rosemary, 356, 357

S

sage, 342

Salsa Verde, 337, 408

salt, 286, 287, 312, 314, 315, 317, 322, 323, 324, 325, 326, 331, 332, 335, 336, 338, 340, 341, 343, 345, 346, 347, 349, 352, 353, 354, 356, 357, 358, 359, 360,

367, 368, 370, 375, 378, 381, 399

Spaghetti, 381, 411

Spicy Salsa, 336

strawberries, 251, 263, 271, 273, 274, 321, 362, 363, 364, 414

Straw-Berry Good Jam, 273

Strawberry Vinaigrette, 362, 413

Sub-Lime Marmalade, 281

T

thyme, 315, 342, 343

Tomato Juice, 345, 408

tomato puree, 344, 352

turmeric, 323, 324, 380

U

unsalted butter, 292

unsweetened fruit juice, 273

V

vegetables, 257, 311, 312, 316, 317, 325, 327, 328, 339, 346, 353, 355, 358, 393, 397, 399, 400, 401, 408

vermouth, 320

vinegar, 257

W

Water Bath Canning, 250, 255, 259, 385, 391, 392, 410, 412, 413

white balsamic vinegar, 320

white onions, diced, 336

white rum, 276

white vinegar, 284, 314, 315, 317, 319, 323, 335, 338, 358, 360, 362, 368, 370, 383

whole eggs, 361

Whole Lotta Whole Tomato, 332

Worcestershire sauce, 340, 349, 382

Y

yellow mustard seeds, 356

Z

zest, 281, 305, 308, 367, 375

Zest Lemon Marmalade, 279

zested, 367

Zoodles, 381

References

10 Fun Facts About Tomatoes | Campbell's Soup UK. (2021, March 31). Campbell's Soup UK. https://www.campbellsoup.co.uk/blog/fun-facts-about-tomatoes/

Adamant, A. (2018a, July 7). *How to Can Mango.* Practical Self Reliance. https://practicalselfreliance.com/canning-mango/

Adamant, A. (2018b, October 15). *Canning Apple Pie Filling.* Practical Self Reliance. https://practicalselfreliance.com/canning-apple-pie-filling/

Adamant, A. (2019a, March 30). *Canning Maple Syrup for Long Term Preservation.* Practical Self Reliance. https://practicalselfreliance.com/canning-maple syrup/#:~:text=Since%20syrup

Adamant, A. (2019b, July 10). *Canning Cherry Pie Filling.* Practical Self Reliance. https://practicalselfreliance.com/canning-cherry-pie-filling/

Adamant, A. (2019c, September 21). *Apple Jam.* Practical Self Reliance. https://practicalselfreliance.com/apple-jam/

Adcock, D. (n.d.-a). *Honey Mustard-canning recipe Recipe - Food.com.* Www.food.com. Retrieved February 13, 2022, from https://www.food.com/recipe/honey-mustard-canning-recipe

Adcock, D. (n.d.-b). *Jalapeno Pickle Relish Recipe - Food.com.* Www.food.com. Retrieved February 13, 2022, from https://www.food.com/recipe/jalapeno-pickle-relish-9407

Amanda. (2011, September 10). *Canning Salsa Verde, Made With Tomatillos • Heartbeet Kitchen.* Heartbeet Kitchen. https://heartbeetkitchen.com/tomatillosalsaverde/

Amanda. (2013, September 12). *Fiery Roasted Salsa: a canning recipe!* Heartbeet Kitchen. https://heartbeetkitchen.com/fiery-roasted-salsa/

Axe. (n.d.). *Tomato Juice - Canning Recipe - Food.com.* Www.food.com. https://www.food.com/recipe/tomato-juice-canning-188981

B, J. (2018, February 16). *Orange Marmalade | The Grateful Girl Cooks!* The Grateful Girl Cooks! https://www.thegratefulgirlcooks.com/orange-marmalade/#:~:text=The%20fruit%20is%20cooked%2C%20sugar

Ball. (2011). *Low Sugar / No Sugar Strawberry Jam.* Allrecipes. https://www.allrecipes.com/recipe/217924/low-sugar-no-sugar-strawberry-jam/

Ball, N. (n.d.). *Smoky-Sweet Barbecue Sauce Recipe by Tasty.* Tasty.co. Retrieved February 13, 2022, from https://tasty.co/recipe/smoky-sweet-barbecue-sauce

Balsamic Pickled Apricots. (n.d.). Better Homes & Gardens. Retrieved February 13, 2022, from https://www.bhg.com/recipe/balsamic-pickled-apricots-/

Barnes, D. (2021, March 17). *These 12 fruits and vegetables contain more pesticide residue than others,*

"Dirty Dozen" study says. USA TODAY. https://www.usatoday.com/story/news/nation/2021/03/17/pesticides-these-fruits-and-vegetables-put-them-dirty-dozen-list/4707708001/

Bauer, B. A. (2016). *Tips to reduce your exposure to BPA*. Mayo Clinic. https://www.mayoclinic.org/healthy-lifestyle/nutrition-and-healthy-eating/expert-answers/bpa/faq-20058331

Bauer, E. (2021a, May 28). *Mango Chutney*. Simply Recipes. https://www.simplyrecipes.com/recipes/homemade_mango_chutney/

Bauer, E. (2021b, November 18). *Apple Butter*. Simply Recipes. https://www.simplyrecipes.com/recipes/apple_butter/

Belk, M. (2013, May 9). *Canning Kiwifruit*. ThriftyFun. https://www.thriftyfun.com/tf/Food_Tips_and_Info/Canning/Canning-Kiwifruit.html

Better Homes and Gardens. (n.d.). *Canned Applesauce*. Better Homes & Gardens. Retrieved February 12, 2022, from https://www.bhg.com/recipe/canned-applesauce/

Blue book services. (n.d.). *Pineapple – Produce Blue Book*. Blue Book Services. Retrieved February 12, 2022, from https://www.producebluebook.com/know-your-commodity/pineapple/#:~:text=Most%20U.S.%2Dgrown%20pineapple%20still

BLUEROWZE. (n.d.). *Nana's Southern Pickled Peaches*. Allrecipes. Retrieved February 13, 2022, from https://www.allrecipes.com/recipe/72126/nanas-southern-pickled-peaches/

Cameron, C. W. (2011, January 18). In Season: Lemons. *The Atlanta Journal-Constitution*. https://www.ajc.com/entertainment/dining/season-lemons/DZmIptJTgAJgrHLYAZo6aL/#:~:text=American%2Dgrown%20lemons%

Canning blueberries. (2015, August 19). Healthy Canning. https://www.healthycanning.com/canning-blueberries

Canning Mixed Fruit - Better in a Jar! - SBCanning.com - homemade canning recipes. (n.d.). SBCanning. Retrieved February 13, 2022, from https://www.sbcanning.com/2013/03/canning-mixed-fruit-better-in-jar.html

Canning Pickled Horseradish - SBCanning.com - homemade canning recipes. (n.d.). SBCanning. Retrieved February 13, 2022, from https://www.sbcanning.com/2013/10/

Canned Rhubarb Pie Filling. (2016, July 6). Healthy Canning. https://www.healthycanning.com/canned-rhubarb-pie-filling

Canning Syrups - Corn Syrup or Clear Jel which is the better texture? - SBCanning.com - homemade canning recipes. (2022). SBCanning. https://www.sbcanning.com/2013/11/canning-syrups-corn-syrup-or-clear-jel.html

Canning Terms Glossary. (2022). Google.com. https://www.google.com/url?q=https://www.freshpreserving.com/ canning-terms-glossary.html&sa=D&source=docs&ust=1644771901875450&usg=AOvVaw2ZB

Centers for Disease Control and Prevention. (2019). *Symptoms*. Cdc.gov. https://www.cdc.gov/botulism/symptoms.html

Chicken wing sauce. (2016, September 14). Healthy Canning. https://www.healthycanning.com

Chihak, S., April 27, R. U., & 2020. (2020, April 27). *Save Your Produce Up to a YearWhen You Master Water Bath Canning*. Better Homes & Gardens. https://www.bhg.com/recipes/how-to/preserving-canning/canning-basics/

Cook, S. (2021, August 7). *Dill Pickle Relish - {Canning Relish}*. Sustainable Cooks. https://www.sustainablecooks.com/dill-relish-canning-recipe-step-by-step/

Delany, A. (2018, March 20). *What Are Tomatillos, Anyway?* Bon Appétit. https://www.bonappetit.com/story/what-are-tomatillos

Easy Hot Sauce. (2016, August 24). Healthy Canning. https://www.healthycanning.com/easy-

Editors, L. C. (2021, August 7). *Peach Salsa*. Leite's Culinaria. https://leitesculinaria.com/105397/recipes-peach-salsa.html#recipe

Educational Resources. (n.d.). *Elevations of the 50 Largest Cities (by population, 1980 Census) | U.S. Geological Survey*. Www.usgs.gov. Retrieved February 12, 2022, from https://www.usgs.gov/educational-resources/elevations-50-largest-cities-population-1980

Elizabeth. (2021, August 3). *Cranberry Sauce for Canning*. The Jam Jar Kitchen. https://jamjarkitchen.com/2021/08/03/cranberry-sauce-for-canning/

Evans, R. (2014, December 24). *Lemon Marmalade - Canning for Christmas*. AT HOME with REBECKA. https://athomewithrebecka.com/lemon-marmalade-canning-for-christmas/

Food labels - Better Health Channel. (2020, February 25). Www.betterhealth.vic.gov.au. https://www.betterhealth.vic.gov.au/health/healthyliving/food-labels#list-of-ingredients

Froment, L. (n.d.). *How Do Cranberries Grow*. Www.westfieldinsurance.com. Retrieved February 13, 2022, from https://www.westfieldinsurance.com/resources/articles/how-do-cranberries-grow#:~:text=Cranberries%20grow%20on%20the%20vines

Garden Vegetable Juice. (2017, September 1). Healthy Canning. https://www.healthycanning.com/garden-vegetable-juice

Garlicky Pickled Mixed Veggies. (n.d.). Better Homes & Gardens. Retrieved February 13, 2022, from https://www.bhg.com/recipe/garlicky-pickled-mixed-veggies/

Homemade Bloody Mary Mix - SBCanning.com - homemade canning recipes. (n.d.). SBCanning. Retrieved February 13, 2022, from https://www.sbcanning.com/2012/07/homemade-bloody-mary-mix.html

Homemade Canned Spaghetti Sauce. (n.d.). Taste of Home. Retrieved February 13, 2022, from https://www.tasteofhome.com/recipes/homemade-canned-spaghetti-sauce/

Horseradish. (n.d.). FoodPrint. Retrieved February 13, 2022, from https://foodprint.org/real-food/horseradish/

Huffstetler, E. (2018, November 21). *Can I Reuse My Canning Lids?* The Spruce Eats. https://www.thespruceeats.com/can-you-reuse-canning-lids-1389094

Jami. (2014, January 23). *Home Canned Pizza Sauce {from frozen or fresh tomatoes}*. An Oregon Cottage. https://anoregoncottage.com/home-canned-pizza-sauce/

Johnston, C. (2020, July 30). *How to Can Diced Tomatoes*. Wholefully. https://wholefully.com/can-diced-tomatoes/

KDP. (n.d.). *Pina Colada Jam Recipe - Food.com*. Www.food.com. Retrieved February 12, 2022, from https://www.food.com/recipe/pina-colada-jam-135040?mode=US&scaleto=5

Kelley. (2014, September 1). *Canning Week 2014 + How to Can Whole Raspberries*. Mountain Mama Cooks. https://mountainmamacooks.com/canning-week-2014-can-whole-raspberries

Kelsey. (2021, October 16). How Many Cups In A Quart, Pint, Gallon (Free Printable). *Bake Me Some Sugar*. https://bakemesomesugar.com/how-many-cups-in-a-quart-pint-gallon/

Kim, A. (2016, May 26). *How To Make Dandelion Jelly*. Homestead Acres. https://www.homestead-acres.com/how-to-make-dandelion-jelly/

Kimberly. (2017, September 8). *BEST Marinara Sauce*. The Daring Gourmet. https://www.daringgourmet.com/best-marinara-sauce-for-canning/

KITTENCAL. (n.d.). *Pickled Beets (For Canning) Recipe - Food.com*. Www.food.com. Retrieved February 12, 2022, from https://www.food.com/recipe/pickled-beets-for-canning-177650

Lampkin, B. (2018, November 14). *10 Pickle Facts to Savor (in Honor of National Pickle Day)*. Mentalfloss.com. https://www.mentalfloss.com/article/71166/10-pickle-facts-savor-honor-

Lee, M., Hutcheon, J., Dukan, E., & Milne, I. (2017). Rhubarb (Rheum species): the role of Edinburgh in its cultivation and development. *Journal of the Royal College of Physicians of Edinburgh*, *47*(1), 102–109. https://doi.org/10.4997/jrcpe.2017.121

Lisa. (2018, September 8). *Homemade Plum Jelly*. The Cooking Bride. https://cookingbride.com/sauces-and-seasonings/homemade-plum-jelly/

Maria. (2017, September 23). *Canning Raw Pack Whole Tomatoes -a step by step guide*. She Loves Biscotti. https://www.shelovesbiscotti.com/canning-raw-pack-whole-tomatoes/

Mel. (2018, September 6). *Homemade Canned Spaghetti Sauce {Step-by-Step Tutorial}*. Mel's

Kitchen Cafe. https://www.melskitchencafe.com/homemade-spaghetti-marinara-sauce-for-canning-or-freezing/

Melissa, A. (2015, May 26). *Secret Ingredients Not Listed on the Food Label.* ThirtySomethingSuperMom. https://thirtysomethingsupermom.com/secret-ingredients-not-listed-on-the-food-label/

Meredith, L. (2021a, May 4). *Homemade Spicy Peach Chutney.* The Spruce Eats. https://www.thespruceeats.com/peach-chutney-recipe-1327510

Meredith, L. (2021b, July 13). *How to Make and Can Sweet and Tangy Pear Chutney.* The Spruce Eats. https://www.thespruceeats.com/pear-chutney-recipe-1327511

Milisa. (2019, July 22). *Sweet Pickle Relish {Easy Canning Recipe}.* Miss in the Kitchen. https://www.missinthekitchen.com/sweet-pickle-relish/

Mobley, A. (2017, November 29). *Homemade Dijon Mustard Recipe.* Flour on My Face. https://flouronmyface.com/homemade-dijon-mustard-recipe/

Mock, S. (2020, August 5). *Candied Jalapeños Recipe (Cowboy Candy).* Savoring the Good®. https://www.savoringthegood.com/candied-jalapenos/

Moreau, N. (2021, September 28). *Largest Cities in Canada by Population | The Canadian Encyclopedia.* Www.thecanadianencyclopedia.ca. https://www.thecanadianencyclopedia.ca/en/article/largest-cities-in-canada-by-population

Myrick, R. (2011, August 11). *Ketchup Fun Facts | Mobile Cuisine.* Mobile Cuisine | Food Truck, Pop up & Street Food Coverage. https://mobile-cuisine.com/did-you-know/ketchup-fun-facts/#:~:text=Heinz%20Company%20back%20in%201876

Nguyen, S. (2021, May 2). *Everything you need to know about when pears are in season.* HappySprout. https://www.happysprout.com/inspiration/pears-in-season-when/#:~:text=Pears%20are%20typically%20available%20from

oldworldgardenfarms. (2021, July 27). *How To Make The Best Canned Salsa - Our Tried & True Recipe.* Old World Garden Farms. https://oldworldgardenfarms.com/2021/07/27/

Patterson, H. (2017, June 6). *What's in Season: Limes - Farm Flavor.* Farmflavor.com. https://farmflavor.com/lifestyle/home/whats-season-limes/#:~:text=Limes%20are%20

Peaches. (2021, September). Www.agmrc.org. https://www.agmrc.org/commodities-products/fruits/peaches#:~:text=As%20of%202017%2C%20peaches%20are

Peterson, S. (2021, February 19). *Water Bath Canning with Printable Checklist. How to Use Your Canner.* SimplyCanning. https://www.simplycanning.com/water-bath-canning/#whatisit

Peterson, S. (2020, April 25). *How to Can Homemade Ketchup: A Safe Recipe for a Water Bath Canner.* SimplyCanning. https://www.simplycanning.com/homemade-ketchup/

Petre, A. (2020, December 14). *How to Meal Prep — A Beginner's Guide*. Healthline. https://www.healthline.com/nutrition/how-to-meal-prep#choosing-meals

Pickled Sweet Onions. (n.d.). Taste of Home. Retrieved February 13, 2022, from https://www.tasteofhome.com/recipes/pickled-sweet-onions/

Preserve, B. H. S., Learn to. (2014, October 21). *Cinnamon Pear Sauce*. USA Pears. https://usapears.org/recipe/cinnamon-pear-sauce/

Blueberry Lemon Dessert Sauce {Water Bath Canning Recipe}. Its Yummi. https://www.itsyummi.com/blueberry-lemon-dessert-sauce/#recipe

Sertich Velie, M. (2018, August 10). *What's the Difference Between Jam, Jelly, Compote, and Conserve?* Serious Eats. https://www.seriouseats.com/difference-between-jam-jelly-compote-conserve-apple-butter-preserves-types

Shawn. (2021, June 1). *Homemade Dill Pickles Recipe*. I Wash You Dry. https://iwashyoudry.com/homemade-canned-dill-pickles/

Strawberry Vinaigrette. (2017, December 21). Healthy Canning. https://www.healthycanning.com/strawberry-vinaigrette

Sweet Chili Sauce - SBCanning.com - homemade canning recipes. (2022). SBCanning. https://www.sbcanning.com/2012/07/sweet-chili-sauce.html

Sweetser, R. (2021, June 29). *Canning for Beginners: What Is Canning?* Old Farmer's Almanac. https://www.almanac.com/canning-for-beginners

The Hale Groves Team. (2019, September 23). *Why are Florida Oranges different from California Oranges? | Farm Fresh Fruit Gifts*. Hale Groves. https://www.halegroves.com/blog/why-are-florida-oranges-different-from-california-oranges/#:~:text=Florida%20and%20California

Traister, L. (2021, September 12). *Canning Cherry Tomatoes (Two Simple Ways)*. Lady Lee's Home. https://ladyleeshome.com/canning-cherry-tomatoes/

Treiber, L. (2017, August 7). *Processing methods for pickled products*. MSU Extension. https://www.canr.msu.edu/news/processing_methods_for_pickled_products

Trowbridge Filippone, P. (2021, December 26). *How to Make Lime Marmalade With 3 Ingredients*. The Spruce Eats. https://www.thespruceeats.com/lime-marmalade-recipe-180811

University, U. S. (n.d.). *Food Safety & Nutrition*. Extension.usu.edu. Retrieved February 12, 2022, from https://extension.usu.edu/saltlake/home-family-food/food-safety-preservation

USDA. (n.d.). *Food Waste FAQs*. Www.usda.gov. https://www.usda.gov/foodwaste/faqs#:~:text=In%20the%20United%20States%2C%20

Wisconsin department of public instruction. (n.d.). *Mango History*. USDA.

Images

Biro-Horvath, R. (2019). [Untitled online image of pickles in a jar]. Unsplash. https://unsplash.com/photos/4MKPaMGIA3U

Chung, Z. (2020). Gardener harvesting apples with daughter in garden [Online image]. Pexels.com https://www.pexels.com/photo/gardener-harvesting-apples-with-daughter-in-garden-5528990/?utm_content=attributionCopyText&utm_medium=referral&utm_

Elijas, E. (2020). Person Pouring Water on Pickled Cucumber Jars [Online image]. Pexels.com https://www.pexels.com/photo/person-pouring-water-on-pickled-cucumber-jars-5503110/?utm_content=attributionCopyText&utm_medium=referral&utm_source

Green, V. (2020). [Untitled online image of dandelions]. Unsplash. https://unsplash.com/photos/i-uBAOo_BBA

Kemper, J. (2021). [Untitled online image of rhubarb plant]. Unsplash. https://unsplash.com/photos/1HHrdIoLFpU

Klein, D. (2016). Fresh Tomato Sauce [Online image]. Unsplash.

K, P. (2019). [Untitled online image of a slice of berry cake]. Unsplash. https://unsplash.co

May, C. (2020). Glass of cocktail with lemon [Online image]. Pexels.com

Medina, F. (2019). [Untitled online image of a fire in a pan]. Unsplash. https://unsplash.com

Melnyczuk, T. (2021). [Untitled online image of lemon marmalade]. Unsplash. https://unsplash.com/photos/RUqnlEBa_7g

Olsson, E. (2018). Meal Prep for Breakfast & Lunch [Online image] Unsplash. https://unsplash.com/photos/P4jRJYN33wE

Pflug, S. Hand Holding Freshly Canned Salsa Photo [Online image]. Burst.

Pixabay. (2016). Clear Glass Mason Jars [Online image]. Pexels.com

Primeau, N. (2019). [Untitled online image of measuring spoons]. Unsplash. https://unsplash.com

Rai, A. (2020). Fresh off the vines [Online image]. Unsplash. https://unsplash.com/photos/6P36fWsCypU

RODNAE Productions. (2020). A Person Putting a Jam on a Bread [Online image]. Pexels. https://www.pexels.com/photo/a-person-putting-a-jam-on-a-bread-5848004/?utm_content=attributionCopyText&utm_medium=referral&utm_source=pexels

Rutkowski, A. (2016). Fresh strawberries [Online image]. Unsplash. https://unsplash.com/photos/GdTLaWamFHwSays, C. (2016, July 20)

www.ingramcontent.com/pod-product-compliance
Lightning Source LLC
Chambersburg PA
CBHW081707100526
44590CB00022B/3682